African Po Elites

Elites

The Search for Democracy and Good Governance

Edited by
Francis Nwonwu and Dirk Kotze

**Africa Institute of
South Africa**

WESTMINISTER
FOUNDATION FOR
DEMOCRACY (WFD)

First published in 2008 by the
Africa Institute of South Africa
PO Box 630
Pretoria 0001
South Africa

ISBN 978-0-7983-0184-8

Publisher: Solani Ngobeni
Project Manager: Rose Bopape
Editorial Assistant: Matau Setshase
Proofreader: Lise-Marie Keyser
Cartographers: Elize van As and Wendy Job
Design and layout by Karen Graphics, Centurion
Cover design by Acumen Publishing

The Africa Institute of South Africa is a statutory body and research organisation, focusing on political, socio-economic, international and development issues in contemporary Africa. The Institute conducts research, publishes books, monographs, occasional papers, newsletters and a quarterly journal, and holds regular seminars on issues of topical interest. It is also home to one of the best library and documentation centres world-wide, with materials on every African country.

For more information, contact the Africa Institute at PO Box 630, Pretoria 0001, South Africa; email ai@ai.org.za; or visit our website at http://www.ai.org.za.

Contents

Abbreviations.. v
Acknowledgements.. ix
About the Editors x
Notes on Contributors... xii
List of Figures xv
List of Tables.. xv

Introduction: 1
Francis Nwonwu and Dirk Kotze

1. Political Leadership in Egypt: The Case of Halt
   Democracy... 21
   Hamdy Abdel Rahman Hassan

2. Egyptian Stakeholders' Perception of the new Partnership for
   Africa's Development (NEPAD) 49
   Francis Nwonwu

3. The Role of Political Elites in the Political Dynamics and
   Reforms in Algeria... 75
   Tayeb Chenntouf

4. Evolution and Nature of Nigerian Political Elites and the
   Realisation of NEPAD's Political and Development
   Agenda 105
   Richard Iroanya

5. Political Leadership in South Africa and the Search for
   Equitable and Sustainable Economic Growth and
   Development 141
   Susan Booysen

6. Political Leadership in Senegal: Clientelism and
    Monopolisation of Power... 181
    Serigne Mansour Tall and Cheikh Gueye

7. Political Leadership and Political Will Contributions to
    Democratic Governance in South Africa 201
    Susan Booysen

Conclusion 255

Abbreviations

AAPS	African Association of Political Science
ACDP	African Christian Democratic Party
AD	Alliance for Democracy
ADS	Afrikaner Unity Movement
AEC	African Economic Community
AFP	Alliance of Forces for Progress
AFRC	Armed Forces Ruling Council
AG	Action Group party
AISA	Africa Institute of South Africa
ANC	African National Congress
ANP	Arab Nasserite Party
APP	All People's Party
APRM	African Peer Review Mechanism
APSS	African Political Science Society
ARIA	African regional integration arrangements
ASD	alternative service delivery
AU	African Union
Azapo	Azanian People's Organisation
BEE	black economic empowerment
BEEE	black elite economic empowerment
BIG	basic income grant
CAEC	Central African Economic Community
CEDEAO	Communauté Economique Des États de l'Afrique de l'Ouest
CODESRIA	Council for the Development of Social Science Research in Africa
COMESA	Common Market for Eastern and Southern Africa
Cosatu	Congress of South African Trade Unions
CSO	civil society organisation
DP/DA	Democratic Party/Democratic Alliance
DSP	central statistical office
ECA	Economic Commission for Africa
ECOWAS	Economic Community of West African States
EFF	extended fund facility

EPWP	Expanded Public Works Programme
EU	European Union
FA	Federal Alliance
FAL	Final Act of Lagos
FAL	Front for Change
FCE	Algerian Chamber of Commerce
FF/FF+	Freedom Front/Freedom Front Plus
FFS	Front des Forces Socialistes
FLN	Front de Libération Nationale
GCIS	Government Communication and Information System
GEAR	Growth, Employment and Redistribution
GNPP	Greater Nigeria People's Party
GNU	Government of National Unity
HABITAT	United Nations Human Settlements Programme
HCA	High Council for the Audiovisual
HDI	Human Development Index
HSGIC	Heads of State and Governments Implementation Committee
ICT	information and communication technology
IFP	Inkatha Freedom Party
IMF	International Monetary Fund
INEC	Independent National Electoral Commission
LDC	less developed country
MDG	millennium development goals
MF	Minority Front
MP	Member of Parliament
MNR	Movement for National Reform
NCNC	National Council for Nigeria and Cameroon
NCOP	National Council of Provinces
NDP	National Democratic Party
NEC	National Executive Committee
Nedlac	National Economic Development and Labour Council
NEPAD	New Partnership for Africa's Development
NEPU	Northern Elements Progressive Union
NGO	non-governmental organisation
NIEO	new international economic order
NMMU	Nelson Mandela Metropolitan University
NNDP	Nigerian National Democratic Party
NNP	New National Party

African Political Elites: The Search for Democracy and Good Governance

NP	National Party
NPC	Northern People's Congress
NPN	National Party of Nigeria
NPP	Nigerian People's Party
NRC	National Republican Convention
OAU	Organization of African Unity
ONEL	National Elections Observatory
PAC	Pan-Africanist Congress
PCAS	Policy Coordination and Advisory Services
PDP	People's Democratic Party
PPP	purchasing power parity
PPP	public private partnership
PRP	People's Redemption Party
PRSP	Poverty Reduction Strategic Planning
PTA	Preferential Trade Area
RADDHO	Africa Meeting for Human Rights
RCD	Rassemblement pour la Culture et la Démocratie
RDP	Reconstruction and Development Programme
SACP	South African Communist Party
SADC	Southern African Development Community
Sanco	South African National Civic Organisation
Sangoco	South African non-governmental organization coalition
SAP	structural adjustment programme
SBA	stand-by arrangement
SDP	Social Democratic Party
SMC	Supreme Military Council
SMMEs	small, micro and medium enterprises
TAC	Treatment Action Campaign
UCDP	United Christian Democratic Party
UDF	United Democratic Front
UDM	United Democratic Movement
UEMOA	West African Economic and Monetary Union
UGTA	General Workers Union of Algeria
UNDP	United Nations Development Programme
Unesco	United Nations Educational, Scientific and Cultural Organisation
UNHCF	United Nations High Commission for Refugees
UN	United Nations

UPGA	United Progressive Grand Alliance
UPN	United Party of Nigeria
URD	Union for Democratic Renewal
Wafd	Egyptian Delegation
WFD	Westminister Foundation for Democracy
WHO	World Health Organization
ZAR	South African Rand

Acknowledgements

Our profound gratitude and thanks go to the following staff of the Africa Institute of South Africa, who conducted the surveys in the respective countries during the course of this study between 2003 and 2004. They are Patrick Rankhumise, who carried out the survey in South Africa and Siphamandla Zondi who, in the company of Edigheji Omano of the African Association of Political Science (AAPS), conducted interviews in Nigeria and Senegal.

Equally important is the support received from the Secretariat of AAPS in Pretoria, in providing links and contacts for country offices and officials during the survey, for which we express our gratitude. Our thanks also go to those AAPS officials or affiliates who collectively and individually contributed to the successful completion of the surveys.

Finally and most importantly, we wish to thank the Westminster Foundation for Democracy (WFD) in the United Kingdom, for providing the necessary funding to complete this research.

About the Editors

Francis O. C. Nwonwu is a Professor and a research specialist: Research Programmes at the Africa Institute of South Africa (AISA). He obtained a Ph.D in Natural Resource Economics in 1983 from Iowa State University, Ames Iowa, USA. He was formerly the Head, Economics and Sociology Division, Forestry Research Institute of Nigeria and Executive Director of FORSEE Consultancies.

He has taught and conducted research in several universities in Africa including the University of Science and Technology Port Harcourt, Nigeria; Egerton Univeristy, Njoro, Kenya; Moi University, Eldoret, Kenya; Kenyatta University, Nairobi, Kenya (part time); National University of Lesotho, Lesotho; and University of the Free State, Bloemfontein, South Africa. He also spent a three-month research fellowship at George August University, Gottengen, Germany, under the German Academic Exchange Programme in 1993.

Francis Nwonwu has attended many local and international conferences world-wide where he read scholarly papers. He has authored many articles in reputable local and international journals and has contributed to many books. His current research at AISA focuses on sustainable development with special emphasis on the millennium development goals (MDGs). In addition, he has a special interest in the application of indigenous knowledge systems and best practices in resource management and development.

His professional services have also been extended to several local and international organizations in different capacities spanning over capacity building, training, research and consultancy services. Among the organizations are the African Development Bank, International Development Research Centre of Canada, Food and Agricultural Organisation, African Academy of Sciences, International Centre for Research in Agroforestry and Swedish Academy of Sciences.

Dirk Kotze is a Professor in the Department of Political Sciences at the University of South Africa (Unisa), and is a graduate of the University of Stellenbosch and Witwatersrand University.

He has been a guest lecturer and Visiting Fellow at numerous overseas academic institutions, and is currently serving as a member of a South African ministerial panel on the ownership of land by foreigners.

He has published widely in the field of both South African and African politics, and is a sought-after commentator on contemporary political affairs in South Africa.

Notes on Contributors

Richard Iroanya is a researcher on Risk Analysis in the West Africa Desk of the Area Studies Research Division at the Africa Institute of South Africa. He holds a B.Sc. degree in Political Science from Nnamdi Azikiwe University in Nigeria and B.A. (Hons) in International Relations from the University of Pretoria, South Africa. He is currently completing a master's degree in Security Studies at the University of Pretoria. He was formerly a sales representative for Joellen Business Enterprises in Pretoria and one time senior staff writer for Hotline International Magazine in Kaduna, Nigeria. He has written widely, contributing to books, journals and conferences locally and internationally. He is a popular political analyst and radio and television discussant on political issues in Africa.

Susan Booysen is Professor at the Graduate School of Public and Development Management (PDM), University of the Witwatersrand. She is President of the South African Association of Political Studies (SAAPS). Her areas of specialization include South African and Southern African politics and political economy, comparative politics and research methodology. In both her academic research and in her work as Johannesburg-based research consultant, she has focused on analyses of South and Southern African politics. Until mid-2005, Booysen was Professor of Political Studies at the Nelson Mandela Metropolitan University (NMMU), Port Elizabeth. At the NMMU, she was programme leader of the Masters in South African Politics and Political Economy. She holds a D.Litt. et Phil. from the University of Johannesburg (formerly the Rand Afrikaans University). She obtained both her Master's and Honours degrees *cum laude*. She has held some major research fellowships, including a post-doctoral fellowship at the Southern African Research Program at Yale University, Connecticut, USA. She was awarded the NMMU Senior Research Bursary in 2001. She has published more than 30 refereed academic articles, chapters in books and monographs. She has concluded more than 25 full-scale research projects and has presented well over 50 papers at national and international conferences in political studies and related disciplines.

She works as media commentator and analyst, is on the editorial board of the *Politikon: South African Journal of Political Studies*, is a research associate of the Africa Institute of South Africa (AISA), and contributing editor to the Johannesburg newspaper *The Star*. Recent specialist work includes projects on public policy processes in South Africa, electoral observation in Southern Africa, peer-review processes and mechanisms in Africa, and political parties and elections in Southern Africa.

Tayeb Chenntouf is a Professor at the University of Oran, Algeria, and Research Director of the Research Project on the History of Algeria, Africa and the Western Mediterranean. He holds a Ph.D, and is a graduate from the School of Political Studies in Paris, France. He was Associate Professor at the University of Nice, France, between 1984 and 1986. He also acted as a study supervisor at the National Centre for Social Research, France, in 1989. He served as an elected member of the Algerian Higher Council of Education from 1995 to 1998. At the same time, he served as a member of the Executive Committee of the Council on Social Science Research in Africa (Codesria) in Dakar, and was the Vice-President of the African Association of Historians. Chenntouf has published the following with the university publisher in Algiers: *Le monde contemporain* in 1983, *L'Algérie politique* (*1830-1954*) in 2003, *Le Maghreb au Présent* in 2003, and *Etudes d'Histoire de l'Algérie* (*18e-19e*) in 2004. He completed another book dealing with *Algeria in the Face of Globalisation*. The book was published in 2004, as part of the Codesria series.

Cheikh Guèye is an Urban Policy Officer at the *ENDA Dialogues et Prospectives Politiques* in Dakar, Senegal.

Hamdy Abdel Rahman Hassan is a Professor at the Faculty of Economics and Political Science, Cairo University, Egypt. He acquired a Ph.D from Cairo University (Egypt) and Maryland University (USA) in Political Science. Hamdy has held several senior academic and administrative positions during his career. He was Director of the UNESCO Chair for Democracy and Human Rights in Jordan and Vice-President of the African Association of Political Science (AAPS) in North Africa. He is a prolific author in his fields of expertise, with more than 40 publications to his name. In 1999, he won the State Prize in

Political Science for his book, *Studies on African Political Systems*. In 2002, he served on a task group formed by the Egyptian Foreign Ministry to evaluate Egyptian African Policy, and in 2003, Hamdy was appointed president of a committee responsible for the production of a new 'Islamic Curriculum' for elementary education in the United Arab Emirates.

Serigne Mansour Tall is a Research Assistant at the *Institut International pour l'Environnement et le Développement* (IIED), Sahel Programme, Dakar, Senegal. He joined the IIED in 1998, where his focus is that of the institutionalisation of participatory methods and approaches in West Africa. He holds a Doctorate in Geography and is fluent in Wolof and French, and has a working knowledge of English.

List of Figures

2.1: Organogram of the Egyptian Government
Structure.. 26

2.2: Number of Egyptian Military Officers Serving
in Cabinet, 1951-1981 32

List of Tables

6.1: Growth, Employment and Redistribution: Trends
in Set and Realised Objectives, 1996-2001 149

6.2: Gini-Coefficient by Race/Population Group –
1975, 1991 and 1996; 1995-1998............................ 152

6.3: Change in Income Deciles for Black South Africans,
1975-1996.. 153

6.4: Percentage Share of Total Income by Race/
Population Group.. 153

6.5: Change in Personal Disposable Income Per Capita
by Population Group, 1995 and 2000...................... 154

6.6: Poverty Levels in South Africa, 1996 –
Comparative Trends, 2000.. 155

6.7: Job Losses or Gains in the Period Between
1991 and 2000 160

6.8: Overall Job Gains and Losses, 1996-1999 –
Select Trends, 2002... 161

6.9: South African Human Poverty Index (HPI) and
Indicators in the Southern African Development
Community Region, 1998.. 166

6.10: Human Development Index (HDI) 168

7.1: Analytical Approach and Operationalisation.......... 205

7.2: Change in National Party Political Representation
(1994-2004) 215

SAMPLE OF COUNTRIES STUDIED

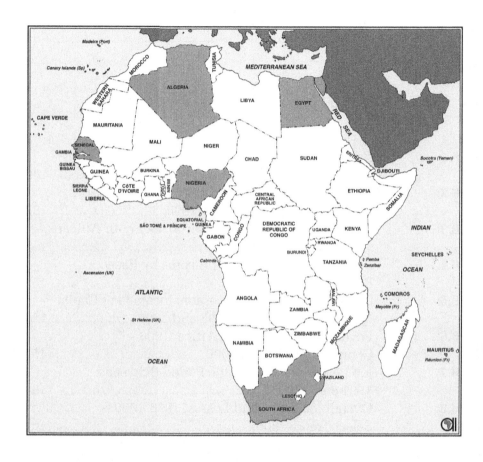

Source: Africa Institute of South Africa, 2005.

African Political Elites: The Search for Democracy and Good Governance

Introduction

Francis Nwonwu and Dirk Kotze

Why study political elites? Interest in elites emerged in the social sciences already in the nineteenth century and continued in the twentieth century in the works of Gustave Le Bon (*Psychologie du Socialisme*), Gabriel Tarde, Scipio Sighele, Pasquale Rossi, Vilfredo Pareto, C. Wright Mills (*The Power Elite*), Gaetano Mosca (*The Ruling Class*), Roberto Michels (*Iron Law of Oligarchy*), Max Weber, Karl Mannheim and Joseph Schumpeter.

By introducing a study on elites, one ought to provide a perspective on the relative importance of such a genre. One can start by looking at the extent of publications on the topic. Tessy D. Bakary compiled a comprehensive bibliography of elite studies in general, and on African power elites in particular. An authoritative publication in political science is the *Annual Review of Political Science,* which has appeared annually since 1998. In their 155 published chapters, not a single one looked at elites as a political science topic. On the other hand, Research Committee 2 of the International Political Science Association concerns 'political elites'. Elite studies have a distinctly individualistic (liberal) undertone, and are therefore challenged today by the theories of communitarianism of Amitai Etzioni and others. Studies of elites tend to concentrate on elites' individual or interpersonal dynamics, especially in decision making, and therefore rely considerably on the theories of rational choice and social actors. Institutionalism in all its forms (e.g. new institutionalism, historical institutionalism), which has become a very popular academic approach, especially in the form of constitutionalism in the context of transitions, is normally excluded from elite studies. From a French perspective – which has in general a more positive look at elites – Bakary identified three motivations to focus on elites in Africa, namely:

1. After independence, African states continued to be directed or governed by a ruling class. The fundamental distinction in those societies was between those who had power and those who did not. It again raised the perennial question: Who governs? For Bakary the question 'who?' is more interesting than the question 'what?'.
2. The number and quality of studies devoted to African politics motivated an increased focus on the 'power stratification' or the relationship between group leaders in African societies.
3. It was also motivated by a theoretical and methodological consideration. The institutional approach to the new states was judged to be insufficient. This view argues that studies about elites ('*le haut*') cannot be reduced to institutional matters such as the constitution, the political system or parties.

Elite studies can either be purely descriptive or informed by assumptions about society and human nature. In its descriptive form, it concentrates on those 'in top positions', normally premised on the assumption that they are the people who matter most, and take the real decisions in a society. Paying attention to others in less prominent social positions would be a waste of effort, because they are not considered as influential in decision making and other political activities. The elites are therefore representative of their societies and are the best reflection of what is happening in their societies. Kotzé and Steyn elaborated on this point by quoting the political scientist David Easton. According to them, Easton asserted that all political decision making regarding the allocation of scarce resources in a political system was made by elites. The relevance of studying elites is therefore justified by their assertion that an understanding of the attitude of elites may provide an explanation of a government's policy preferences and performance judgements regarding certain policy issues.

Elites studies can also reflect pertinent views on society and the sociology of politics. It was originally intended to discredit, refute or replace the Marxist theory of class conflict. Mosca, Pareto and Michels developed a doctrine of rule by an elite of superior people. At the same time, it was an attempt to revive power relations and social hierarchy similar to those in the feudal period, to counter the new democratic ideas of equality. Michels' *Iron Law of Oligarchy* for example, postulates the inevitable emergence or presence of a small group, who will inevitably control political power in any society. The formal organisation of bureaucracies unavoidably leads to oligarchy. All such organisations are eventually dominated by a small, self-serving group, who achieve positions of power and responsibility. Michels believed that this oligarchy would become enthralled with its elite positions and would increasingly take decisions that protect its power, rather than address the interests of the constituencies, which they are supposed to serve. Ultimately, it believes that it is indispensable and more knowledgeable than those it represents.

Michels commented on Pareto's view of elites, especially his notion of 'circulation of elites'. According to Pareto, no association can function without a dominant class. However, this class is not guaranteed longevity and is unavoidably subject to decay; a new dominant class arises from the people. Michels maintained that people can never govern themselves democratically but their rulers (elites) change continually. Michels differed from Pareto in the sense that Pareto described an absolute change in leadership, while Michels saw a perennial amalgamation between old and new elite elements. According to Michels, the old aristocracy (elites) does not disappear and does not make way for new groups of rulers. It always remains at the head of nations, which it has led for centuries.

However, the old aristocracy does not rule alone but is forced to share this status with new rulers. The aristocracy of birth is accompanied by the aristocracy of government clerks, money and knowledge, to constitute the new ruling class. This observation is particularly relevant for many societies in Africa, where independence, liberation and democratisation have not necessarily replaced one set of elites with another. Instead, the two sets of elites often strike a compromise and function as a new unit of rulers.

The first set is a deterministic view that political society is unavoidably hierarchical in nature, irrespective of the political system, democratic or autocratic. Often the expression is used: "some are born as leaders and others as followers". In its most extreme form of bio-determinism, it is a justification for fascism: racial superiority is used to rationalise a racially determined political hierarchy and elite, while at the bottom, ostensible racial inferiority is a justification for the other's subjugation. Leadership (Führer and Il Duce) is an extension of this logic. Elite studies are therefore not necessarily a value-free exercise, and those involved in this exercise should make the rationale for their choice of study explicit from the start.

In the latter part of the twentieth century, Karl Mannheim and Joseph A. Schumpeter reinterpreted the concept of elites in an effort to reconcile the ostensible contradictions between democracy and elites. Mannheim maintained that the actual shaping of policy was in the hands of elites. However, this is not inherently undemocratic, because individual citizens have the opportunity to make their aspirations known at certain intervals. Schumpeter, for his part, was the political free-marketer. In his view, democracy was an institutional arrangement to arrive at political decisions by means of individuals' free choice to decide in a competitive environment, whom they wished to support. Politics is therefore competition between elites for the support of the electorate. People have the right to accept or reject the political leaders who rule them, based on free competition among aspirant leaders for the vote of the electorate.

Marxism provides another perspective on elites. Its economic determinism is the foundation of a social configuration based on classes. Class struggle is per definition a contestation of the economic structure and its associated class structure. Elites are therefore, firstly, defined by their ownership of a nation's means of production. These ownership patterns are symbiotically related to the concentration of power in a society. It follows that a change in the structure of ownership implies a change in elites. Some might therefore argue (quite dogmatically) that by embracing elite studies as a research endeavour, this endorses a capitalist mode of thinking.

Ironically, the 'dictatorship of the proletariat' in Leninism is a continuation of the elite mode of thinking, and in ideological terms, will only disappear in a classless, communist society. Socialism has become embedded in the notion of elites. During the Stalinist period, for example, elite formation reached the point of what Milovan Djilas referred to as 'a new class' of privileged state bureaucrats.

In modern Marxism, as a social science, the hierarchical configuration of the class structure, as essentially a bipolar concentration of political and social power, is questioned. The classical Marxist notion of economic classes evolved effortlessly into a political, dominant class and a subjugated class. These overlapping concepts became useful analytical tools for dissecting the colonial situation. Frantz Fanon, in particular, utilised this for his concept of the 'national middle class'. Also the French Marxist, Louis Althusser, analysed society in terms of four sub-systems (i.e economic, political, ideological and theoretical). According to him, the manner in which they are combined determines the mode of production or social system. The state is a function of the specific manner in which these sub-systems interact with one another. These sub-systems constitute a diversity of power centres in a society and each one relates to the elite in question.

Elite studies are also a bone of contention in postmodernism. Studies of elites are often accused of applying the assumption that 'it is only important men who create history'. By studying Churchill, Mao, Hitler, Gandhi, Ataturk or Nkrumah, one studies the history of Britain, China, Nazi Germany, India, Turkey or Ghana. Postmodernism emphasises relativism and the uniqueness of each person. Elites are therefore not necessarily representative of their societies. The ordinary person is not less significant than the important man. Postmodernism is therefore decidedly anti-elitism.

Reaching the point of a generally acceptable definition of elites is understandably a difficult task, because it is partly determined by the aforementioned approaches. Joseph LaPalombara described the elite as a group of people who, "at any one time, and for continuing periods of time, more or less determine the major public policies and how they will be implemented". Higley and others (1976) defined elites as "those persons who, individually, regularly, and seriously have the power to affect organizational outcomes". Burton concentrated his definition on authority and influence, and defined them as "a body of people holding positions of authority or influence in a major institution of society; individual members of an elite were called opinion leaders, opinion makers, or policy makers depending on the nature of the institution". Hennie Kotzé (1991) consolidated these definitions by describing the national elite as

> all those people who occupy strategic and influential positions in society and in organizations which can use their organizational power in the political process. In most studies on national elites, this group is defined operationally as comprising those people who fill the top positions in the 'largest and most resource-rich' political, governmental, economic, military, professional, communications and cultural organizations and movements in a society.

These definitions raise another dimension of elites: how can we concretely identify them in any society? LaPalombara referred to persons involved in policy decision making; Burton referred to those with positions of authority or influence; and Kotzé concentrated on those in top positions. Operationalisation of the concept, for the purpose of identifying elites, can be done in at least five different ways, namely:

1. The 'positional' approach: employees' institutional positions in the organogram of their working environment determine who are in the 'top positions' and therefore qualify as elites.
2. The 'reputational' approach: a person's reputation amongst others, as a person of influence or authority, irrespective of his/her official position, is the definitive factor. Two classic examples of this operationalisation are the approach used by Soviet-watchers to determine the internal dynamics in the Kremlin, and the role played by Deng Xiaopeng in China until 1997, as *de facto* leader, while only being the Chairperson of the Central Military Commission.

3. The 'social stratification' approach (Warner 1949): this emphasises the notion that the elite is a class of influential persons, often referred to as the 'ruling class', 'political class' or 'dominant class'.
4. The 'decision making' approach: it focuses on those who take decisions or those who are influential and close to the decision makers.
5. The combined 'reputational' and 'decision making' approach.

According to Kotzé (1991), the positional indicator has become the dominant operational instrument in identifying the elites. He used the works of Robert Putnam, Higley and Moore, and Moyser and Wagstaffe in support of this conclusion.

If one moves the focus to the African continent, elites become an even more contested focus point. According to Manghezi (1976), the study of elites in Africa dates back to the 1950s, with the work of J. E. Goldthorpe. He was followed by S. F. Nadel and Peter Lloyd. Lloyd concentrated on West Africa and mainly on Nigeria. He divided societies in Africa into two categories: the elites and the masses. The elite, he divided into the elite proper, marginal sub-elites and earlier traditional elites. He described the elite as a small, homogenous and cohesive group with a similar background. He added that the elite members came from a humble social background and continued to maintain links with their villages, but were Westernised; they resided in the national or regional capitals and lived well. He noted that they also shared a common educational experience and belonged to the same formal organisation. In 1956, Nadel's appreciation of the elites in Africa differed markedly from Mosca and Pareto's view of the same:

> The elite is looked up to, and imitated, because it is credited with important gifts and desirable attributes. Thus the elite, by its very manner of acting and thinking, sets the standards for the whole society, its influence and power being that of a model accepted and considered worth following.

Nadel's presentation of the elites in the 1950s supported the perception that they constituted (and even continue to represent) a transplanted Western phenomenon and a colonial legacy, primarily responsible for the political ills in Africa, including the 'failure of the state'. In support of the notion that the elite is a foreign phenomenon, the argument is used that traditional African societies were egalitarian and therefore without elites. In the absence of private ownership of land, no social classes were formed. The argument is that colonial capitalism and colonial public administration established a social hierarchy, which cultivated national elites. Abner Cohen (1981) challenged this view and concentrated on the mystique of power as the foundation of eliteness. He argued:

> In stratified societies, power groups seek to validate and sustain their elite status by claiming to possess rare and exclusive qualities essential to the society at large. In some cases these claims are rejected by the rest of the society; in others they are accepted in varying degrees; and in yet others they are developed and bestowed by the society. In closed and formally institutionalized systems of stratification, these qualities are explicitly specified and organized. In more liberal, formally egalitarian systems, on the other hand, the qualities tend to be defined in vague and ambiguous terms and objectified in mysterious, non-utilitarian symbols and dramatic performances, making up what amounts to a mystique of excellence.
>
> ... The mystique is not just an ideological formula, but is also a way of life, manifesting itself in patterns of symbolic behavior that can be observed and verified. The ideology is objectified, developed, and maintained by an elaborate body of symbols and dramatic performances: manners, etiquette, styles of dress, accent, patterns of recreational activity, marriage rules, and a host of other traits that make up the group's lifestyle.

As a general and simplified observation, the study of elites in Africa remains relatively underdeveloped and not many publications have appeared in recent years. A notable exception was Codesria's 2003 Session of its Governance Institute, with the topic: 'The African Power Elite: Identity, Domination and Accumulation'. The formal rationale for this focus is that

> the challenge of systematically studying the African power elite and the mode by which it governs has become urgent not only because of the conceptual/theoretical dead-ends to which much of current received wisdom leads, but also because a better understanding of

the nature, composition and renewal of the elite is critical to our understanding of the governance of the public sector.

The unfulfilled promises of democratisation and the continuing susceptibility to violent conflicts point to power as the main concern: the way in which the rulers or elites appropriate, accumulate, structure, legitimate and reproduce this power.

Another exception in the literature of elites in Africa is the recent study conducted by Hennie Kotzé and Carly Steyn (2003) about elite perspectives on the African Union (AU) and New Partnership for Africa's Development (NEPAD) in Nigeria, Senegal, South Africa, Algeria, Kenya, Uganda and Zimbabwe, based on surveys conducted in October and November 2002. Their choice of states coincides considerably with that of this publication, and therefore provides a convenient point of reference. The two authors used a positional sampling method to identify the elites in eight societal sectors in each of the states. Their samples included variables on gender, age, country of birth, education levels, first-generation elite or inherited elite-status, and place of upbringing (urban or rural).

Contemporary studies of politics in Africa are quite often concerned with transitions or the breakdown of democracy. In these studies, the premise is predominantly that structural or systemic factors (such as economic growth rates, ethnicity or violence) are the main explanatory variables for these phenomena. In the research on the relationship between democracy and development, it has become increasingly clear that democratisation cannot solely depend on enhanced economic growth, constitution making, elections or greater respect for human rights. Increasingly, it is acknowledged that the role of powerful political actors (elites) deserve more attention. Important determining factors for democratisation are therefore the values, skills and decisions of elites and the unification of divided elites.

Several of the 'third wave' studies of democratisation in Africa in the 1990s, presumed that political mismanagement and the lack of economic development were primarily the result of poor leadership (elites). Therefore, the solution would constitute good governance by good leadership. Structural deficiencies in the economy and society, and inefficient or inappropriate political institutions, were therefore made subject to a predominantly individualised, social actor explanation. Gorbachev and F. W. de Klerk, and later Nelson Mandela, epitomised this emphasis on a leader's personal convictions and personality, in contrast to defining attributes of their predecessors. Much of the developmental paradigm, applied in most recent years, since the discrediting of the economic structural adjustment approach, is premised on good leadership or political and public management.

South African constitutional negotiations in the early 1990s, however, served as a widely quoted model for a structuralist or institutional approach to conflict resolution. These negotiations provided an impetus to designing a standard formula for conflict resolution, in the form of a package consisting of political democratisation and constitution making, plus economic development. NEPAD combines this package with good governance, in the form of the African Peer Review Mechanism (APRM).

The divergent views on leadership (elites) versus structural explanations of economic and political successes and failures in Africa can be reduced to the agency-structure dichotomy explored in most social sciences. For the purpose of this introduction, the importance of elites serving as agents in their political systems, should be considered. The debate about who or what should be blamed for the socio-economic and political ills in Africa, and therefore how Africa should or could be modernised, depends partly on how the agent-structure debate is understood in the African context. Questions that emerge from this discussion relate to whether it was the state (structure) that failed or the leadership (agents) who failed, and what the solution to this might be, such as a restructured state with a new constitution and new institutions, or better leadership (new agents) in these states.

The dialectical relationship between the structure and agency is encapsulated in Anthony Giddens's theory of structuration. He prefers to see them as two sides of the same coin (duality) instead of two separate coins, which are both externally related (dualism). Duality means that social structures are constituted by human agency and are, at the same time, the medium of this constitution. They are internally related through social practices. Structures, therefore, do not exist on their own, but depend on the agents' knowledge about what they do.

Margaret Archer made an attempt to overcome shortcomings identified in Giddens's work, by incorporating an analysis of time into the relationship. She noted that structures have properties, which cannot be reduced to social practices. She also focused on the time gap between the original formation of structure, interactions then taking place within it, and the modified structure, that emerges from it. Her perspective on the dialectical interplay between structure and agency is therefore not only dualistic but also sequential, working with endless cycles: structural conditioning > social interaction > structural elaboration > structural conditioning...

The notions of the 'failed state', 'weak state', 'collapsed state' or 'soft state' have become an established paradigm in African studies. Its premise is based on either of the following:

1. The social contract as a mutual agreement for the state to monopolise power and force, and therefore to provide security for its citizens, which has failed; or
2. The Weberian notion of the state, consisting of institutions with the capacity to provide public goods to its citizens, which has failed.

Structure

Failure of the state, as an institution, is therefore reduced to the legacy of colonialism, the dependency of neo-colonialism, the inappropriate nature of the post-independence constitution, the artificial demarcation of the national state, and an unevenly developing economy. A new social contract is therefore a core requirement to address social dissent in the form of secessionist movements, rebel movements and internal wars, as well as military regimes. Democratisation, multiparty elections, national conventions or inclusive dialogues, a new constitution and governments of national unity, are the political institutional (structural) remedies. Economic growth, liberalisation and deregulation of domestic markets and becoming part of the globalised community, are but a few elements in the basket of economic restructuring. The agents (government leaders) are neutral factors, as long as they receive their institutional positions by constitutional means (i.e. elections). The election in Kenya, in 1991, was a good example of this approach. The election was part of an IMF-induced structural adjustment and 'democratisation' package, which disregarded the *content* of democratisation – especially the political leadership – and concentrated only on its *form* (multi-party contestation). The common wisdom that conflicts in African states are most effectively resolved by new constitutional frameworks and therefore by procedural democratisation, demonstrates an understanding that the essential nature of Africa's future is dependent on new social contracts and a Weberian state – in other words, a newly structured state.

Agency

Moeletsi Mbeki diagnosed the problem as that of the agents. In his mind, a predatory political elite has been primarily responsible for corruption and poverty in Africa. According to him, after colonialism, most African states were beset by elites, who saw the state as a means to acquire personal wealth. Mbeki's approach is to diversify the elites and emphasise the role of private sector producers (economic elites).

> While NEPAD may address some of the worst excesses of the political elites, it does not address the fundamental problem: the enormous power imbalance between the political elite and key private-sector producers. If the driving force behind sub-Saharan Africa's underdevelopment is the structural powerlessness of producers and therefore their inability to retain and control their savings, there will be no development in sub-Saharan Africa.

Mbeki's emphasis on agency is supported by a network of NGOs working in Africa, the African Human Security Initiative (AHSI). They observe that while external considerations, such as the international political-economic environment ("a structure"), provide an explanation for Africa's woes, they do not explain why some states have fared better than others. Their view is that "domestic factors such as the choices and actions of local political elites compounded rather than moderated the external factors in Africa's economic decline". One of the explanations for this crisis is that post-independence elites appear to have been overly concerned with their own uniqueness as liberators, therefore assuming a self-gratifying and imperial right to rule these states. Most Africans, therefore, sought to avoid 'the state' and to resort to 'informal' economy and politics. Implicit in this view is the assumption that change in formal structures will not short-circuit the endemic social and economic problems. New approaches to leadership and their association with institutions of the state, appear to be a necessary requirement for a more efficient state structure – a conclusion similar to Archer's theory of time and structure.

The interaction between structure and agency will not be conclusively clarified in this publication. This volume's main emphasis is on agency (elites) but the assessment of structures (AU and NEPAD) and their impact on democratisation and economic development, as a blueprint for Africa's modernisation, forms an important component of this study. NEPAD's Peer Review Mechanism is – at least in theory – an important instrument to bring the agency (good governance by the political and business elite) as close as possible to the structure (economic restructuring and development).

Composition of the Book

Scholars were commissioned to write opinion chapters on the political elites in Egypt, Algeria, Senegal, Nigeria and South Africa. Apart from discussing the peculiarities of each country from political, social and economic viewpoints, the chapters in this publication specifically address some of the key issues, which lean towards the notion that political elites are generally reluctant to practice democracy and good governance. Specific issues addressed in this volume include:

- The historical evolution of the political elite in the country
- The factors that contribute to a lack of political will among the elite to promote sustained growth, development and democratic governance
- The historical developments that gave rise to the conditions identified above
- The current socio-economic and political reforms being undertaken, if any, to achieve the goals and objectives of both the AU and NEPAD

- Mechanisms for managing access to the state and political succession, including party politics
- Institutional capacity of the state, relations between different branches of the state and the role of different tiers of government
- The current socio-political and economic situations in the country, as they affect the ideals of democracy and good governance;
- The scope and constraints of political participation of members of society with regard to ethnicity, race, gender, and religious beliefs
- The compatibility of the country's political culture, with regard to the requirements of NEPAD's African Peer Review Mechanism and code of conduct for leaders.

This volume presents current and immediate past factors that underpin African political elites' lack of commitment and political will to promote equitable distribution of resources; their persistence to cling to power, to suspend all democratic means of governance and to suppress the rule of law. It also examines the extent of commitment to good corporate governance and transparent democracy, which serve as preconditions for political stability. The latter, in turn, acts as the propeller and accelerator of economic growth, which proffers solutions to sustainable development. This, in turn, acts as a diagnostic barometer for assessing the performance of African political elites against the background of Africa's chequered history of political instability, economic stagnation and subsequent condemnation to the colossus of political, socio-economic and technological vicissitudes. Hopes are high that through this investigation, a pattern of political conduct will emerge and offer clues to a process of developing assessment indicators for measuring African leaders' ownership of a quantum of political will, or lack thereof, in promoting good democratic governance for equitable and sustainable growth and development.

This volume is presented in seven chapters. In Chapter 1, Hamdy Abdel Rahman Hassan presents and discusses the historical evolution of the Egyptian political elites from the post-revolutionary era under Nasser, to the neo-liberal economic and liberalised autocratic political regime of Mubarak. It highlights the intermediate Sadat rule as the era in which the Egyptian political system was transformed from a strong presidential system to a near presidential monarchy. During this period, influential relatives overwhelmingly became members of the ruling elite. The strong role of the military in Egyptian politics is stressed in this chapter. This political involvement climaxed with the military's assumption of power in 1952, and its continued maintenance of strong influence in the executive, up until 1977. The Mubarak era is marked by an attempt to amalgamate the policies of its predecessors to maintain some continuity, with the infusion of liberalism in the political and economic systems.

Chapter 2, authored by Francis Nwonwu, gives an account of the perceptions of both the political elites and civil society in Egypt on a number of new African initiatives, such as the transformation of the OAU to AU, NEPAD and the APRM. Respondents featured in this chapter spanned political elites within the government and the opposition, as well as academics, both serving and retired diplomats, the organised private sector, women's groups and non-governmental organisations, domestically and internationally based.

In Chapter 3, Tayeb Chenntouf presents an account of the roles of political elites in the political dynamics and reforms in Algeria. The chapter outlines the dynamic efforts made by the political elites in establishing a series of reforms, from economic reforms (1980-1985), to the inclusion of political and educational reforms from 1989 onwards, instituted by the incumbent President Abdelaziz Bouteflika. It is on record that he has subdued terrorism to a minimal level and that political stability is seen to have triumphed in Algeria. Currently, Algeria boasts three discernible and distinct political eras, namely the era of the 1950-1960s, the era of the 1980-1990s and the current period of reform that came to power in 1988 through the multi-party politics involving trade unions and political parties. This chapter, however, admits that a reproduction of authoritarianism seems to be simmering and reflects the lack of political will to accept change among those of the 'old brigade', or former political elites.

Chapter 4 discusses the structure and conduct of the political elites in Senegal. In the chapter, Serigne Mansour and Cheikh Gueye pose questions that portend some skepticism about the acclaimed excellence of the unique Senegalese democracy, for which the country is cited as being the ideal model in the sub-region. The chapter argues that democracy should not merely be perceived as the absence of coups, and that a smooth political transition should not be treated as the panacea of democratisation, because these are not indicators of a competent and accountable ruling class. The authors of this chapter contest that even with the perceived adoption of democratic principles, multi-partyism is interpreted as the sheer existence of various parties. Yet, citizens cannot participate fully in the political procedures, as they are heavily burdened by illiteracy and poverty. The chapter reveals a paradox of clientelism; excessive liberal democracy with numerous but somewhat ineffectual political parties; a free and independent press; as well as an active mass media in Senegal. The authors further query the kind of multi-party democracy in which citizens lack the moral courage and financial liquidity to actively participate. While the chapter lauds the contribution of Senegal in the birth of NEPAD, it questions whether this new initiative is another gimmick for milking states dry, or a positive paradigm shift. Whereas they endorse NEPAD as a new window of opportunity for Africa, they are skeptical about the top-down approach in its formation and dissemination.

In Chapter 5, Richard Iroanya discusses the dynamics of the Nigerian political elite, which has been marked by intermittent civilian *cum* military regimes. The post-independent Nigeria scarcely survived a decade of civilian rule before the onslaught of military intervention in January 1966, which led to the fall of what is historically referred to as the First Republic. The period between 1966 and 1979 was inundated by military coups and counter coups, and culminated in the civil war of 1968-1970. The second post-independence civilian regime, otherwise referred to as the Second Republic, lasted from 1979 to 1983. The emergence of another military regime, with its characteristic palace coups, counter coups and change of batons, took place between 1983 and 1993 and marked the birth of the Third Republic, with military dictators as heads of state and civilian professionals as technocrats, joining as cabinet members, when and where deemed appropriate, at both federal and state levels. The Fourth Republic started in 1999, under the leadership of a civilian head of state, following a general election in the same year. The current head of state, Olusegun Obasanjo, is one of the architects of a number of current African development initiatives, and the New Partnership for Africa's Development, in particular. It is argued in the chapter that for several reasons, the Nigerian society built much hope on and expected much political benefit from President Obasanjo. Firstly, he was the first-ever military head of state to voluntarily bequeath power to civilians in 1979. Secondly, he had suffered political incarceration under the notorious dictator Sani Abacha. Thirdly, he originates from the south, which is seen to have been politically marginalised and dominated by the north, both under the military and civilian regimes.

In Chapter 6 Susan Booysen assesses the impact of the apartheid and post-apartheid elites' political will and governance, in terms of socio-cultural development in South Africa. It reviews the political transformations from apartheid to democracy, and the change undergone by the African National Congress (ANC), from a liberation movement to a political party. Furthermore, it assesses the political will of the ruling elite to accede to democracy, good governance, the establishment of competitive electoral systems, and the adoption of the rule of law.

Chapter 7 is the final chapter of the volume. Susan Booysen discusses the role of the political elite in South Africa, in terms of economic management and the pursuit of sustainable economic growth and development. The chapter reviews the macro-economic policies and strategies adopted to address some of the nagging issues of unemployment, income inequity, education, service delivery and poverty. It highlights some economic policies and development initiatives by the post-apartheid government, such as Black Economic Empowerment (BEE) and the Growth, Employment and Redistribution (GEAR) macro-economic programmes. These programmes, among others, aim at improving the economic well-being of the previously disadvantaged sectors of the South African society, including black people, as laudable of the initiatives of government. However, some skepticism is expressed that their effectiveness is contingent upon the effectiveness of the democracy, and the commitment of the political elite, in translating these programmes into practical instruments of positive change.

Notes and References

1   Tessy D. Bakary, *Les Elites Africaines Au Pouvoir: Problématique, Méthodologie, Etat des Travaux,* Talence: Centre d'Etude

d'Afrique Noire, Institut d'Etudes Politiques de Bordeaux, 1990, pp 53-117.

2 Stephen Mulhall and Adam Swift, *Liberals and Communitarians*. Oxford: Blackwell, 1995; Amitai Etzioni, *The Spirit of Community: The Reinvention of American Society*. New York: Touchstone, 1993.

3 Bakary 1990, pp 4-5

4 Hennie Kotzé and Carly Steyn, *African Elite Perspectives: AU and NEPAD: A Comparative Study Across Seven African Countries*. Johannesburg: Konrad-Adenauer-Stiftung, 2003, p 2.

5 Alpheus Manghezi, *Class, Elite and Community in African Development*, Uppsala: Scandinavian Institute of African Studies, 1976, p 70.

6 Spunk Library, http://www.spunk.org/library/places/germany/sp000711.txt, 27 July 2005.

7 Roberto Michels, *First Lectures in Political Sociology*, New York: Arno Press, 1974, pp 63, 75-76.

8 Manghezi 1976, p 70.

9 Milovan Djilas, *The New Class: An Analysis of the Communist System*, London: Thames and Hudson, 1957.

10 Hennie Kotzé, *Elites and Democratization: An Exploratory Survey of South African Elites*, Stellenbosch: Centre for South African Politics, University of Stellenbosch, 1991, pp 2-3.

11 Wright C. Mills, *The Power Elite*, New York and London: Oxford University Press, 1956; Kotzé and Steyn 2003.

12 F. Hunter, *Community Power Structure*, Garden City, New York: Doubleday, 1963.

13 Robert A. Dahl, *Who Governs? Democracy and Power in an American City*, New Haven: Yale University Press, 1961.

14 Robert V. Presthus, *Men at the Top: A Study in Community Power*, New York: Oxford University Press, 1964.

15 Robert Putnam, *The Comparative Study of Political Elites*, Englewood Cliffs, New Jersey: Prentice-Hall, 1976.

16 L. Higley and G. Moore, 'Elite Integration in the United States and Australia', *American Political Science Review*, vol 75, no 3, 1981.

17 G. Moyser and M. Wagstaffe (eds), *Research Methods for Elite Studies*, London: Allen & Unwin, 1987.

18 S. F. Nadel, 'The Concept of Social Elites', *International Social Science Bulletin* (UNESCO), vol 8, no 1, Fall 1956.

19 P. C. Lloyd, *The New Elites of Tropical Africa*, London: Oxford University Press, 1966.

20 Quoted by Manghezi 1976, p 74.

21 Abner Cohen, *The Politics of Elite Culture: Explorations in the Dramaturgy of Power in a Modern African Society*, Berkeley: University of California Press, 1981, pp 1-3.

22 CODESRIA, 'The 2003 Session: The African Power Elite: Identity, Domination and Accumulation', http://www.codesria. org/ Archives/Training_grants/governance/governance_inst03. htm, 23 August 2005.

23 Kotzé and Steyn 2003, pp 2-3.

24 Kotzé 1991, p 2.

25 Andreas Bieler and David A. Morton, 2001, 'The Gordian Knot of Agency-Structure in International Relations: A Neo-Gramscian Perspective', *European Journal of International Relations*, vol 7, no 1, 2001, pp 7-10.

26 For example, Patrick Chabal and Jean-Pascal Daloz, *Africa Works: Disorder as Political Instrument*, Oxford: James Currey, 1999; William I. Zartman, *Collapsed States: The Disintegration and Restoration of Legitimate Authority*, Boulder, Colorado: Rienner, 1995.

27 Moeletsi Mbeki, *Perpetuating Poverty in Sub-Saharan Africa: How African Political Elites Undermine Entrepreneurship and Economic Development*, London: International Policy Press, 2005, p 9.

28 AHSI, *Human and State Security in Africa – A Conceptual Frame work for Review* (Draft 3), http://www.africanreview. org/forum docs/Theorydraft3.doc, pp 12-14.

29 Mark Cooper, 'The Demilitarisation of the Egyptian Cabinet', *International Journal of Middle East Studies*, vol 14, 1992, pp 203-225.

NORTH AFRICA

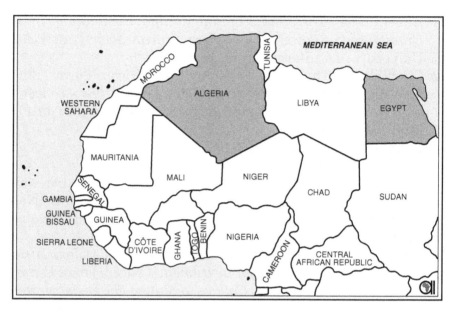

Source: Africa Institute of South Africa, 2005.

1. Political Leadership in Egypt:
The Case of Halt Democracy

Hamdy Abdel Rahman Hassan

Introduction

Egypt's political elite is a unique entity. In spite of the changes in the political orientation of the ruling elite throughout the past four decades, the elite itself did not undergo any radical changes, keeping its basic traits, thus almost violating the established theoretical approaches and paradigms.

One of the most important traits of the Egyptian political elite is the pivotal role played by the institution of the presidency. An analysis of the structure of the ruling regime in Egypt and the mechanisms of inclusion into the political elite reveals that the legitimacy of the system is grounded in the persona, or the post of the president. The evolution of the Egyptian political elite has been directly related to the institution of the presidency. Ever since Egypt's adoption of a republican system, the president has been elected through a popular referendum. Thanks to this mechanism, the president has enjoyed absolute legitimacy and a great deal of authority. None of the Egyptian presidents occupied this post because of a majority vote. They all came to power because of a near consensus.[1]

In spite of the general traits, which have characterised the Egyptian political elite ever since the 1952 revolution, one cannot make an assessment of the sincerity of the current elite's support of a new participatory approach, reflected in the introduction of political and economic reforms, without first studying the origins and evolution of this elite. The need is expressed to examine the elite from the point of view of its social background, its renewal and its contribution to the development process, its confrontation with external challenges (the structural changes of the new world order) and internal problems including political corruption among others.

The Development and Structure of Egypt's Political Elites

The Origins and Evolution of the Post-Revolutionary Elite

On the eve of the Nasserist regime, Egypt's political elite comprised a small minority of pre-revolutionary elements and a great majority of technocrats, bureaucrats and army officers. The small pre-revolutionary minority diminished considerably for failing to adequately understand the sources of its new legitimacy. Family ties, class origins and political expertise ceased to be solid sources of legitimacy. The formulation of policies and its effective implementation became a function of these close ties, which connected members of the elite with the president, rather than public acceptance and political as well as social support. Acceptance and support became directly related to the legitimacy of the president.[2]

Nonetheless, the military establishment represented the most salient source of the political elite during the Nasser era. Trusted army officers were assigned ministerial and important bureaucratic posts. The intensive representation of the army within the government did by no means insinuate that the military establishment had imposed its control over the president or the political elite. It was normal to draw on the army official base in occupying leadership positions within the state, in view of the fact that the regime, which had relinquished power in the aftermath of 1952, had done so because of a military coup. However, military officials did not assume their positions due to their efficiency. The military establishment, on its part, did not exert any pressures on the president to ensure its privileged status. Trusted military officers were assigned governmental posts based on their loyalty to the president, with the aim of reinforcing the military protection of the new regime. Some senior officers who helped Nasser make the revolution were entitled to be consulted in decision-making processes; many of them served as powerful vice-presidents. However, the real challenge to Nasser's charismatic leadership came from Field Marshal Abdul Hakim Amer, his close colleague and the number-two-man in the regime. Amer came close to making the army his personal 'fiefdom'. After the suspicious death of Amer, those who challenged Nasser were purged and generally, he (Nasser) enjoyed nearly unquestioned presidential authority. As soon as Nasser's regime ensured its power, the role played by the military personnel began to wane gradually. Nonetheless, the military establishment played a salient role in the late 1960s, as well as in the 1970s and 1980s in backing the executive authority.[3]

Thus, the civilian or military character of the ruling elite had not been the most important attribute characterising the country's political elite. The most important trait had been the network of personal and mutual utilitarianism, which regulated the inclusion process into the ranks of the elite, a quality that is of vital importance in providing a full and comprehensive understanding of the Egyptian elite structure. The recruitment of elite members in Egypt is embedded within a network of unofficial loyalties, which had turned the political system into an entity that was based on personal bases rather than on an institutional structure. This recruitment process has guaranteed a certain degree of political and ideological homogeneity within the ranks of the elite. Objective criteria for the inclusion within the ranks of this elite have receded, pushing personal loyalties to the fore, which would inevitably have repercussions, in terms of the technical and professional efficiency of the state apparatus. Against this backdrop, institutional regulations and regulated political competitiveness diminished considerably. Owing personal allegiance to the ruler of the Egyptian political elite, the head of state was not subjugated to any kind of official supervision.[4]

The Sadat Era

The personalised character of rule persisted throughout the rule of Sadat, who managed to prevent the emergence of any organised opposition within the ranks of the political elite, notwithstanding the disagreement voiced by some of its members. Sadat succeeded in purging the political elite from the pro-Nasserist ideological factions. The elite, quite aware of its inability to intervene in the decision-making process and to voice any kind of opposition, turned into a silent docile entity. The president's powers were cemented by the 1971 constitution, which augmented the president's hegemony over each institution. The president stands on top of the executive authority, which in its turn presides over the ministerial council, whose head is assigned by the head of state. The president makes the ultimate decision regarding the assignment of ministers. He is also entitled to assume the presidency of the ministerial council, to summon extraordinary cabinet meetings and to preside over its sessions in the presence of the premier.

The president's authority is interlinked with the legislative authority. He has the right to issue decrees, which have the effect of law. As per the constitution, the president has direct authority to issue resolutions and to sign agreements after obtaining the approval of a two-third majority from the legislative council. Thus, enormous powers were vested in the presidential institution. Frequent cabinet reshuffles during the Sadat era were a reflection of his attempt to reinforce and augment his hegemony, which stands proof to the marginal role played by the political elite in the decision-making process in his era.[5]

Despite Egypt's move towards political liberalisation since the mid-1970s, the presidential establishment dominated its regime heavily. The president has enormous constitutional and legal power in a society that has a long tradition of a paternalistic political culture. It was clear that almost all influential bodies of the state machinery were affiliated to the presidential office, either formally or informally. In order to implement any project in Egypt, it has to be endorsed by the presidential institution.

As Ayyubi notes,

> Any important policy or project must normally have the blessing of the
> president before it can proceed with a reasonable prospect of suc-
> cess.[6]

One can describe the Sadat years of power as a tumultuous decade,
disrupted by a war with Israel in 1973, prolonged military tension
(1970-1973 and 1974-1978 respectively), economic upheaval, including bread riots in 1977, and isolation from Egypt's Arab allies
(1978-1980). Sadat responded frequently by employing coercion – he
arrested opponents and brought tanks into the streets when his power
was threatened.[7]

Sadat succeeded in transforming the presidential establishment
into a sort of presidential monarchy. He formed a kind of royal family
of influential relatives in his entourage. He also resurrected the traditional legitimacy by insisting on his role as the lord of the Egyptian
family. However, how did Sadat ensure his longevity and survival in
power? He was actually able to consolidate his power through the
establishment of a strong client network of politicians, who enriched
themselves by the often-illicit manipulation of the economic opening
his policies afforded.[8]

The Mubarak Era

During the Mubarak era, no drastic deviations from the Sadat years
were sensed. An important change though was introduced through
the means and measures adopted for the implementation of these
policies.

The most important aspects of the ruling Egyptian elite (the president and the ministerial elite) during the Mubarak era were the continued and vital role played by the president of the republic in
political processes. In addition to the constitutional and legal framework, the structure is predicated on a very important base of power,
namely the leadership of the ruling National Party – a fact that
cemented Mubarak's hegemony over both the legislative and the
executive authorities.[9] Demands were repetitively made for a refor-
mation of the constitution, especially concerning the article on the
reelection of the president. Those demands, which insisted on

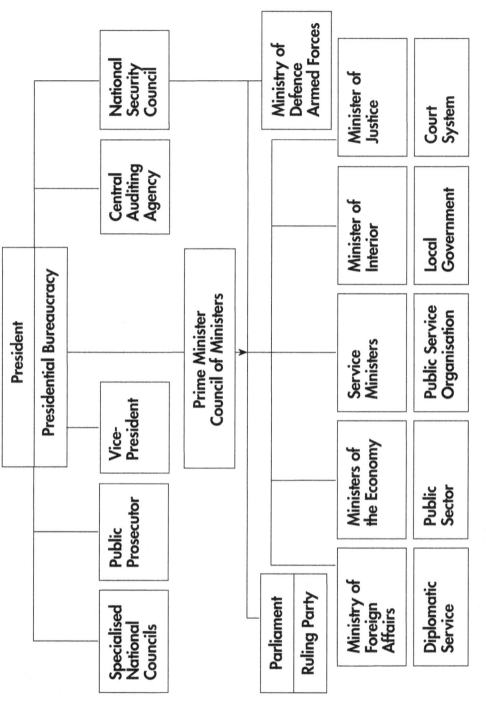

Figure 2.1: Organogram of the Egyptian Government Structure

restricting the tenure of the president to two terms, were practically ignored, with the main justification being the absence of an acceptable alternative, which in its turn, reflected a crisis in the recruitment process within the political elite.

Opposition parties asked the president to relinquish his leadership of the National Party, noting that this state of affairs presented the National Party with a relative advantage in the political domain and confined the political elite within its boundaries. However, one should note that the monopoly of the elite National Party did not necessarily reflect its success in recruiting prospective elite members. Rather, it reflects the party's ability to lure members of the elite into becoming leading elements.[10]

Apart from this, another important issue remains within the spotlight and raises doubts more often than not, namely President Mubarak's insistence on not assigning a vice-president, ever since he assumed power. His basic justification was the difficulty of locating a suitable candidate for that post – a fact that raises fears of the possibility of the eruption of an eventual power struggle. The president, in his turn, waved these fears as irrelevant, asserting that the proper mechanisms for the transfer of power had been explicitly defined by the constitution.[11]

A number of studies indicated that the true reason for this position could be the desire to avoid troubles, which might arise as a result of choosing a vice-president with a certain background or orientation. Would the vice-president, for example, be civilian or military? The assignment of a civilian vice-president for the first time since 1952 could possibly arouse the fears of the military establishment. The enrollment of a military vice-president, on the other hand, could give rise to criticism regarding the truth about democratic reforms in Egypt.

There has been a diminishing number of military personnel among the ministerial elite (around 15% from 1981-1995; 25% during the Sadat era, compared to 34% during the Nasser era). This, however, does not signify a move away from the role of the military establishment in the political system, noting that the president himself is of a military background, and is vested with enormous powers by the parliament, not to mention the continued role of the military establishment in a number of civilian domains. The armed forces represent the backbone of the system, providing support and protection in times of crisis. The crushing of the rebellion staged by the Central Security Forces in 1986, attested to this role.

The retreat in the representation of the military personnel within the ministerial elite was coupled with a continued increase in the numbers of academics, bureaucrats and technocrats – the academics occupying top rank, followed by the technocrats, the bureaucrats and the military personnel. Thus, the ministerial elite during the Mubarak era was predominantly bureaucratic and technocratic. The great majority of the elite members were enrolled in accordance with professional criteria that had nothing to do with political and ideological affiliations.

The ruling elite during the Mubarak era has thus included elements of continuity and elements of change, compared to the ruling elite during the reign of his predecessors. The most salient of these continuity elements are the continued pivotal role played by the president and the ongoing importance of the military institution for the ruling regime. Elements of change, on the other hand, are reflected in the diminished number of military personnel within the ranks of the elite and the refusal by the president to assign a vice-president, not to mention the absence of a challenge from within the ranks of the elite.

The Social Origins of the Egyptian Political Elite

The Egyptian official elite has drawn its members, since the 1950s, from the middle and lower-upper classes, who had the financial means to create professional and academic elements, capable of assuming higher administrative, political and military positions. Several studies indicate that the only change, which affected the Egyptian institutional elite within the executive apparatus, was the change in the background of its constituent members, from military to technocratic personnel. The social origins, however, remained unchanged.[12] The elite kept its ties with its middle class origins, which did not imply, however, that this elite represented the interests of its class of origin. Ever since the 1950s, Egypt's political elite ceased to become a distinctive class of homogenous social and political orientations. The years of socialist transformation had witnessed differences and disagreements among the members of the elite, regarding social and economic transformations and the augmentation of state control over means of production, as opposed to the encouragement of the private sector. In a nutshell, the ranks of the elite witnessed a left-right schism.[13]

The right-wing embarked on enhancing its position within the political system, especially in the aftermath of the 1967 defeat, which caused cracks in the legitimacy of the regime, affecting its control over society. The most important elements of this right-wing were the leaders of the political, bureaucratic and technocratic organs at the top of the state apparatus, who made use of their position to accumulate material wealth, political influence and a huge network of utilitarian connections. Members of the elite exploited their high political posts within the state apparatus and the public sector to accrue such wealth. They made a sudden transformation from one social stratum to the other, making their affiliation to the middle class rather dubious. This social mobility caused a transformation of affiliation, loyalty and social, as well as political alliances among members of the elite, who exerted enormous pressures to effectuate the transformation of the political regime towards the end of the Nasser era, augmenting these orientations during the Sadat regime.

All of the above could provide an explanation of the controversial policies adopted by the official political elite, which stood in stark contrast to the interests of the classes they originally represented. The elite gradually began to represent the interests of the capitalist class, which then struck an alliance with the elite, as manifested in the mutual interests and even social and marriage ties.[14]

Keeping in mind the vital role played by the president in the transformation of the regime, one cannot ignore the fact that this official elite had been in charge of implementing policies and had played an undeniable role in formulating these policies. The elite also remained an indispensable source of information, which had undeniable effects on the decision-making process.

This right-wing was augmented by the business elite, which, in spite of its crisis during the years of socialist transformation, had retained its importance within the economic sector. The medium-sized landowners elite, who had inherited the top of the social hierarchy within the countryside, subsequent to the removal of the large landowner class in the aftermath of the agrarian reform laws, could not be ignored either.

This right-wing exerted pressure on the state to encourage the private sector, and to put restrictions on the activities of the public sector. It criticised the nationalisation experience and demanded an end to state control of economic activities, encouraging increased cooperation with the West. During the Sadat era, a number of decisions had been reached, which reinforced this trend and proclaimed the right-wing victory over the leftist wing, especially after the proclamation of the economic open door policy, which entailed the reinstitution of traditional capitalist, bourgeoisie and bureaucratic elements as the cornerstone of the social base effecting this transformation.[15]

The influence of this right-wing increased even further by the mid-1980s. A number of examples display the regime's response to the demands extended by this wing, whose effectiveness was predicated on the fact that its interests coincided with the policies and pressures exerted by the international financial institutions, which intervened to reinforce this trend.[16] It is clear that Egypt under Mubarak witnessed a growing private sector. Therefore, the Egyptian Businessman's Association representing this sector has sought to influence the government's economic policies by establishing institutional links with the government, just as the profession's syndicates and labour unions have sought to influence government policies.[17]

The Military and the Political Elite

The political role played by the military is a salient issue in the analysis of Egypt's political elite, noting the undeniable political role played by the military over the past decades, which ended in the assumption of power by the military in 1952. The crisis of the political and social system before 1952 has led to an assumption of power by young officers, on behalf of the rebellious middle class, whose political organisations had largely contributed to the political socialisation of the officers.[18]

While it had taken Nasser only two years to confront his civilian opponents, he was unable to fully control and de-politicise the army for almost five years. Nonetheless, the army remained a parallel power to Nasser's civilian authority, which became entrenched after he had cast off his military attire. Even though Nasser had grounded his legitimacy on socialist achievements and his revitalisation of Arab nationalism, he resorted to the military to accomplish the mission. The reconstruction of a robust army, with the support of the Soviets, was one of Nasser's cornerstone Arab policies, particularly in light of his preparation for an imminent military confrontation with Israel. Nasser also depended largely on the armed forces in implementing his social transformations. Army officers thus occupied top positions within the government and the economic institutions.

However, the first half of the 1960s witnessed some poignant changes, manifested in the heterogeneous character of the official political elite. This elite contained civilian and military elements, as well as noting the role played by the technocrats in the implementation of economic and social development programs. The defeat of the army in 1967, however, paved the way for public dialogue of the ills and fiascos of military leadership. Political reforms thus became imperative.[19]

Under the rule of Sadat, the military character of the Egyptian political system became even more diluted. Out of 35 persons occupying the top positions of the ruling political hierarchy, only 8 were of a military background (22.8%) – an ongoing trend during the Mubarak era. It was therefore natural for the political role played by the army to undergo drastic changes under the multiparty system, inaugurated in 1976, in spite of the limitations on the freedom of party politics. One should, however, note that after 50 years of the army's monopoly of power in 1952, and after more than 25 years of multi-party politics, every single president and vice-president was of a military background.[20]

This significant political role played by the army was strongly criticised. Demands were made for a disclosure of the budget allocated to the armed forces, and the subjection of the army budget to the Central Auditing Apparatus. These actions rejected ties between the army and the ruling National Democratic Party (NDP), on the one hand, and those connecting it to the presidency on the other. The military legitimacy of the ruling party and the presidency became the target of opposition voices, which cynically referred to the assignment of military personnel as governors in almost all governorates. Defence strategy, military expenditures, in addition to privileges reserved for the military, all became a focal point of disagreement between the civilian elite on the one hand, and the ruling military-civilian elite on the other.[21]

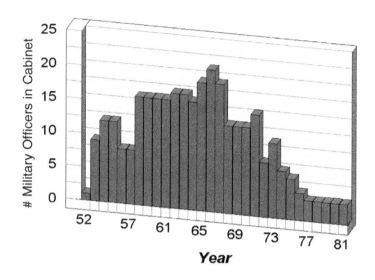

Source: Mark N. Cooper. "The Demilitarization of the Egyptian Cabinet", *International Journal of Middle East Studies*, vol 14 (1982), pp 203–225.

Figure 2.2: Number of the Egyptian Military Officers Serving in Cabinet, 1951-1981

Towards the end of President Nasser's rule, and because of the military defeat in the 1967 war, the number of senior military officers in government positions and cabinet positions began to decline. Yet, in spite of the diminishing number of military personnel within the official political elite, the military establishment remains the most important political structure within the state. It represents the president of the republic, who presides over all aspects of political life. It enjoys a separate budget comprising loans, external military grants and profits amassed by the expanding military enterprises. The military has proven to be the most capable and reliable institution, in terms of management and discipline, against a background of chronic crises, which the civilian institutions failed to confront over the past few years.

Since the 1970s, the Egyptian military has played an expanding role in economic issues in Egypt. President Hosni Mubarak has a vision of the beneficial role the military could play as an engine for economic growth and development. This led to what Robert Springborg refers to as the horizontal expansion, in terms of the role of the military, into the Egyptian national economy. The military's role in Egypt's economy is represented in four primary sectors: military industries, civilian industries, agriculture, and national infrastructure. [22]

On the other hand, because of the lack of deep public support and genuine political legitimacy, the Mubarak regime depends heavily on the military. It provides him with security, support and guards his interests in society. As a result, many officers came to play an increasingly important role, enriching themselves and becoming more and more prominent in their role as members of the state elite.[23]

Renewal and Replacement Within the Egyptian Political Elite

The Egyptian political elite is a closed but relatively inclusive elite, which is one of the reasons for its survival. This elite managed to make use of its diversity to guarantee its seclusion, controlling all channels of political nomination and recruitment. The relatively large size of the elite has enabled the ruling regime to enjoy political legitimacy, which helped augment the feeling that alternative elites or elite rotation was dispensable.[24]

The structure of the simultaneously closed and inclusive elite has proven to be an obstacle to elite circulation. This circulation was also hampered by a multiplicity of factors. First, there was the supremacy of personal and unofficial ties, as the determinants of inclusion into the elite. Second, there was limited political accountability of the executive elite in Egypt, noting that they are not elected officials and do not represent any particular interest group. This elite does not participate in the making of policies and is thus not held politically accountable. They remain, despite this, accountable to the president.[25]

On the other hand, the circulation of elites (in the sense of redistributing posts among its members) guarantees the continuity of the official political elite in Egypt within the executive, legislative and bureaucratic organs. Re-circulation remains the cornerstone of the continuity and survival of the elite in Egypt, as it gives a false impression of real elite circulation.

Elite transformation is always a function of the presence of a viable political opposition, which confronts the existing elite and expresses its demands through the official channels or via more clandestine ways, either in a peaceful manner or by the use of more violent means. The absence of a viable opposition in Egypt has led to the hegemony and continuity of the elite. Ever since the adoption by the regime of a multi-party system in 1976, some form of legitimate but decorative opposition was allowed, within the framework of what was known as *façade democracy*. Meanwhile, the regime kept an iron fist over the making of policies and the recruitment of the elite. While the entry into the official political elite is restricted to those who do not engage in any opposition activities, the ruling regime works diligently to prevent the transformation of those who leave the ranks of the elite, into opposition forces. Those departing the elite are assimilated into the wider elite circle, occupying various upper-posts within the different state organs. Forces and organisations, apart from the opposition parties, are subjected to certain limitations, which prevent their transformation into counter-elites. Professional syndicates are monitored and their loyalty is guaranteed through the recruitment of their members or the control of its elections.[26]

The Contribution of the Elite to the Development Process

The development policies adopted by the Egyptian government since 1952 focused largely on the economic and social spheres. Economic and social development had precedence over political development. The passage of five decades notwithstanding, one cannot claim that these two domains have scored reasonable success points.

In spite of the numerous factors that led to this unfortunate state, the political leadership shoulders a great part of the responsibility for the deterioration of development levels, noting the failure of the political elite in the aftermath of 1952 to adopt a comprehensive national development programme.[27] Prevalent development ideologies in the Nasser era had depended largely on a socialist orientation, predicated on a state-controlled economy. The Sadat epoch, on the other hand, reflected a capitalist orientation based on economic liberation, the encouragement of the private sector and the withdrawal of the state from economic activity. The first decade of the Mubarak era, for its part, witnessed an attempt to combine the two ideologies of his predecessors. President Mubarak stressed the continuity of the major policies adopted by Sadat, reforming them though, in accordance with the orientations prevalent during the Nasserist era.[28]

Economic Crisis

In spite of this compromise, the development process did not proceed at an acceptable pace throughout the 1980s. The crisis became even more acute in a number of sectors and was further exacerbated in the 1990s, in spite of the initiative to drop the foreign debts made by some nations (United States, Saudi Arabia, Qatar and the United Arab Emirates) in the aftermath of the second Gulf War. The most significant manifestations of this crisis were an increase in unemployment and a higher inflation rate, not to mention slow growth, unbalanced development programmes and economic dependency on the outside world. Egypt was forced into starting negotiations with the International Monetary Fund (IMF) regarding the initiation of an economic reform programme predicated on the rules and regulations defined by the Fund. Egypt launched a reform programme in 1987 under the sponsorship of the IMF. However, this programme was not comprehensive enough to alleviate all prevalent economic problems. From the very beginning of 1990s, the economic situation was exacerbated by the political turmoil in the Gulf.[29]

The Egyptian economy heavily relied on four financial sources: oil, tourism, the Suez Canal revenue, and workers' remittances, mostly from the oil-rich Gulf countries. During the years 1990-1991, Iraq's sudden invasion of Kuwait and the subsequent Gulf War dealt a serious blow to all Egyptian financing sources. The return of around 700 000 workers from the Gulf countries, together with declining tourist numbers, compounded all the existing economic problems. Adding to these was the heavy service burden of the debt, totalling US$46 billion, which became an imminent threat to the economy.[30]

The Liberalisation of the Economy

The Egyptian government once again signed a reform programme in April 1991, the most important principles and policies of which had been the liberation of the economy, affording a free hand to the market economy, cutting public expenditures, restricting the economic role of the state, and accelerating the privatisation process in an attempt to encourage the local and foreign private sector to contribute to the development process. The necessary facilities and guarantees were extended to make sure this programme was enforced. Thus, the capitalist approach to development had been pushed largely to the fore under Mubarak.

Nonetheless, a number of public policies adopted by the Mubarak regime reflected some elements of continuity, such as the inconsistency of some public policies, which revealed a general sense of confusion and a lack of clear-cut objectives, not to mention the frequent cabinet reshuffles and the ineffective implementation of the policies.

At the economic level, the state seemed hesitant in adopting an integrated economic policy to deal with the crisis, whether in legislative terms or in the implementation mechanisms. The state did not adopt the economic reforms programme until the early 1990s, under the pressure of deteriorating economic conditions, and thanks to the economic and financial facilities granted to the Egyptian government, as a reward for its position during the second Gulf War, as well as being due to the pressures exerted by the IMF.[31]

The first phase of the economic reforms programme implemented during the first half of the 1990s, took off with the unification of exchange rates, the reduction of the deficit and the materialisation of a commercial exchange surplus, as well as the increase in state foreign currency reserves. Those economic achievements notwithstanding, they were accomplished at a very high economic and social cost, shouldered greatly by the low-income sectors. The monetary reforms had repercussions on the prices of commodities and services, as well as the reduced subsidies and the tax increases, which contributed to a widening gap between the haves and the have-nots, largely affecting the marginalised communities. This phase had, as a result, a host of problems and negative economic repercussions, first among which were the increased poverty rates, unemployment, the reduced per

capita share of the Gross Domestic Product (GDP), as well as the accu-
mulating economic and social burdens, which the poor had to
endure. Manifestations of administrative and financial corruption
were also visible.

Research

The regime's handling of other aspects of the development process
did not deviate largely from the aforementioned pattern. In the field
of scientific research, a host of drawbacks are visible, first being the
negligible budget allocated to scientific research (not exceeding 0.2%
of the national income), which is rather trivial, even compared to
other Third World nations. Another manifestation is the absence of a
tangible scientific strategy defining priorities of scientific research
and coordination between the various research centres, as well as the
lack of prerequisites for scientific research (such as laboratories,
equipment, updated references and databases). The great majority of
research institutions suffer from the absence of a rational management system, noting the supremacy of bureaucratic criteria. Research
institutions also suffer from the absence of appropriate policies and
plans that meet the needs of the different sectors, thus, resulting in a
divorce between the research community and the executive organs.
Proposals offered by the former are rarely translated into practical
policies and resolutions.

The technological policies, on the other hand, suffer from similar
shortcomings, such as the absence of a clear-cut technical strategy, as
well as the absence of integrated plans for the development of domestic technical capacities. Priorities in the fields of research and development are not crystallised, which is, in its turn, reflected in the
technological dependency on the outside world, as well as the impor-
tation of inappropriate technologies.

Politically, the Mubarak regime is still carrying the same traits
manifested by his predecessors' regimes, from 1952 onwards.
However, evidence suggests the gradual expansion of the political
domain, which has started to include some active players, who had
hitherto been excluded. Some analysts regard the Mubarak regime as
more flexible and less inclined to the kind of individual rule, which
had become so obvious during the rule of his predecessors. One could
safely say that political pluralism had resulted in a limited democracy

that experienced moderate expansion during the Mubarak era. This state of affairs had several manifestations. First among them is the relative freedom enjoyed by the press, as well as the independence of the judiciary and the larger number of political parties that came into existence, as well as the rejuvenation of the civil society. These manifestations, however, are not proof of a real democratic transformation. They refer, rather, to the mixed nature of the system, which manifests democratic traits side by side with authoritarian ones. The fledgling democracy is still subject to the restrictions of the authoritarian political traditions, as well as the personalised nature of authority and the inappropriate constitutional framework to democratic transformation. Other manifestations are visible and include the continued enforcement of martial law, among other freedom-limiting legislations, the absence of a real multiparty system, noting the hegemony of the ruling party, headed by the president, the limited freedom enjoyed by the press and the rigged elections. Some of these violations remained, even after the imposition of judicial supervision on election proceedings. The lack of independence of civil society organisations and their abstaining from political participation remain visible manifestations of restricted democracy.

Thus, while the Egyptian government embarks on its structural adjustment policies, the democratic reforms seem to be fluctuating and the possibilities of elite circulation remain remote in the absence of real structural changes.[32]

Confronting Developmental Challenges

Political and Administrative Corruption

President Mubarak's campaign to purge the state organs of corruption and to fight malpractice, culminated in the trial of a number of corrupt personnel who had amassed considerable fortunes during the Sadat era. These measures did not decisively put an end to the phenomenon, which reemerged to become one of the most salient problems haunting Egyptian society today.

According to Ibrahim, there are two interpretations of the phenomenon of political corruption within Egyptian society, under the rule of Mubarak. The first stresses that political corruption is an international phenomenon and that the manifestations of corruption in Egypt are individual incidents that do not constitute a phenomenon. The government, according to this interpretation, is adamant on pursuing the culprits and on trying them. The second interpretation, on the other hand, emphasises that administrative and political corruption has become a public phenomenon and that in spite of the integrity of the Egyptian judiciary, organs, which are in charge of collecting data and investigating cases of corruption, manifest negligence and inefficiency.[33]

Evidence attests to the proliferation of the phenomenon of political and administrative corruption within Egyptian society (nepotism, embezzlement, fraud and the abuse of the public office) to the interest of a small minority, not to mention the misuse of public funds.

The phenomenon of political and administrative corruption in Egypt is characterised by the following views.[34]

First, that political and administrative corruption is connected to the state organs, whether directly or indirectly, thus weakening the governmental capacity to put a leash on the phenomenon. The involvement of high officials in corrupt practices spills over into the lower echelons of the state organs. Thus, it turns corruption into an indivisible part of the operation process of a score of state organs and institutions. Within the generally corrupt political and administrative climate, some social groups climbed their way up directly and indirectly into influencing state organs and using this influence to amass considerable fortunes, usually through illegal means, leading ultimately to the entanglement of wealth and authority within Egyptian society.

Second, corruption is not confined to the central state organs, but extends to municipalities. Corruption has also extended to some non-governmental organs, such as political parties, syndicates and the voluntary sector. Many factors induce corruption, among these are: the inefficiency of auditing and accountability mechanisms; the waning of respect for the law; in addition to the state refusal to abide by court rulings. They also include the deteriorating economic and living conditions of a large sector of state employees, due to the economic and social transformations, as well as the absence of proper control mechanisms.

Third, some warning voices were raised in anticipation of the proliferation of political and administrative corruption in Egypt because of the implementation of economic reforms predicated on privatisation. The sale of public enterprises to the private sector, both domestic and foreign, opens the door wide to corrupt practices. These conditions exacerbate, even further, the acquisition by multinational corporations of former public enterprises.

Fourth, the phenomenon of political and administrative corruption has a score of negative repercussions, such as the increased economic and social discrepancies, the mismanagement of national resources, the loss by the political regime of its legitimacy, noting that a large sector of the population accuses the leadership and the elite of being responsible for the proliferation of corruption. Political and administrative corruption creates a fertile ground for the growth of political and social opposition, which rejects the status quo and seeks change. The sectors affected by such practices, manifest a willingness to oppose the system.

Despite attempts by the ruling regime to confront corruption, the problem seems to persist. Corruption cannot be effectively confronted without first addressing the economic, social and political problems which create the appropriate environment for the expansion of this occurrence. Measures of accountability and the rule of law should be activated to put an end to the phenomenon.

Challenges from the International System

The New World Order has imposed certain challenges on the elites' management of the development process in more than one way. These include the continued pressures exerted by the International Financial Institutions on developing nations, including Egypt, to adopt economic reforms policies. Egypt has embarked on the implementation of an economic reform programme since the early 1990s, in response to pressures from the IMF and World Bank condition. Regardless of the degree of commitment displayed by the Egyptian government to some elements of the programme, the government is undeniably responsive to the criticisms and recommendations issued by the IMF regarding its economy. This attitude has been clearly reflected in the accelerated privatisation process implemented by the Egyptian government over the past few years, in response to the repeated criticisms voiced by the IMF regarding the slow rate of privatisation.

The economic achievements scored by the Egyptian government during the first phase of the programme have been at an enormous social cost, shouldered mainly by the poor and the low-income sectors. The adopted policies are expected to manifest a visible positive effect on those affected classes and are aimed at creating new employment opportunities. Furthermore, the policies should expand the economic base over a reasonable time span. Unless these expectations are met, the repercussions of the implementation of these reform programmes would be sure sources of social tension and political instability. This would most likely occur if the manifestations of political and financial corruption and the economic and social discrepancies persist.

On the other hand, economic reforms programmes implemented by the Egyptian government, in agreement with both the IMF and the World Bank, pave the way for the intervention of multilateral corporations and their acquisition of Egyptian assets, thus affecting economic evolution dynamics. The activities of these corporations are also greatly stigmatised by corrupt practices, particularly in view of the inefficiency of the state's management of the privatisation process, and the ineffective accountability and transparency processes. All these factors would inevitably augment the dependency of the Egyptian economy on international corporate capitalism and would lead to the proliferation of political and administrative corruption.

Egypt Within the Unipolar Context

Egyptian-American relations are among the most important elements of the external environment affecting Egypt's economic and political development. In its relationship with Egypt, the US administration alternately makes use of the carrot and the stick approach. The overall American aid to Egypt is estimated at around US$1.2 billion annually, not to mention the partnership agreement between the two countries. In a certain view, the American administration repeatedly resorted to threatening the country with cutting its aid or by cancelling it altogether, in an attempt to exert pressure on the Egyptian government. The Egyptian leadership has reiterated more than once that Egypt does not expect an incessant inflow of aid. Prospects for an interruption of this aid were great, noting the Egyptian government's disclosure that Egypt was not the only beneficiary, referring to the US profits resulting from the conditionality clauses and the strings attached to this assistance.

The Communication and Information Revolution

The great developments achieved in the field of communication and information, as well as the incessant inflow of information, ideas, humans and capital across the boundaries, imposes on the Egyptian leadership a new set of challenges and dictates a renewed interest in structural developments, which are more responsive to such challenges. Manifestations of globalisation make economic, political, cultural and technological adjustments imperative to maximize the profits and minimise losses.

The Egyptian state, under Mubarak, has failed to meet the political needs of development. Public developmental policies were greatly marred by shortcomings, which negatively affected its effectiveness in achieving development. The state has also failed in tackling the distributive crisis. Policies of structural adjustment have led to an increased economic and social gap, including the proliferation of financial, political and administrative corruption. Manifestations of economic dependency on the outside world have had their political, economic and social repercussions domestically. As noted by Korayem, the Egyptian economy is "still suffering from low per capita income, high unemployment, and abiding political instability".[35] To eliminate these maladies as soon as possible could be the most important and ultimate target of all economic policies at the present moment and in the future.

Conclusion

Egypt is a presidential state which, despite an ongoing democratisation process, is still characterised by a dominant rule of the presidential establishment. All authoritative and influential bodies of the state machinery are necessarily affiliated to the presidential office, either formally or informally. It seems that the old paternalistic and pharaonic relationship in Egypt perpetuated the hegemony of the Egyptian presidency. Almost every Egyptian ruler is aware of this cultural and historical element. Sadat himself affirmed his role as a pharaoh in the political system. He told Ahmmad Baha'aul Deen, a prominent writer:

> O Ahmmad, Abdel Nasser and I are the last Pharaohs. Did Abdel Nasser need any written rules to follow? I don't need such rules either!

The rules, which you are talking about, have been issued for our successors. Ordinary presidents such as Mohammed, Ali and Omar will follow us. And of course, they will need these rules.[36]

There is no doubt that Sadat conceived the democratisation process as his initiative and domain of action. He tried to control the whole political arena by establishing his own laws, such as the shame law and the law of 'protecting Social Peace'. Thus, Sadat believed that he was a democracy-giver. He once warned his political opponents that "democracy has sharp teeth".

The 1971 constitution affords the Egyptian president enormous authority, with the potential of reaching tyranny. When this constitution was amended in May 1980, the pivotal role of the president was enhanced. For example, according to the amended Article 77, "The term of the presidency shall be six Gregorian years starting from the date of the announcement of result of the plebiscite. The President of the Republic may be re-elected for other successive terms."[37] Mubarak enjoyed this amendment, and has been the official head of state for almost 25 years, officially longer than any Egyptian ruler since Mohammed Ali.

The procedures for the choice of new president remain the same, through the People's Assembly (Article 76). In fact, there is a continuing hegemony of the ruling NDP over parliament. As Mubarak is the president of both the republic and the NDP, he chooses NDP candidates for the People's Assembly. This means that the Assembly, despite its enormous constitutional powers, is a mere rubber stamp in the hands of the president and that of his executive.

According to the constitution, the president determines the general policies for his executive. He also possesses great influence over the military institution. Thus, to suggest or implement any new project in Egypt, the president or anybody affiliated to the presidency must endorse it. It is well known that the credibility of any governmental achievement is rendered to "the wise guidelines of the president".[38] In addition to this, "...if any danger threatens the national unity or the safety of the motherland or obstructs the constitutional role of the state institutions, the President of the Republic shall take urgent measures to face this danger, direct a statement to the people and conduct a referendum on those measures within sixty days of their adoption".

This tendency of authoritarianism continued to shape the type of political culture of the Egypt in modern times. Hence, the present Egyptian constitution of 1971 afforded the presidential institution enough powers to overshadow and overrule the other legislative and judicial institutions of the country.

Recommendations

Several questions continue to be posed on the effectiveness of the current political elite and its ability to bring about democracy and good governance as viable instruments for Africa's development. One such question is: what are the future prospects of this authoritarian political structure? The challenges faced by Egypt and the South in general, make the introduction of radical changes imperative, especially regarding the redistribution of wealth and power. Three basic demands are indispensable. These include:

- The introduction of constitutional changes to strike a balance between the state and society, on the one hand, and to redress the imbalance within state institutions, on the other. It should be mentioned that these constitutional changes are strongly requested by official and un-official opposition forces.
- Working diligently to redress the inherited cultural moulds and patterns, which ascribe absolutist attributes to the ruler, who is cast in a holy light, and remedying the imbalance manifested in the central role played by the state *vis-à-vis* the civil society institutions.
- A new generation of political leadership, which is more responsive to the challenges of the present phase, should emerge. A new generation of leadership, with a clear-cut vision of the future, has become imperative to introduce the necessary radical changes to the decision-making processes.

Notes and References

1 It was Gamal Himdan who explained the nature of the central state in the context of ancient Egyptian civilization. He believed that Egypt's hydraulic society produced a social contract, which

was based on the Nile waters. This contract between the ruler (Pharaoh) and the ruled dictates: "Give me your land and hard labor and in return I will give you my water". It was not odd for absolute autocracy to be a natural feature of pharaonicism. For more details see, Gamal Himdan, *The Personality of Egypt: A Study on the Genius of Place*, Cairo: Dar al-Hilal, 1993 (in Arabic); Nazih Ayyubi, 'Government and the State in Egypt Today' in Charles Tripp and Roger Owen, *Egypt Under Mubarak*, London: Routledge, 1989; Karl A. Wiyyfogel, *Oriental Despotism*, New Haven: Yale University Press, 1957; Ahmad Sadeq Saad, *Social and Economic History of Egypt: In the Framework of the Asiatic Mode of Production*, Beirut: Ibn Khaldun, 1979 (in Arabic) and Maissa al Gamal, *The Political Elite in Egypt* or *al Mustakbal al Arabi*, no 166, December 1992, pp 38-41.

2   *Ibid.*, p 42.

3   See P. J. Vatikiotis, *The History of Egypt*, Baltimore: Johns Hopkins University Press, 1980, pp 383-385; Ibrahim Aoude, 'From National Bourgeois Development to Infitah: Egypt 1952-1992', *Arab Studies Quarterly*, winter 1994, vol 16, no 1, pp 1-23.

4   Maissa al Gamal, *The Political Elite in Egypt: A Case Study of the Cabinet Elite*, Beirut: The Center for the Study of Arab Unity, 1993, pp 51-56.

5   *Ibid.*, pp 107-128.

6   Nazih Ayyub op. cit., p 2.

7   For more details about the tumultuous decade of Egypt under Sadat, see Kirk J. Beattie, *Egypt During Sadat Years*, New York: Palgrane, 2001, pp 60-79.

8   The patrimonial and arbitrary hand of Sadat can be illustrated by his murkier decisions made in the year prior to his assassination, namely to forbid the sale of meat in Egypt for a month, to bury the pharaonic mummies in Egypt and the attempt to force Egyptian shop owners to open for business during European hours (9:00am-5:00pm) rather than Egyptian hours (9:00-1:00pm and 5:00-9:00pm, with a break during the hottest part of the day) see Aoude, op. cit., pp 5-7.

9   Hassanin Tawfik Ibrahim, *The State and Development in Egypt*, Cairo University: The Center for the Study of Developing Countries, 2000, p 230.

10 Abdel Salam Noweir, 'The Political Elite in Egypt, The Third Annual Conference of Young Scholars: The Political Elite in the Arab World', Cairo University: The Center for Political Studies, November 1995, pp 12-13.

11 For more details about the crisis of political succession under Mubarak see, George Ziad, 'After Mubarak', *Middle East*, October 2000, no 305, p 17.

12 Maissa al Gamal, *The Political Elite in Egypt*, op. cit., p 45.

13 Abdel Salam Noweir 1995, op. cit., p 21.

14 Samia Said, *Who Owns Egypt: An Analytical Study of the Social Origins of the Open Door Policy Elite within the Egyptian Society 1974-1980*, Cairo: al Mustakbal al Arabai, 1986, pp 226-227.

15 *Ibid.*, p 117.

16 Abdel Salam Noweir, op. cit., pp 25-26.

17 See A. K. Banerji, 'Egypt Under Mubarak', *Round Table*, January 1991, no 317, p 7.

18 Egypt maintains a large and professional army, which numbers 500 000 personnel – comparable in size to the armies of Syria, Iraq and Iran. In the context of Egypt's peace with Israel, the size of its military greatly exceeds that of its most likely opponents – Libya (70 000 personnel) or the Sudan (118 500 personnel). See, The International Institute for Strategic Studies, *The Military Balance 1994-1995*, London: Brassey's, 1994, p 125.

19 Ahmed Abdallah, 'The Armed Forces and the Evolution of Democracy in Egypt', in Ali al Din Hilal (ed.) *The Egyptian Political system: Change and Continuity*, Cairo University: The Center for Political Studies, 1988, pp 212-214.

20 Robert Satloff, 'Army and Politics in Mubarak's Egypt', Washington DC: *The Washington Institute for Near East Policy*, 1988, p 14.

21 Ahmed Abdallah., op. cit., pp 215-216.

21 For more details see Robert Springborg, *Mubarak's Egypt: Fragmentation of the Political Order*, Boulder: Westview Press, 1989, p 107.

23 Since the rise of Islamic fundamentalism and political violence in the 1980s and 1990s, the military has intervened directly in Egyptian society. Its power has extended by the emergency law, in place since 1981, which blurs the fine line that divides the military from the civil sphere in society. See also, Larry P.

Goodson and Soha Radwan, 'Democratization in Egypt in the 1990s; Stagnant or Merely Stalled?', *Arab Studies Quarterly*, winter 1997, vol 19, no 23, p 9.

24 Maissa al Gamal, *The Political Elite in Egypt: A Case Study of the Ministerial Elite*, op. cit., pp 50-51.

25 *Ibid.*, op. cit., pp 213-214.

26 *Ibid.*, pp 215-218.

27 *Ibid.*, op. cit., p 220.

28 Aoude 1994, op. cit., p 5.

29 Alia El Mahdi, 'Aspects of Structural Adjustment in Africa and Egypt', Cairo: Center for the Study of Developing Countries, 1997.

30 Karima Korayem, 'Egypt's Economic Reform and Structural Adjustment', Working Paper No 19, Cairo: The Egyptian Center for Economic Studies, October 1997; Joseph Licari, 'Economic Reform in Egypt in a Changing Global Economy', OECD: Development Center, Technical Papers, December 1997, no 129.

31 Hassanein Tawfik Ibrahim 2000, op. cit., p 240.

32 Hassanein Tawfik Ibrahim, *The Political Economy of Economic Reforms*, Cairo: The Center for Political and Strategic Studies, al Ahram, 1999, pp 54-68.

33 Hassanein Tawfik Ibrahim, *The State and Development in Egypt*, op. cit., pp 240-256.

34 *Ibid.*

35 Korayem 1997, op. cit.

36 Ahmmad Baha'al Deen, *My Dialogues with Sadat*, Cairo: Dar Al Hilal, 1987, p 64.

37 The Egyptian Constitution as amended in 1980.

38 For further discussion on this subject see, Mona Makram-Ebeid, 'From Single Party Rule to One Party Domination: Some Aspects of Pluralism Without Democracy', Lopez Garcia and Gema Munoz (eds), *Elections, Participation and Transitional Politics in North Africa*, Madrid: Instituto Internacional de Cooperación con el Mundo Arabe, 1991.

EGYPT

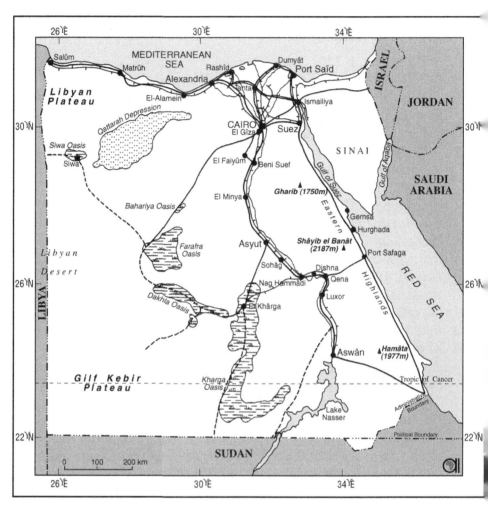

Source: Africa Institute of South Africa, 2005.

African Political Elites: The Search for Democracy and Good Governance

2. Egyptian Stakeholders' Perception of the New Partnership for Africa's Development (NEPAD)

Francis Nwonwu

Introduction

The generation gap in the Egypt's politics is rapidly closing. This, because the new generation of political elites has acceded to democracy, while the older generation is inadvertently compelled to accept the new dispensation. The overall effect is that there have been improved democratic principles and a more practical democracy in Egypt. Some centres of excellence, among them the Centre for Arab and African Studies, assist with the integration of African development initiatives, such as the African Union (AU) and the New Partnership for Africa's Development (NEPAD), into civil society, as a mechanism for creating fuller participation and a sense of belonging in the African forum and its many development initiatives. The Centre for Arab and African Studies plays a dynamic role in the activities of the African Political Science Society (APSS). Some ten years ago, one of its directors was the president of the APSS. Indeed, the centre also publishes the Arabic version of the APSS's newsletter.

A number of the new generation politicians, especially in the National Democratic Party (NDP) are very committed to the promotion of democracy and good governance in the country. They, however, admit that democratisation takes time and in the case of Egypt, they envision three to five years for the full transition into democracy. On the other hand, the traditional leaders are not keen on joining the transformation and the democratisation process. To them, even 20 years are not long enough to achieve full democracy. In 2002, the NDP held its fifth yearly conference, in which it looked at a new structure for the party, assessed new leaders and new organisations. The committee, which was set up to reorganise the party, is led by none other than Gamal Mubarak, the son of the president himself. Under his dynamic and youthful leadership, the party is seen to be more democratic and more creative, in terms of hatching new initiatives. Under this new dispensation of young leadership, the party has established the National Council of Human Rights, pursued more democratic policies and agendas, and introduced greater transparency in the business of government. Other parties are taking a cue from the NDP, following its fast pace in adopting democratic reforms. Among the 17 democratic parties in Egypt, those which have distinguished themselves most in this pursuit of democracy are the Arab Nasserite Party (ANP), Wafd Party and the Right Party.

The political leadership in the country is highly rated by the society, especially among academics, who are usually very critical and oftentimes have put the government on the firing line. This chapter investigates the views of the Egyptian society, including serving and retired politicians, intellectuals, university academics and research organisations, diplomats, the mass media, non-governmental organisations (NGOs) and civil society, on the performance of the country's political elites. It also assesses the commitment of the Egyptian elite to African initiatives, especially in terms of NEPAD. The account given in this chapter follows a ten-day survey conducted in Cairo, in August 2003. The aim of the survey was to seek the views of selected political elite members and other stakeholders in the governance of the country on issues such as democracy, governance, the AU, as well as the NEPAD initiative. Oral interviews were scheduled and conducted with selected members of government, private researchers, development agencies and NGOs for the purposes of this research.

The chapter is structured in four parts. The first section provides an overview of the Egyptian political structure and the political elite in relation to democracy, freedom of the press and gender equality. The second section examines the opinion of both the ruling elite and the rest of Egyptian society on a number of African political initiatives, particularly NEPAD. The third part examines the roles and attitudes of different social and professional groups in the country, including university dons, research organisations, NGOs and the international development organisations, especially the United Nations Development Programme (UNDP). The fourth and final section delivers a summation of the aforementioned contents and conclusions reached.

Political Systems and Governance in Egypt

Egypt operates a multi-party democracy with as many as 15 active political parties. There is a functional judicial and legislative system and a constitutive supreme court on the one hand, and the executive and legislative arms of government on the other. The country operates a presidential system of government with strong executive power resting on the president. The government rules through constitutional means and holds general elections, as prescribed in the constitution. However, there is very limited competition in presidential elections.

The current multi-party system of democracy in Egypt is a departure from the historical and feudal system of leadership under the pharaohs. The transformation from the pharaoh era of the country's history to the Nasser regime is not fully documented but Hamdy[1] gives an account of the chronology of transformation from the Nasserian epoch to the present period.

This process of transformation is indicative of the substantial existence of political will to imbibe and entrench democracy in Egypt. It is a widely held view that the political system of Egypt has evolved and changed for the better and stands the test of time as regards its stability and sustainability. The observation is that there currently exists good security and stability in the country, which complements the political will of the elite for the establishment of good governance.

Speculations are rife that the right-wing or conservative elite, who sees the political transformation as inimical to the perpetuation of its conservative ideology, resorts to some unorthodox means to attempt to intimidate the democratic elites and the government. Religious fundamentalism and fanaticism, as well as political extremism, have served as instruments for expressing disapproval of current views on democracy and political modernisation as advocated by the political elite. In Egypt, there is no discernible demarcation between politics and religion. This unholy union of the two interests tends to breed elements of mistrust, as well as act as an instrument of reprisal between people and groups of different political followings. The ruling elite faces the daunting task of holding together its fragile democracy within the ethics and tenets of its religious beliefs, and at the same time, protecting its sovereignty and security, which it fears threatened by foreign insurgents. The country now enjoys a sense of stability, freedom and liberty, having beefed up security to prevent the infiltration of foreign terrorist insurgents, who have been accused of attempting to destabilise the government and taint the image of Egypt in the eyes of the global community.

Spotlight on the Political Elites in Egypt

Democracy and Governance

Many schools of thought among academics, and a crop of past members of the diplomatic corps, believe that the government and current politicians are deliberately keeping some political and intellectual elites from participating in the business of government. These critics believe that those in power feel threatened by the cadre of people outside the government and therefore keep them at bay in order to avoid threats to their privileged positions. This view is complemented by scholars, who posit that the ruling elite is composed of a circus of close political relatives and associates, who see opposition as a threat to its hegemony. The government of Egypt is very much a part of a good social governance objective, and is involved in disease eradication, through the adoption of better health delivery systems, undertaking comprehensive educational reforms, the creation of employment, and creating better job opportunities for young graduates.

Mayek[2] expressed the view that the political elite should be awarded a clean bill of health on the parliamentary elections, which he passed as free and fair. While he believes that elections are free, he seems to limit this assertion to elections in sub-Saharan Africa, and adds that in the Arab north, such conditions of free and fair elections do not stand, as government fears the political parties and seizes every opportunity to suppress the opposition, in order to retain power.

The Afro-Arab relations demonstrate the difficulties in the pursuit and achievement of good corporate governance. While the intent and the will have been expressed through the setting up of necessary organs, the practical reality of its successful implementation is a problem confronting the respective states within the sub-regional bloc.

The political system in Egypt is far from sliding into a dictatorship, as expressed by the majority of people outside the government because the political elite in the country is committed to democracy and the democratisation process. The political leadership is considered very responsive to the tenets of democracy and good governance. For instance, the leadership has been highly ranked on the key area of good governance, under the sub-sections of Commitment to Democracy (90%); Accountability (70%); Transparency (90%); as well as Equitable Development (100%) by the academia in the country.

There is also independence of the judiciary, as courts of justice conduct open trials irrespective of the offenders. Elections are held as prescribed by law, with the exception that sometimes the conduct of the overall procedure receives criticisms. There is limited freedom of association, in the sense that groups or associations still need to obtain permission before being allowed to meet. This restriction on freedom of association was contested at the African Committee on African Charter, as it challenged the fact that the law could not deny citizens the right to associate and the law was overruled.

Press Freedom and Freedom of Expression

On human rights and freedom of the press, the elite claims that there is indeed freedom of the press, with many print and media houses in existence, most of which are very critical of government.

The press in Egypt is thus considered free and lends its voice to the discourse on democracy and good governance by writing and airing topical issues. For instance, the *Cairo Times* discusses freely some of the sensitive issues on economic and political reforms. There is also Islam On-line, which is an on-line media house. While it has limited coverage on the specific areas of democracy, political governance, it informs on a wide range of issues particularly Islamic laws and religion in the social context.

Electoral System

The electoral system is reported to be improving gradually with the increased injection of equity and transparency. However, some negative aspects still persist, such as the occasional amendment, in favour of the ruling party. For instance, the voters' list is not always prepared and this has implications in the monitoring of the election and in assessing its fairness and transparency.

Participation in Political Activities

One of the grey areas in Egyptian politics remains the limited participation of citizens in active politics on grounds of gender and religion. The political culture in Egypt is not particularly relevant to the values of democracy. The politicisation along religious (Islamic and Christian) divides tends to perpetuate certain religious groups in power, and aids and abets poverty in the society. The desire to gain access to resources, rather than political principles, is still seen as the factor that drives politics in the country.

Other non-governmental bodies, such as the civil society organisations, are increasingly making significant contributions towards good governance in the country. The media, especially the *Al-Ahram* newspaper, is quite critical of government and helps expose malpractices, such as corruption and non-transparency where they exist. These media groups also defend human rights and support the need to involve women in all aspects of governance and human endeavour.

Parliamentary Oversight on Executive Organs of the State

The parliament plays a significant role in controlling the powers of the executive and the other organs of the state. There is also the Central Accounts Service, which, despite being connected to the presidency, plays an important function in investigating relevant organs of the state. It prepares a report for all its investigations, which is subsequently presented to parliament for debate and ratification.

Gender and Socially Disadvantaged Groups

Gender equality is becoming a sensitive issue on the geopolitical agenda of African political elites. The Centre for Statistical Survey and Applications, at the Faculty of Economics and Social and Political Science, Cairo University, has been involved in conducting research on issues of critical importance in the country. One of its latest studies was on "Political and Economic Governance", which was commissioned by the Economic Commission for Africa (ECA). The study focused solely on the public sector and specifically on governance. In this study, 13 African countries, 26 governments,[3] 2 000 households and 100 people from the political, social and economic elites were chosen to be interviewed. Initially, the survey was deemed not to have involved enough women and an additional questionnaire was created by ECA to cater for the gender disparity. In addition to the gender sensitivity of the survey, the interest of the next most vulnerable members of the society, namely children, was specially included. The rights of children and the need to end child abuse were given special recognition and coverage. The issue of homeless children received national attention, with the First Lady, Mrs Mubarak, leading the campaign for the rehabilitation of homeless children. To this end, the National Council for Motherhood and Children was established to serve as the focal point for the pursuit of this objective. The former Egyptian Ambassador to South Africa, Her Excellency Mushira Khattab, currently heads the Council.

In further support of the gender consciousness of the government, Egyptian female political elites are of the opinion that greater involvement of women and youths in government is the panacea for the political problems in Africa. It is their view that with the increased participation of women, some of the social and economic problems that derail African development will receive better leverage. They argue that if attention is focused on women, especially mothers, the society will be made to cultivate the culture of peace and love, the way mothers love their children. Such a gesture and attitude will pass on from mothers to their children and will undoubtedly develop a solid foundation for a peaceful and stable environment, respectful of constitutional human rights and sustainable development in Africa.[4]

The leader of a youth organisation in Cairo, Abdel Kader Ismael, outlined the major problems facing Africa and its development as those of civil wars, HIV/AIDS, corruption, illiteracy and famine. These natural catastrophes are the menacing worms that burrow deep into the social, political and economic fabric of the continent. He argues that much can be achieved in development by promoting employment for the youth. This, he suggests, could be done through the investment in small, micro and medium enterprises (SMMEs).[5] He reported the ruling party's attempts at forging this promotion of women and youths in the country as a vehicle for economic development. The ruling party adopts two strategies to achieve this objective. The party has formed the National Council for Women to cater for the interest in and the empowerment of women. The SMME programme also targets the youth. Plans are being made to amalgamate the two bodies for more comprehensive coverage of the social and economic aspects of development and the stakeholders.

According to the views of some leading academics, globalisation is helping to facilitate better communication and technological advancement. NEPAD could also be a good avenue for pursuing the Millennium Development goals (MDGs) in the country. Mayek believes that with the NEPAD initiative, Africa is moving in the right direction. His views on good governance are that there is much corruption in the continent as a whole, and this is perpetrated by the presence of multinationals and their foreign governments.[6] He sighted the role of Belgium, France and the United States in Zaire under the rule of Mobutu, when they aided and abetted Mobutu in plundering that economy. He also cited the role played by the United States (US) in the conflict in Angola, in which the US supported Jonas Savimbi. He singled out the issue of human rights as one of the biggest challenges facing African states. He stressed the need to empower people to develop their fundamental and inalienable rights as a precondition for development. He stressed the importance of promoting the rights of the society and specified in particular women rights, including their right to participation in all activities at all levels; their right to education; empowerment; as well as the right to participate in policy-making through the parliament. According to him, in the Arab world, the problem of women is not created by the government but by the society. It is the society that tends to impose some of the discriminatory laws and standards that preclude women from active participation in politics. Politics is considered one of men's chauvinistic domains.

Views on the African Union (AU)/the New Partnership for Africa's Development (NEPAD)/ African Peer-Review Mechanism (APRM)

Potential and Prospects of the NEPAD Initiative

On 12 January 2003, the Egyptian government set up a unit specifically responsible for the NEPAD programme. The body was to produce a first report in June 2003 to parliament. Outside the parliament, a programme on NEPAD does not exist in the country. Academia and the political elite see the AU/NEPAD programme as a very prospective instrument for the comprehensive development of Egypt and Africa in general. NEPAD is seen as a new foundation for democracy in Africa and democracy is seen as a prerequisite and a *sine qua non* to economic development. It is an effective institution for capacity building in the continent. A cross-section of society believes that there is strong political will to adopt the AU/NEPAD agenda as a point of departure for African development. This commitment is mostly seen in the objective of condemning the practice of the non-constitutional removal of governments and the illegal seizure of power.

In the words of a seasoned politician and diplomat under Nasser, the continent of Africa needs a slogan that will provide a 'catch-word' for all to apply and use as a tool for the 'African Renaissance' – a strategy that was adopted during the decolonisation struggle. 'Pan-Africanism' was the slogan that became the magic wand, which transformed pre-colonial Africa to the present day post-colonial and independent Africa.[7] It is his strong view that today, the catch-word or the slogan in vogue is that of 'NEPAD'. He admonishes however that countries must aspire to be economically independent before aspiring for political independence. Any effort in the contrary will be tantamount to placing the cart before the horse. He is of the opinion that the creation of the AU is a good idea, as it represents one conglomerate of states with a common agenda. He nevertheless does not endorse or favour the creation of the regional blocs. According to him, smaller countries within the regional blocs are always afraid of the larger countries among them. However, under the AU, the influence of regional superpowers is diluted to the advantage of the smaller countries. At the same time, the AU provides the much-needed larger market, which the World Economic Order strives to create through the globalisation initiatives. The view is somewhat a departure from current paradigms and philosophies on Africa's economic integration. The transformation from the Organization of African Unity (OAU) to the African Union (AU) is predicated on new concepts about African economic integration, which prescribe the use of the regional economic blocs as the building blocks for Africa's integration.[8]

The interest of Egypt in NEPAD was further demonstrated in a conference held in 2002, specifically on NEPAD, at the Centre for Developing Countries Studies in Cairo. The conference was organised principally to further inform the elites about the NEPAD initiative and the prospects it holds for the involved states and for the development of the continent and its people. The conference invited ambassadors from Senegal, Algeria, Mauritius, and deputy ambassadors from Nigeria and South Africa. Others invited included the Egyptian foreign minister and the minister of state in the ministry of foreign affairs, as well as senior academics from Nigeria and South Africa. Before the meeting, the NEPAD issue was scarcely known or comprehended, even among the political elites. It was only after the conference that a flurry of commitments to NEPAD followed, starting with the Egyptian foreign minister attending a meeting on NEPAD in Nigeria. Later, President Mubarak attended the meeting of the G8 in Avian. Currently, it is required of Egyptian students to conduct research and write their dissertations on NEPAD. Furthermore, some Egyptian students in the American University in Cairo were sent to South Africa for a more in-depth study on NEPAD.

There is, however, general apathy on some issues that relate to Africa. For instance, the Egyptian political elites and academics expressed their dismay at the slow pace of transformation of the OAU into the AU. They particularly derided the influence of Muammar Gadafi on the transformation and they queried the suitability of Libya to host the African parliament when the country had no parliament of its own. Libya has held front position to host the African parliament.

The government of Egypt remains committed to the ideals of NEPAD, and has expressed concern over the African Peer-Review Mechanism. While other African countries observed the election in Egypt, the secretary-general of the election monitoring committee was later arrested. Scepticism over the implementation of the APRM and the arrest of the secretary-general reveal a dead end on the part of the government, as it seems to be uneasy about strangers in its backyard. On the economic environment linking Egypt and the rest of Africa, the government welcomes economic integration. It is in this light that the country joined the Common Market for Eastern and Southern Africa (COMESA) with Egyptian businesses being active members and playing vital roles. The Egyptian International Economic Forum also held a conference on COMESA with Egyptian businesses actively undertaking business in East and Southern Africa.

The Egyptian government aspires to institute corporate governance in its political agenda. In this regard, the Egyptian representative at NEPAD, Abu Musa has been involved in setting up a social, economic and political task force that will serve as an instrument to enlighten the people. The report by the task force has, among other things, dwelled on how Arab nations could contribute to the continental initiatives, including NEPAD. It is the view of some serving political elites and group activists that the divide in Afro-Arab interests is a major obstacle to implementing some of the African initiatives in Egypt. A woman diplomat highlighted two key problems that limit the capacity of the Arab nations, including Egypt, in successfully implementing the development programmes that target Africa. First, the primary allegiance of Arab nations is to the Arab League, rather than Africa as a continent. Second, is the problem of inadequate financial resources to execute the pro-Africa and development initiatives.[9]

On financing, she reiterated that the Arab Bank for African Development, established to finance development programmes in Africa, is located in Khartoum, Sudan. The bank provides loans and technical assistance for African development. Furthermore, the Arab Fund for Technical Assistance for Africa has serious financial problems, in the sense that Arab countries do not pay their contributions to the fund, which makes it cash-strapped. Among the programmes financed by the Fund are training courses, agricultural projects, irrigation and the provision of experts in key strategic fields, such as political, economic and social development. Apart from the dearth in funds, some of the developmental attentions of the bank seem to be directed to the Arab League rather than the continent-wide agenda.

Overall, it is indicative that Egyptian and Arab interest in African affairs is waning and the enthusiasm of the post independence era of the 1960s and 1970s is being replaced with some sense of apathy and nostalgia. The country currently seems more committed to the Middle East and Arab League affairs and problems, than the African continental issues.

Many Egyptian pundits still think that NEPAD is an ambitious programme because the money involved in its implementation is enormous. However, they laud it as a tool for self-development in Africa. As a new tool for development it has its own challenges, which have to be pursued to a logical and successful end. It is prescribed that for its survival, it should claim ownership of the initiative and the resources intended for its implementation. In other words, it should lay full claim on the resources of Africa, which are immense and sufficient to cater for the execution of the new development agenda. Due recognition is given to the fact that in many respects, Africa lacks the capability to truly make NEPAD wholly its own without external assistance, especially with regards the phenomenon of corruption, which is a major destabiliser and seems to be very deep-rooted in Africa.

It is the feeling among the elites in Egypt, among them Ambassador El Asaal, that membership of a country in the AU and NEPAD is not enough. There must be a demonstrable degree of commitment and participation to accompany the membership. As part of this demonstration of commitment, the elites suggest that the appointment of people to central continental bodies such as NEPAD and the AU should be done with careful scrutiny and not just merely filling positions for the sake of it. They condemn any act that depicts nepotism, such as the appointment of a high elitist or a sensitive position on the grounds of friendship with people in authority or who share a close relationship with an influential person. This practice, if left unchecked, would worsen such vices as corruption and lack of accountability, which are already causing serious damage to the democratisation and good governance objectives of NEPAD.

The ambassador put forward the following recommendations on how he conceives NEPAD's chances of attaining its shared objectives towards African unity, growth and development.[10]

Egyptian businesspeople can finance and invest in some of the programmes that will drive the NEPAD initiative forward, but first they need to 'know' the African, which to his mind, these Egyptians do not know much about. This is against the invitation to foreign investors, who are now beckoned to provide financial assistance. This move is seen by African elites as an indirect way of inviting neo-colonisation and further plundering of our resources by the past colonial masters.

The Egyptian elites need to be re-directed and better informed on the new African initiatives. In the first instance, they question why the OAU was changed to the AU. In their view the Charter of the OAU should have been amended and not completely changed.

They also suggest that certain slogans that do not sound pragmatic need to be changed, in order to reduce their intractability and the nightmare involved in trying to come to terms with them, for the purposes of achieving success in their implementation. Among the slogans that demonstrate this ambiguity are: good governance and gender equality. Good governance is ambiguous and very subjective and lacks practical and measurable indicators. Gender equality is alien in the Egyptian socio-cultural system, especially in the domain of the Islamic religion.

Criticisms of NEPAD

The position of Egypt in the geopolitical map of Africa is still a major factor in Afro-Arab relations. It is not yet certain as to what the inclination of Egypt is, whether in the Middle East or Africa, and this doubt and uncertainty hangs over the country's orientation and loyalty to the African Union and its initiatives. It is the view of the doubters that Egypt's active participation and involvement in NEPAD is crucial in shaping the future of the African political landscape. Egypt is looked upon from both sub-Saharan Africa, on the one hand, and the Arab League, on the other, as a liberal state that can act as a durable link between the sub-Saharan region and Arab North Africa.

One of the main criticisms levelled against NEPAD is that it is an initiative conceived and hatched hurriedly by a handful of African heads of state. It is further seen as a top-down approach to policy formulation and governance, which reduced the relevance and contribution of the grassroots, civil society and a host of other stakeholders.[11]

The NEPAD initiative is also criticised as a bogus and ambitious plan, for which the initiators lack the financial capability and political power and morality to implement. For instance, the expectation that with its implementation, the economy of the AU member states would grow at an annual rate of 7% by the year 2015 and that the rich nations would pump in a whopping US$64 billion towards the operationalisation of the initiative, are indicators of this ominous ambition. The economic optimism and expectations of the creators of NEPAD was dampened by the G8 only approving a mere US$6 million in additional investments for the African continent during their meeting in Canada in 2002. According to Olukoshi,[12] for an initiative, which hopes to raise US$64 billion annually to finance the development of the continent, a correction in the terms of trade bias, which the continent suffers, could have yielded roughly the same amount in resources. At the same time, it would eliminate the uncertainty of aid and foreign investment flows at the level that is projected. In spite of the variety of myths that have been woven around NEPAD, it would seem to be fraught with shortcomings which, if not addressed, might block the realisation of its most basic objectives, even in the terms in which they are outlined.[13]

Although NEPAD is seen as an improvement on the Lagos Plan of Action of April 1980, the critics of the initiative seem to argue that NEPAD is merely the same wine in a new cellar. While the Lagos Plan of Action was not formulated entirely by Africans and relied on outside donors to finance it, the new initiative is formulated by Africans, but still depends on foreign donors for financing its envisioned programmes. NEPAD is accused of being another form of introducing the notorious structural adjustment programmes (SAPs) in another guise. In this regard, African states have defined the conditions as those of good governance, good democracy, transparency and a mechanism to eschew corruption and accede to peer review. Nevertheless, analysts argue that the same donors to whom the hands of partnership for Africa's development are stretched, are the same colonial masters that plundered the continent's economies and natural resources and used them to develop their own economies. It is the same group that is still engaged in plundering the economies of developing countries, under the New World Order of globalisation and new economic order.

It is argued by the experts that good governance, in its central connotation as initially introduced by the World Bank, has focused on what makes institutions and rules more effective, including transparency, responsiveness, accountability and the rule of law.[14] In addition, a number of World Bank studies include the aspect of popular participation in the selection of government. The main definition of governance in World Bank literature refers to the traditions and institutions by which authority in a country is exercised. These include: the process by which governments are selected, monitored and replaced; the capacity of the government to effectively formulate and implement sound policies; as well as the respect of citizens and the state for the institutions that govern economic and social interactions among them. This definition is not different from the IMF's definition of governance. In this description, the IMF refers to the aspects that portray the way a country is governed, including its economic policies and regulatory framework, thus concentrating on promoting good governance by ensuring the rule of law; improving the efficiency and accountability of the public sector and tackling corruption, as essential elements of a framework within which economies can prosper.[15]

The political democracy and governance initiative of NEPAD does not offer any such local value or anchorage in domestic political processes or structures. Indeed, the entire process leading to the production of the NEPAD document has been bereft of systematic public debate and consultation within Africa – a serious deficit, which is not mitigated by the fact that the initiative is an almost exclusively governmental and donor affair. It is little wonder that many have challenged the top-down approach that has underpinned the introduction of the initiative and the path that is being followed for the realisation of its goals. Many schools of thought among the political elites believe that the African problem lies more in the continent's peace and security realm, which has been found to be wanting with many civil wars and political unrest in Africa. It is therefore their opinion that Africa must channel its resources into achieving peace and security as the first step towards democratisation and good governance. The African initiative and intervention in Burundi is lauded and recommended as a model of our commitment to African development, by initiating and conducting peace missions and conflict resolutions. To this school of thought, the NEPAD agenda is patterned under the European Union and Canadian culture and is therefore not applicable to Africa. NEPAD is seen as the project of the future, for its standards and requirements are far ahead of the present African socio-economic and political status. It is their thinking that for NEPAD to work, its programme needs to be phased in accordance with the prevailing level of education, consciousness and awareness of Africa. The elites feel that NEPAD was hurriedly put together by heads of state and governments, with minimal contribution from diplomats, and this is why the initiative resembles a square peg in a round hole.

The authors of the NEPAD document seem to assume that there is one universal, ideal model of democracy and governance, against which African and other experiences can be abstracted from the current practices of Western countries, as though these practices themselves are not problematic and diverse. The consequence is that the creativity and originality that could have been brought to bear on the quest for a political framework that is in time with liberation and empowering the peoples of Africa, are not explored. Instead, emphasis is placed on the NEPAD document on 'good' governance as opposed to democratic governance. And yet, the content of the governance framework, which is espoused, borrowed as it is from the World Bank, seems too functionalistic, managerial and technocratic. However, sustainable African development, if it is to be realised, must proceed from a premise, which treats politics as a legitimate arena, integral to the developmental process and development itself, as an equally legitimate terrain of politics. By definition, this is one that necessarily assures the integrity of the review process; all such review systems are subject to bias, abuse, problems of interpretation, and in the case of political leaders, strategic choices tied to definitions of national interest. Zimbabwe is a living example of the difficulties and dilemmas that are posed by the ambiguity of "good governance".

A hint of this was gathered in the run-up to the Zimbabwean election, when the leading Western countries put pressure on African governments to take action against the Mugabe regime or support sanctions against it, as a decisive test of the NEPAD commitments being made. A foretaste of this selectivity was offered by Robert Fowler, the Personal Representative of the Canadian Prime Minister for the G8 Summit African Plan when he stated, in November 2001, that NEPAD offers the Western powers the prospect of "concentrating engagement on those countries that are prepared to take political and economic decisions necessary to make this new plan work".

The Role of Local Research Organisations

Both the university and independent research organisations conduct research on political, social and economic issues that impact and shape the political architecture of the country. The Centre for Statistical Applications at Cairo University, and the Centre for Arab and African Studies, among others, contribute towards political governance and democracy through research on national, regional and continental issues that guide the political, social and economic interests of the country.

The intellectual elites in academics and research created a new agenda to combat the hostility under the leftist Nasser regime. They saw private sector involvement in research as the true avenue for transparency and accountability in information procurement and dissemination. In light of this, a private sector research centre was established to cater for the interest of intellectuals on pan-Arabism and to guard the security of the public sector, which is very sensitive and apprehensive of foreign research invasion; to enable scholars to conduct research and publish on Arab matters; in addition to encouraging gender equality and the protection of the rights of women. The intellectuals had become disillusioned with foreign donors who had their own external agenda, which they tried to impose on the states in Africa. For example, the architects of the research centre believe that the United Nations agenda has been hijacked by the United States, such that it is principally the United States agenda that is pursued by this international body. The notorious SAP and the Council for the Development of Social Science Research in Africa (Codesria) are some of the programmes that are resented as inimical to African development and renaissance.[16]

They further decry the general absence of democracy, of freedom in exercising political freedom, as well as freedom of association and expression. Marshall law took centre stage against democratisation and there was serious political polarisation into the leftist Islamists, on the one hand, and the Progressives, on the other. Open meetings could not be held without prior permission from the government. Security was very tight and there was little or no freedom to conduct research; it took long and bureaucratic procedures to obtain permission to execute research, and the granting of permission was contingent upon the de facto authority and status of the permit seeker.

The Egyptian intellectuals assert that Egypt is not very committed to African issues but rather leans more to the Arab and Middle East groups. Thus, for them, NEPAD could be quite popular among academics and civil society but not among intellectuals. In their view, it is yet another avenue for developed countries to invest in Africa to pursue their selfish interests. The intellectuals further believe that the government is not using them effectively. It is their view that since Sadat, the Egyptian government has been extremely Euro-centric. Consequently, there exists an identity crisis in pan-Arabism, in which there has been a dramatic shift towards capitalism, as witnessed and practised in Europe and North America. This has weakened pan-Arabism and the experts believe that a viable option would be to revive the Afro-Arab cooperation in banking and industry and to lean more towards the emerging economies, such as in Asia and South Africa.

It is at the peak of this scenario of apparent injustice to some of the segments of society that the Arab and African Research Centre was born in 1987. The centre established its own agenda and pursued progressive ideologies that involved a study of the peasantry and the civil society as its main research agenda. It has largely practised and achieved this objective.

While apathy and despair appear to be the new paradigm among the old generation politicians, enthusiasm and a zealous desire to integrate with Africa seem to be the aura among the new breed and youth in politics. Two children of the former head of state of Ghana, Kwame Nkrumah, have established an African Centre in Cairo, which attracts great crowds in all its events and activities. The role of the Egyptian youth in the fight against apartheid in South Africa is remarkable. Students from Cairo University and the American University in Cairo massively signed petitions and maintained sustained pressure for the release of Nelson Mandela while imprisoned on Robben Island. Egyptian human rights activists enjoy observer status in African Human Rights Charter summits and there is close cooperation between the Egyptian Human Rights Organisation and the African Human Rights Charter. The same organisation cooperates closely with the pursuance of reparations.

The Role of NGOs

The UNDP Commitments

The UNDP is of the opinion that on the performance of development projects, the Millennium Development Goals (MDGs), as implemented in Egypt, lack measurable indicators and benchmarks for assessing the fulfilment of their objectives. The organisation recommends that the Ministry of Planning should incorporate the MDGs into its structure and provide a set of indicators to be used in monitoring and evaluating the performance of the programme in the country. At the Egyptian state level, the organisation has had some dialogue with the Ministry of Planning and policy-makers through seminars and workshops. It suggests that the policy unit introduce the MDG framework and adopt it for its policy formulation. Egypt is not part of the Poverty Reduction Strategic Planning (PRSP) programme. Membership of PRSP is a conditionality for the less developed countries (LDCs) to acquire development funding. The UNDP has lobbied Egypt to put a Plan of Action in place and to enter into dialogue with the donor agencies, as a strategy for procuring all the necessary financial and technical assistance it needs in the pursuit and successful implementation of the country's MDG programmes. Egypt is Africa's highest ranked recipient country and the world's tenth-ranked in MDG and development loans. The country is currently negotiating a loan of US$1 billion from the International Monetary Fund and the African Development Bank.

The UNDP and NEPAD

The United Nations Development Programme (UNDP) office in Egypt acknowledged that it is outside of its mandate to finance NEPAD directly but could support country programmes that are geared towards the implementation of NEPAD projects. The organisation reported that they have signed a support of US$2 million over a period of one and a half years in the following areas for the support of the NEPAD secretariat:

- Establishment of NEPAD and implementation of the MDGs
- Monitoring of the activities of NEPAD
- Developing communication strategies
- Popularising the initiative among the African public
- Setting up an advisory board for the future
- Involving the intellectuals, academicians and the civil society organisations (CSOs)
- Making further commitments in raising additional financial support.

Country Operations of the UNDP

At the country level, the modus operandi of the UNDP is such that NEPAD is not in the priority list. In Egypt, the organisation has two main offices, namely the Regional Bureau for Africa and the Regional Bureau for Arab States. These two bureaux perform their duties and coordinate the development programmes of the country together with the UN headquarters. The main task of the country and regional offices is that of organising seminars, conferences and studies related to the mandate of the organisation in the country or region. However, special units of the UN regional offices handle specific projects directed at special initiatives, such as the NEPAD. In this respect, the FAO agency of the UN would coordinate agricultural projects or programmes designed to tackle the poverty eradication objective of NEPAD. Other specific tasks, such as the MDGs, dealing with provision of clean water, shelter and good health are directed to special units of the UN, such as the Word Health Organization (WHO) for health, the UNDP for clean water supply, and HABITAT/United Nations High Commission for Refugees (UNHCF) and the UN Human Settlements Programme.

In general, the focus of the UN falls into three main categories:[17]

1. Overall support for governance, through the provision of statistics and in the monitoring and evaluation of relevant projects. It also includes the formulation of policies on education, health and employment.
2. Management of natural resources, which includes the environment, natural assets, water management and biodiversity conservation.

3. Poverty eradication among groups and locations which are considered to be highly impoverished. In light of this stratification and discriminatory support, the areas and groups supported in Egypt include the following:

    a. The Upper Nile region, which is regarded as the most impoverished region in the country, is chosen for the poverty eradication programme in the country. Second, women and youth are targeted in the preservation of the right of the socially disadvantaged or underprivileged members of the society.

    b. Women and children are also supported through involvement of women in the work of the UN agencies. In addition, the UN helps set up the National Council for Women, which works closely with the national line ministry to formulate and execute programmes, and projects that will protect the rights of women and children, empower them and provide them with employment opportunities. It also builds the technical and institutional capacity of the council to make it effective for the implementation of the task for which it has been set up.

    c. Youth and child rights, with special emphasis on the girl child. The National Council for Motherhood and Childhood caters for the interests of women and children in the country. Specifically, the areas the organisation focus on include illiteracy, enrolment in schools, child labour, and population issues such as fertility rates, population growth and mortality.[18]

Summary and Conclusion

This chapter surveyed the political structure in Egypt and assessed the views of a cross-section of the country from academia, politicians, mass media and NGOs. The express objective was to assess the performance of the government with respect to democracy, governance and commitment to some of the continental institutions and initiatives such as the African Union and the NEPAD. The results indicate that there are convergent views regarding Egypt being a functional democracy. However, views are divergent on the legitimacy of the Egyptian democracy. Although the country operates some semblance of multi-party democracy with regular parliamentary elections, the latter is less competitive than the general elections. The ruling elite seems to be a caucus of successive royalties. It is a strongly held view among academics and intellectuals that the ruling elites feel their positions remain precarious in the hands of the former, who the elites feel deliberately keep them from the helm of political affairs. On the contrary, some diplomats and others who still have close relationships with government laud the leadership and give the ruling elites a clean bill of health, for the most part, on democracy and good governance. They believe that Egypt is an example of a fully-fledged democracy, demonstrating human rights, freedom of speech and freedom of expression, as well as a very free and independent press.

The political elite in Egypt has reached a milestone on key sustainable development issues, such as gender sensitivity, the protection of women and youth, and has established special organisations on motherhood and youth affairs to pursue the agenda. It is the view of the proponents and advocates of gender equality and youth involvement that the concept of democracy, good governance and sustainable development will take its roots in the upliftment and empowerment of the family through youth and motherhood organisations. These organisations create and nurture the machineries and instruments for grassroots participation in democratic and development processes.

On the wider continent agenda, opinions differ on the performance of the AU, especially with regard to the NEPAD initiative. Some schools of thought consider the programme a hot potato, which, if not carefully handled, might backfire and become counter-productive. Others see it as a disguised structural adjustment programme, which will again lead to arm-twisting of the countries of Africa, with the poorest bearing the full brunt of its negative impact.

On the positive side, many analysts, including past politicians and diplomats in Egypt, endorse the NEPAD initiative and approve of the stance of the Egyptian government on the African political pursuit. They believe that it is a homegrown initiative in which the future of Africa stands to be transformed, if the programme is given adequate local and international support. Support seems to be flowing in, as many organisations, both locally and internationally, appear to have made serious commitments in support of NEPAD and its objectives.

Whether NEPAD is the long awaited centrifugal force that will pull Egypt and other Arab African states towards the centre of Africa, rather than maintaining the Pan-Arabic Movement's agenda, which pulls Egypt and its north African Arab states away from continental representation, is yet to be seen. Much is expected of Egypt to play the reconciliatory and integrating role between the Arab north and the rest of Africa, south of the Sahara.

Notes and References

1   Hamdy Abdel Raman Hassan 'Political Leadership in Egypt: The Case of a Halt Democracy', see chapter 2 in this book.
2   Mohammed Mayek, oral interview in Cairo during the survey.
3   Kamal El-Menoufi is the Dean of the Faculty of Economics and Political Science at Cairo University. He outlined the commitment of the Egyptian Government in pursuing the gender equality as enshrined in the UN Millennium Development Goals (MDGs) during a personal interview in Cairo.
4   Dr Able Soltan is a woman member of parliament, who pursues the gender equality programme in government. She gave the study team an interview on the role of women in politics at the Cairo University campus during the study.
5   Abdel Kader Ismael is Head of the Youth Employment Association, Division of the Ministry of Cabinet; a personal interview was conducted at the Cairo University Faculty of Economics and Social and Political Science.
6   Mohammed Mayek, personal communication.
7   Mohammed Farkah, the Former Director, Division of Presidency, under Nasser. The former Secretary-General for the Arab Human Rights Organization, spoke to the author during a personal interview in his home in Cairo.
8   Francis Nwonwu, 'The formation of an African Economic Community' in S. K. B. Asante, F. O. C. Nwonwu, and V. N. Muzvidziwa, *Towards an African Economic Community*, Pretoria: Africa Institute of South Africa, pp 22–41, 60.
9   Samia Bibars is a top official in the Ministry of Foreign Affairs and a gender equality activist. She granted this interview in her office during the survey.

10 Ambassador El Ashaal, Professor of International Law at Cairo University made these submissions during the oral interview in Cairo.

11 Iraqi Sherbini, 'NEPAD and the African development strategy: A critical review of some major issues' in El-Sayyid (ed.), *Neo-Liberalism and African Development Strategies: Prospects of the New Partnership for African Development, Development Issues*, no 27, 2003, pp 49-73.

12 Adebayo Olukoshi, 'Governing the African development process: The challenge of the New Partnership for Africa's Development (NEPAD)' in El-Sayyid (ed.), *Neo-Liberalism and African Development Strategies: Prospects of the New Partnership for African Development, Development Issues*, no 27, 2003, pp 19-48.

13 *Ibid.*, p 34.

14 Rawia Tawfic, 'Reviewing good governance in NEPAD: Towards a methodology for the African Political Peer Review Mechanism', Monograph.

15 International Monetary Fund, 'The IMF and good governance: A fact sheet', available online at http://www.imf.org /external/ np/ exr/facts/gov.htm, April 2003.

16 Helmi Sharawy, expressed these views at the Arab-African Research Centre in Cairo during an oral interview in the course of the survey.

17 United Nations Development Programme, 'Report on the Millennium Development Goals at the Country Level', UN Resident Coordinator, Cairo, p 39.

18 Michelle Ribotta, 'The involvement of the UNDP in the New Partnership for Africa's Development', personal interview in Cairo, August 2003.

NORTH AFRICA

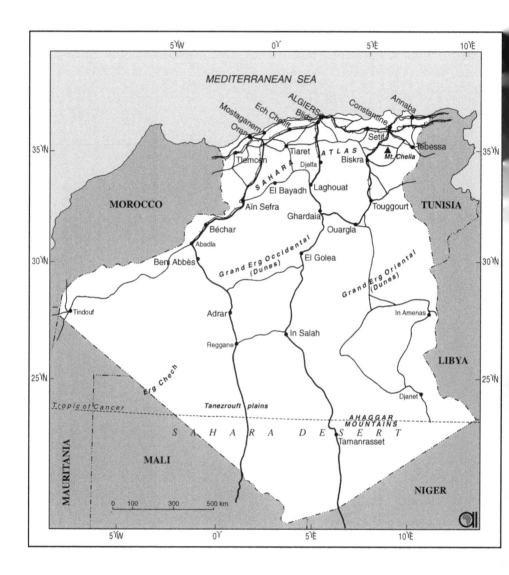

Source: Africa Institute of South Africa, 2005.

3. The Role of Political Elites in the Political Dynamics and Reforms in Algeria

Tayeb Chenntouf

Introduction

The question of political elites has both practical and theoretical aspects and has become a central issue in Algeria, and forms the focus of various debates.[1] Paradoxically, little has been written on the subject. University research in Algeria has neglected the issue until recently. Such research should usually orientate towards an analysis of policies, industrialisation and development.

In a more diffused than systematic way, theories of the "non-capitalist development path" and of "national democratic construction" are privileged. From these perspectives, elites are considered avant-garde. The vigorous industrial policy pursued since 1970, however, hints towards the existence and management of industrialisation by a "techno-bureaucracy", a role afforded to engineers in industry. An extension of this approach would suggest that the notion of "state capitalism" is the most relevant. In the political arena, Harbi uses the concept of "bureaucracy" to characterise the *Front de Libération Nationale* (FLN), which emerged from the war of independence. This self-management regime established itself in the agriculture, industrial and services sectors by decrees in March 1963.

Outside of Algeria, a few rare American researchers (Quandt and Zartman) and a few French researchers (Leca) in the 1970s, looked at the role of elites in the war of independence (1954-1962) and the years to follow.[2] The Algerian political system was linked to "sultanism" and the subsequent struggles, which led to "factionalism". Political elites then emerged as a significant problem and an issue of concern for the social sciences after October 1988. Empirical studies focused on developing the biographies of those who fought for national liberation. Blin analysed elites from the angle of their renewal and the tensions, which they survived between 1991-1992.[3] The notions of "neo-patrimonialism" and "clientelism" became key concepts in English sociology and anthropology. Finally, the central role of the state in the accumulation and the "prebendary" character of political actors were underlined. The Algerian political system was seen as a "rentier bureaucratic" or "populist" system. In these two perspectives, elites used the state for their own enrichment.

The importance of the decisive position and role of elites in the political system, which is well known in all the social sciences, has formed the basis of various theories.[4] For Larry Diamond, Juan Linz and S. M. Lipset, "The directors in place ... act within the constraints of the structural framework which they have inherited but the structures and institutions, especially the political ones, are built by their actions and choices".[5]

Literature on African political elites is relatively abundant.[6] Political elites share a dual character: they exercise an "authoritarian", "charismatic" sense of "personal power". On the other hand, their conservatism is opposed to any risk-taking, such as reforms and changes in the mode of governance. The most recent theoretical writings are now focusing on their ethics.

This chapter intends to take up the question of political elites in Algeria, which has become more pressing since October 1988. The point of departure is the work of both historians (Chaussinand-Nogaret and Charles) and sociologists (Bourdieu and Foucault).[7] The past weighs heavily on political elites in Algeria. The composition and complexity of this grouping can be traced back to the periods of colonisation and decolonisation, and even to pre-colonial times; at the same time, the dynamics of the present are also pertinent. Algeria underwent many transformations in the years 1988-2002, which almost disrupted the entire social structure. While some elites fall, others rise, and still others plot for the future.

The question is less of the replication (Bourdieu) of elites than of finding out how a social group becomes autonomous and professional, politically speaking.[8] It is also important to understand the habits and positions occupied by its members, as well as the strategies, which they put in place to improve – or not improve – their governance. In the end, this chapter evaluates the chances of reform and identifies the reformers.

Emergency Elite Documentation

Research into political elites is extremely difficult in any country. Researchers freely admit the shortfalls of such research. Without being completely impossible, it is difficult to undertake and source materials. Written sources must be carefully selected and established. Official documentation can always be summarised as a simple list of names of government members or other political institutions. Biographies, memoirs and first-hand accounts are more useful. In Algeria, since October 1988, 'mouths have opened'. A number of politicians have written historical or political essays, as well as autobiographies, memoirs or accounts of their participation in the anti-colonial struggle and the national liberation war. They have been privileged by their access to a wealth of data and material. The press, in both languages (French and Arabic), is also indirectly a useful source, as the question of leadership is often used in political struggles to criticise or defend one or another member of the elite. However, journalistic commentary rarely proceeds to the level of a systematic treatment, rather providing multiple images of elites and their activities.

Thus, it is necessary to take into account the current hesitation in Algeria between reforms and the status quo. The habits of elites is one of the factors hampering reform and leading to authoritarianism. However, keeping in mind that elites are not totally homogeneous, two questions must be answered: which section of the elite would be most susceptible to promoting reforms, and what indicators can be used to evaluate the government's reform measures?

Post-Reform Algeria: Standing Still or Moving Forward?[9]

Algeria is engaged in a global reform programme that touches all aspects of society and its institutions, and represents a veritable 'revolution' of the system established after independence. However, after some years, no changes have taken place and the chances of real reform are slim in the immediate future. They date back to 1979 and were not yet complete by 2002. Coupled with this immobility in all areas is the temptation to return to the previous system. The planned reforms in Algeria are not like the big-bang, which has been witnessed in several countries. They were set in motion, in fact, in 1979 after the death of Bourmediène. The period 1988-1992 saw intense legislative activity meant to signal a break with the past. From 1992 to 1998, security and political problems gained importance as the government tried to deal with terrorism and violence. A structural adjustment plan was nevertheless implemented at this time. After 1998, economic reforms gained momentum again with the privatisation of public enterprises and the prioritisation of three areas: education, justice, and state services.

Economic Reforms

The first set of reforms was economic, between 1980 and 1985, aimed at restructuring enterprises to improve their performance. The petrol shock and decline of the dollar in 1985-1986 led to a new series of measures, which aimed at reducing state involvement. The right to perpetual tenure on agricultural land was granted to workers, and a more liberal investment code was promulgated. The independence in management of non-agricultural state enterprises was proclaimed in 1988.

The coming to power of Hamrouche as the head of state in September 1989 led to an acceleration in the reforms process. A new law on money and credit guaranteed the autonomy of the Central Bank from political interference. The monopoly on external commerce was abolished, while foreign investment was sought after and encouraged. Prices were liberalised and salaries were no longer fixed by the administration. These reforms were now economic and political, and affected freedom of the press and that of information.[10]

There was hardly any slowing down of reforms between 1992 and 1998, which saw the peak of drastic economic measures. In April 1994, the government signed a stand-by arrangement (SBA) with the International Monetary Fund to reschedule its public and private debt, after negotiation with its creditors. This was followed by an extended fund facility (EFF), April 1995-March 1998, and the implementation of a structural adjustment programme (SAP), which involved the devaluation of the dinar; general deregulation of prices; liberalisation of foreign trade; raising interest rates; as well as the restructuring and privatisation of public sector enterprises.[11]

Political Reforms

The liberalisation of the political field was equally spectacular. Between 5 July 1989, the date the law relating to political associations was promulgated, and 30 July, the date of the government parties meeting, 49 political associations were registered. Fifteen more were registered before the end of 1989, a further 10 in 1990, and 16 in 1991. However, after not conforming to the organic law of 6 March 1997, 30 were dissolved in 1998.

The law on information of 3 April 1990, led to the emergence of 550 newspapers between 1990 and 2000. Of these, 150 are still in operation. The circulation and readership of daily newspapers rose to 1.5 million copies per day, or 46 copies per 1 000 people. The norm established by United Nations Educational, Scientific and Cultural Organisation (UNESCO) is 100 per 1 000 inhabitants. Twenty local radios and 2 more television channels were given the green light to broadcast; the opening of cyber-cafés has also been extremely rapid. However, the state broadcasting organs have been criticised for shortcomings in their public service mission. On the whole, the local media is known for poor credibility, in comparison with the success of foreign information media.

Social Reforms

During his presidential election campaign in 1999, Bouteflika announced a set of reforms that he would undertake if elected. When elected, the new president set up a National Commission for justice reforms on 20 October 1991, and installed a National Commission to reform the educational system on 13 May 2000. On 25 November 2000, a committee to reform the state's structures and missions began its work. Between February and March 1997, the government announced the revision of the family code. The work of the three commissions has not led to any public debate, partly because the reports, which are submitted to the president of the republic, remain confidential. But the press has regularly reported on the work and contents of the reports.

Indeed, the reform process is regularly analysed by the press, political parties and personalities on their anniversary dates. The evaluations tend to emphasise the poor results in all areas. No problem has been completely resolved and the conditions for introducing reforms are no longer the same. Nonetheless, three aspects have been judged positively. Diplomatic policy since 1999 has "enabled Algeria to break the isolation in which it found itself and to reconcile itself with the international community".[12]

Evaluation of the Reforms

The security situation has improved and terrorism is declining, as noted by Human Rights Watch (2003), "political violence has declined on the whole but continues to lead to an average of 125 deaths per month, mostly civilians".[13] The number of armed terrorists, which reached 27 000 in 1992, dropped to 10 000, according to the chief of state and leader of the national popular army.[14] The same source reported that the war resulted in 52 000 deaths.

The results of debt rescheduling and the structural adjustment plan have also been good. On the eve of reforms, the Algerian economy was characterised by an absence of growth; an inflation rate of 29%; currency reserves of US$2.5 billion; a deficit in the balance of payments of US$4.4 billion; and debt which absorbed more than 45% of foreign exchange. The application of the SBA (1994) and the EFF (1994-1998) re-established macro-economic balance and improved Algeria's financial situation.

The social consequences, however, have been brutal: poverty has spread and social disparities have deepened. The evaluations of the National Economic and Social Council reveal growing unemployment, a social protection system in crisis, and social instability, which arose from the closure of 815 economic enterprises of which 83% were local and 16% public. At the end of 1999, these closures forced the retrenchment of 326 678 workers, among whom 66 932 – or one worker in five – opted for voluntary retrenchment.[15] The reversal of these successes can be seen in the growing number of social movements and the democratic deficit, while problems of identity and economic development remain.

The phenomenon of unrest is becoming more common, even affecting the previously peaceful southern regions (of Djanet, Abadla, Aïn Salah, and El Goléa). In 2002, 40 out of 48 *wilaya* (regions) were affected. Rioters have taken to the streets to protest against water shortages, the distribution of social housing, and the abuse of public services.[16] The street demonstrations, which are growing increasingly violent, have become the only form of communication between the state and its citizens. They have become the "language of correspondence between institutions and society".[17]

Unrest, often spontaneous or anarchic, overwhelms the theoretical mediators of society such as parties, elected representatives, trade unions and associations, which are distracted from their function of representation: 'The people realise that their only recourse is collective action, action which must be sufficiently noisy to penetrate the deaf ear which is usually turned to their grievances. The gap between the state and society widens more and more by the day".[18]

In effect, the democratic deficit blocks any possible regulation. Political society, like civil society, is on the wane. Multi-partyism is in a state of crisis. Several political parties are waiting to be registered, while others are created without knowing if they will be recognised by the Ministry of the Interior. The active parties are, on the whole, plunged in a crisis that is "threatening the very idea of multi-partyism".[19]

Exercising one's trade union rights is difficult in the face of legislative and practical barriers and the harassment of union representatives. Independent unions are falling victim to the constraints of labour law. They are not recognised as social partners during negotiations and are forbidden to meet and their offices are constantly closed. The right to strike is not respected and this leads to violence. "Labour pluralism has been systematically broken down" according to a report by the International Federation of Human Rights.[20] The General Workers Union of Algeria (UGTA) continues to be considered the only representative organisation and spokesperson for labour rights. Union pluralism, which is enshrined in the constitution, is barely recognised. Independent unions start all the strikes.[21] According to the Labour Ministry, in 1996, 441 strikes involving a total of 127 300 workers were organised; in 2001, the number fell to 176 and a total of 50 000 workers, or a 40% decline.[22]

The union movement, for its part, is going through a critical phase. After twelve years of existence, it "is still at the primary phase. It is not managing to play its role, given the multiple problems, particularly financial and legal, which confront it".[23] With regard to human rights, a considerable deficit is underlined by the National Consultative Commission for the Promotion and Protection of Human Rights. They complain of "totally negative attitudes towards these rights, including the most basic sometimes".[24] Problems of identity have led to riots in Kabylie since April 2001. Associations have been created and have adopted, at El Kseur, a list of demands that they present as "sealed and non-negotiable". The crisis has remained at boiling point in spite of attempts at dialogue and repression.

Progress in the field of economics is not much better. Reforms have not been implemented, and growth is not taken place, while no economic development projects have been designed for the future. Four years after the 1999 presidential elections, none of the envisaged economic reforms have been achieved. Privatisation has not advanced. Banking and fiscal reform has not moved beyond promises. The 2002-2004 plan of action earmarked the sum of US$7 billion without taking into account serious economic repercussions.[25] The Algerian Chamber of Commerce (FCE) sees the 1993 finance law as "a purely formal scenario of the development of some economic and trade variables". The aim "remains, as it has been for the past ten years, to preserve a certain macro-financial stability". They add that the government tends to "get caught up in the ideology of structural adjustment".[26]

The Confederation of Algerian Economic Operators has evaluated the past twelve years of reforms in a 30-page report. They analysed the causes of the economic and social crisis, and the reasons for the failure of economic reforms, and proposed solutions to the crisis. The growth rate has seen an annual average of 2% since 1990, despite an improvement in the financial situation and the slowing down of demographic growth.[27] "All the reforms undertaken since 1990 have failed," according to the Confederation.[28] The FCE deplores "The absence of any serious economic projection for the economic and social development of the country." They advocate "a planning phase ... over the medium and long term ... resulting from a consensual debate involving all the economic and social actors".[29] The Confederation targets the political and administrative environment as a serious handicap and recommends as a priority, reforming the structural property, monetary, financial and capital markets.[30]

The crisis is translated into a profound political disaffection among Algerian citizens. In spite of the uncertainties affecting electoral statistics, electoral participation has been declining since 1995.[31] The two elections in 2002 – legislative and local – confirm the profound lack of interest among the electorate. This apparent political apathy does not spare any parties, trade unions or associations, including the opposition. Political mobilisation is becoming increasingly weak.[32]

The mitigated results of the reforms can be attributed to the absence of political will and to mis-management. The present immobility may in time fall into backsliding – a return to the previous system and the restoration of the 'strong state'. Attempts may be made to restore the presidential regime and to forge a conservative political coalition.

President Bouteflika, after his election, has shown some interest in amending the 1996 constitution. The idea of a new constitution was envisaged as a return to presidentialism rather than a semi-parliamentary regime. Although this idea was abandoned, day-to-day politics has considerably strengthened the powers of the president. Anti-constitutional infringements are common, and in fact, have led to the resignation of Benbitour, the previous head of government:

> A leader brought up in the atmosphere of a single party, Bouteflika has never hidden his aversion to the idea of multipartyism, preferring a system which maintains the traditional general philosophy, but brought up to date, inspired by the Tunisian model that assures the pre-eminence of the President of the Republic, who has all power and

is served by a dominant, omnipresent party, with various satellite political formations.[33]

The re-establishment of the FLN as the primary political party after the results of the 2002 election, raises the fear that "it is the whole system as well as a supportive column thereof, which is gaining confidence in its destiny and is beginning to reconstitute its essential components".[34]

Proposals to revise the legislation relating to political parties, trade unions and associations are regularly raised. New parties are however denied access to amenities. The Minister of Labour would like to abolish the notion of unlimited strikes, while the representativeness of independent unions has also been questioned.[35] A new and more restrictive text, governing the associative movement, is in the pipeline at the Ministry of the Interior.[36] The national consensus project has led to overwhelming tensions. In its spirit, it is seen as the successor to the *Rahma* (pardon) adopted by President Zeroual. The civil concord law was adopted by Parliament in July 1999. On the occasion of the celebration of independence, President Bouteflika announced clemency measures for those involved in support networks and for those found guilty of participation in terrorism. On 19 September 1999, the proposal was adopted, with 95.63% of the vote after a referendum.

While its contents are not publicly known, the national concord raises fears that a conservative coalition, which is opposed to reform, could be created. The president is suspected of devising this strategy, which would have an effect on the presidential elections of 2004. The most radical critiques are coming from the democratic parties and those involved with the union, UGTA.

The Reproduction of Authoritarianism

At the end of 2002, change was not palpable. A fortiori no systematic rupture could be discerned. Nearly fifteen years after the start of reforms, authoritarianism continued. The political elites were at its foundations and the principal actors in its reproduction. Whether they campaigned on the basis of social origins, education and training, or political experience, the members of these elites showed that they were not open to change, although they also did not openly demonstrate their orientation towards authoritarianism.

The principal characteristic of political elites in Algeria, as compared to other countries, is their context of nationalism and the struggle for national liberation. With few materials, capital or symbolic resources in the 1950s, they managed to take absolute control of almost all resources by placing them under the control of the state.

Structure of the Algerian Elite

The identification and statistical breakdown of the elites is problematic, more for reasons of documentation than uncertainties surrounding the definition of an elite. Their composition reveals, in fact, three distinct chronological generations.

The *Dictionary of the Algerian Political Class from 1900 to-Date* notes the "lack of credible written sources and the impossibility of comprehensiveness". Without delineating, the criteria used to pick out the members of the elite; it mentions 700 principals behind political movements and groupings.[37] The (non-official) *Political Annual of Algeria of 1999* listed 235 historical and political personalities, again without clarifying the criteria used to collate the list.[38] In France, Blin *et al* published a list of the "200 men of power in Algeria".[39] And, in a speech published during the summer of 1999, Bouteflika described the existence of an index of "national skills" which is kept by the President of the Republic.

Independent of the questions of identification and number, the political elites can be grouped in three generations of politicians. The first took part in the anti-colonial struggle and the war of independence. They acceded to power in 1962. Today still, many important political functions are carried out by those who entered politics during the 1950s-1960s.

The 1980s-1990s coincided with the arrival of a new generation of actors. This generation was born after independence and had no experience of colonisation or the anti-colonial struggle. Rather, they were the product of the Algerian educational system and were trained in the new programmes, almost always in Arabic. Their composition is extremely heterogeneous, but all aspire to power. Indirectly, they pose the dual problem of their political integration and the renewal of elites, which leads to tensions with the 'November generation'.

The third generation is now seeking to enter political life. They began to gain power in associations, trade unions and political parties after October 1988, within a context of multi-partyism. The framework of the Kabylie Citizens Movement is representative of this generation, which is only just beginning. The centralisation of resources, under the control of the state, was realised in 1962-1963, and later in 1971 and 1975. The political, economic and cultural domains belonged exclusively to the state and its representatives, who intervened to regulate or control private activities.

The old political grouping lost legitimacy after 1954, when it failed to take an active part in the war of independence. In 1962, the political service and top administrative posts were reserved for those who had been active in the struggle for independence. Special accelerated legislation was adopted to facilitate access to universities and the public service for ex-Moudjahidine (combatants). The notion of a 'revolutionary family' emerged in 1993-1994, including the National Organisation of Moudjahidine, the FLN and the associations created in their wake. Access to employment, credit and property was facilitated for children of the *Chahid* (martyrs) and descendants of the Moudjahidine.

There were few economic elites in trade and industry at the time of independence. They were at first not threatened, and developed on the fringes of the public economic sector, thanks to the state markets. The codes regulating investments and state monopolies on foreign trade, however, seriously limited their positions. The agricultural revolution in 1975 was the first real attack on the economic elites. It affected landowners, who managed large agricultural holdings or accumulated property while in public office. In 1962-1963, the previously colonial lands had been nationalised and managed by workers' collectives. The nationalisation of hydrocarbon in 1971 placed the primary wealth of the country under the control of the state.

The cultural and traditional religious elites were disqualified by the massive schooling of children, and distribution, by the state apparatus, of religious discourses from the Oulema Association. Accused of being archaic and conservative, they had to make way for elites linked to the *Nahda* (Renaissance). Certain religious orders were even accused of having sided with the colonisers.

The centralisation of resources led to the almost complete elimination of the elites that emerged during the colonial period. The renewal was brutal and rapid. The new elites, educated in the wake of nationalism and the war of independence, subordinated all sectors of social life and dominated the political sphere. With exclusively political resources, they constantly sought ways to keep themselves in power and ensure their continued control. Their education and training served to reinforce their authoritarian tendencies. The patriarchal family was strongly unsettled by the agrarian laws in the second half of the nineteenth century. The migratory movements of the twentieth century and the industrialisation after independence only deepened the crisis. The system lost power, but only in the urban areas and in a narrow social class, giving rise to the nuclear family in its stead.

Elsewhere, the cultural model transmitted by the family was largely authoritarian: authority of parents over children, boys over girls, and father over all: "The frequency of paternal authoritarianism, this metaphorical 'sultanate', has had a lasting effect up until today, thus reducing the 'civic space'".[40] Relations within the family were above all, relations of authority, domination and dependence. The supreme authority of the father was based on punishment. "Familial repression is implacable. [The child] is raised to be obedient, subordinate to those who are above him, father, older brother, chief of the clan, president".[41]

Mothers, themselves, prepare their daughters to accept the roles that have traditionally been defined for them.[42] A founder member of the collective *Femmes du Printemps Noir* (Women of the Black Spring) confirms the difficulties women experience in fighting for equality and liberty: "Kabylie society is a patriarchal society, it is not easy for a women to engage in this combat with much ease. The sociological nature of the arch-ancestors does not make the task simple for women to participate fully and entirely".[43]

Obedience and submission run the risk of violence towards women and children. Women belong to all, and most socio-professional categories accept violence by husbands towards their wives.

> In stead and place of affective implications of respect and shared affection is found the over-determination of the macho image of the ideal spouse, of the man who is himself the troubled and sexist imaginary of a society still stuck in archaic structures; and a conjugal space where repression, domination, stifling, collapse, imprisonment and tyranny all mingle together.[44]

In 2002 the legal and psychological monitoring centre of the Association of Women in Distress received more than 10 000 calls from married women who were victims of conjugal violence. The age of the affected women ranged between 5 and 70 years.[45]

Socialisation, education and training in the educational system, from primary school to university, are also not exempt from authoritarianism. The massive school attendance of children (boys and girls) is one of the most remarkable achievements since independence. The educational policy put an end to colonial education and mobilised education for national construction and economic development. However, these programmes, coupled with rapid Arabisation and the pedagogic teacher-pupil relationship, tend to reinforce authoritarian relations built up in the family. The creation of new programmes is primarily linked to new contents, especially in history and philosophy. Religious education is introduced at a young age, and is centred on learning the Qur'an. However, the interpretation of the Qur'an remains the monopoly of religious functionaries, whose exegesis is based less on the sacred text itself than on the traditional commentaries which followed it.

The Arabisation of teaching, proclaimed in the nationalist programme before 1962, has been vigorously and rapidly implemented since independence. Classical Arabic, used in the schools, is closely linked to literacy and classical culture on the one hand, and to the Qur'anic model on the other. The Qur'anic context dictates the rules for using the language and provides the structures of thought.[46] It imposes on the learners and the teachers themselves. Rapid Arabisation has had the consequence of a massive recruitment of new teachers in Algeria and other Middle Eastern countries (Egypt, Syria, Iraq). They come from a traditional teaching background that has hardly been affected by modernisation. Their training emphasises the "traditionalisation" of teaching.

The pedagogic relationship creates little room for the learner or even for pedagogy itself. Rather, it reproduces the traditional *kuttab* (school) based on the authority of the teacher and 'rote learning' among the pupils. Rote learning, based on memorising and not encouraging questioning, is the norm. The teacher or professor's monologue places the accent on consensus, excluding any difference or questioning by the learner. Algerian schools in the year 2003, adopted peculiar methods of teaching. They used the so-called "methods of another age, completely obsolete, dominated by an authoritative, univocal and dogmatic discourse" and produced learners who demonstrate "complacent deference, blind obedience to the little zaïm, which prefigures the later unreserved obedience to larger zaïms". There is little space for among other things "the free will of the learners, these future citizens are completely torn apart from the state, which sees itself as the law".[47]

The entry into politics as an adult does not substantially change this education and training. In fact, the contrary would be more true. The political experience of elites is the most difficult area to document, particularly for post-independence generations. Since October 1988, various biographies, as well as memoirs have been published by men of the "generation of 1st November". Political experience was more open, paradoxically, before 1954 than between 1954 and 1962 and after that date. Compared to Morocco and Tunisia, Algeria had lengthy experience of political pluralism between 1919 and 1954 within the limited framework of colonial legislation. Many militants of the period today evoke the anti-colonial political debates and struggles. Electoral contests were open, including those among nationalist parties.[48]

The first turning point came in 1954, when Bouhara, a teacher in Constantine, became part of the *maquis* in eastern Algeria and was later integrated into the ALN troops stationed in Tunisia near the Algerian front. He provided portraits of the officers with whom he collaborated, dividing them into three profiles. The first generation was essentially political. It emerged from the political parties that led an armed struggle. The second was the "warriors" – they came after 1956 and took part in military combat themselves. The third includes the cadres formed during the armed struggle in the military academies of the Middle East (Egypt and Iraq).[49] Djillali, who belongs to the post-independence generation, devotes long passages to the historical role of the "1st November generation" and the consequences of the armed struggle for the formation of elites:

> The Algerian Revolution acted as a strong factor in the selection of men whose psychological profile conformed with the norms imposed by the war. The men who became commanders or directors of the opera-

tions, and who formed as a result the political and ruling elite of the country, had more need of character and motivation than of university instruction or openness of spirit.

After independence, "with no experience of the state ... no political culture or technical training, certain of them twisted power like sorcerers' apprentices. The state was created out of chaos".[50]

The Post-Independence Generation

For the post-independence generation, political experience can be found in state institutions and in the sole party and its mass organisations. The usual official channel for recruiting elites is to poach university graduates. Engineers, doctors and economists are given political functions after a career of managing public enterprises and administration. Between 1985 a nd 1990, 1 800 nominations by decree were made, although fewer than a thousand posts follow this procedure. In five years, the entire top personnel of the state were twice renewed.[51]

According to General Nezzar, "in no case was there a real recruitment process. Appointments were made any how".[52] A top official places the criteria for access to high-level posts in the following hierarchy: "There are first of all personal relations, family ties, regionalism, common interests, corruption and finally partisan or political affiliations".[53] Competence "is sometimes considered in fourth position; it has been third and even second but never first". The culture of high-level officials is ambiguous. They have the experience of the necessary and rational conduct of the state's business, but have to submit to the constraints of allegiances among the top political personnel, who proceed from cooptation to promotions.

The other recruiting channel, as stated previously, is represented by the sole party and its mass organisations. This conduit is used by the young, Arabisers, and local and regional representatives. It is not frequently discussed or publicised, with the exception of Bouchama, who has written various works that trace his political career and activities.[54] He started by becoming active in the National Union of Algerian Youth, as an official and then a member of the central committee of the FLN, and finally Minister of Youth and Sports, before October 1988. His deliberately optimistic texts are a defence of the FLN at a time when the policy of centralisation, and Article 120 were subject to harsh criticism in the press. This fraction of the elites sought a political experience marked by the absence of democratic debate, by conformity, and, for some, by populist demagogy.

Lacheraf is one of the rare politicians to criticise the archaic consequences of nationalism and the national liberation struggle. Even today, these have not entirely disappeared. A weekly newspaper noted in 2003, that "the morals of our rulers are based on ruses, lies, arbitrariness and impunity".[55] It also argued that the "absence of a tradition of debate is a historical deficit". The opposition political parties are just as guilty. In fact, political pluralism since 1989 has revealed how unprepared the elites are for the democratic management of public affairs and for the pursuit of economic development. Political education, training and experience are dominated by the central figure of the father (the patriarch). In family life, at school, in business and in political life, the will of the superior (biological father, principal, political leader) is absolute. It creates a "forced consensus based on ritual and coercion".[56]

Chances for, and Indicators of, Reform

Among the most commonly asked questions in the Algerian political discourse are: Can the current immobility around reforms continue? Do reforms have a future? Will the political elites choose the uncomfortable status quo or will they take the risk of opening up and changing? Do they prefer an increasingly unacceptable present to an unpredictable future? Will governance improve? What are the most pertinent indicators to evaluate public policies?

Existing conceptions and indicators of governance are not always adequate to evaluate the necessary policies for deepening reforms.[57]

Apart from a purely formal evaluation, it is important to identify possible (elite and social) coalitions that could be used to construct a new historic bloc in place of that of nationalism, which declined in the decade 1980-1990.

The opposition between traditionalists and more modern elites, frequently discussed in the literature, does not take into account the extreme complexity of the composition, positions and strategies of elites. Many disagreements fragment the two so-called camps and make the identification of pro-change groups more complex. The difficulties of a political analysis are recognised by researchers in the social sciences, as well as political actors. There are three main difficulties.

The opacity of the political system is very strong. It does not only concern the taking of decisions (by whom? according to what procedure?), but also the political engagements of members of different institutions. W. B. Quandt notes that, "Some claim to see complex struggles between factions among these powerful personalities, and that is no doubt true. But this area of Algerian politics remains inaccessible to the ordinary Algerian and almost entirely to the outside world as well".[58] This lack of transparency is the source of many rumours and suppositions that are spread in the press and discussions over coffee.

Second, the reversibility of political engagements and the circulation of elites is remarkable. This is true among political organisations and trade unions, as well as politicians. The Rally for Culture and Democracy (Rassemblement pour la Culture et la Démocratie) RCD supports, primarily, Bouteflika's policies before proceeding to a more radical critique. On the other hand, the Socialist Forces Front (Front des Forces Socialistes) FFS was in opposition to Bouteflika in 1998 before reconciling and participating in the local elections of October 2002, after having boycotted the legislative elections. Upcoming elections regularly provide an opportunity for politicians to move from one party to another. Differences among their programmes are ignored when given the opportunity to be listed as a candidate.

Finally, the weight and pursuit of political violence (terrorism) clouds real political choices by moving economic, social and cultural issues on to the back burner. The term "reformers" is intended to designate, on the one hand, the small group of experts and high-level officials who drew up the texts of reform, between October 1988 and 1991, at the level of the presidency; on the other hand, it also refers, chronologically, to the policies of the Hamrouche government.[59] It is seldom used in political discourse because of these connotations. The head of state, an Abdesselem, following concerned reactions from the press and certain parties, used the term "secular assimilationists". He does not define precisely who the secular assimilationists are, nor does he state what they oppose in the political domain. The Islamist parties isolate these 'Westernised' groups (Djaballah and the Movement for National Reform, MRN) or the 'Hizb França' or 'Frenchified' groups (Nahnah and Hamas). The opposition between 'eradicators' and 'reconcilers' is more radical, linked as it is to terrorism and Islam's place in society. The opposition between 'Islamo-nationalists' and Republican democrats is undoubtedly less polemical, yet more meaningful.

Economic and social problems are less responsible for these dichotomies than cultural and political issues. Everything continues as if all the political parties and elites were in favour of the market economy and liberalism, with the exception of the Labour Party, whose programme is a scathing critique of the economic reforms and the World Bank. The reform of the petrol company SONATRACH and the legal statute on nationalised land, which has recently risen, is leading to unexpected political disputes. These may be considered a good indicator to distinguish those for and against reforms.

The opposition between the dominant and the dominated is, in fact, not mentioned in the programmes or discourse of the political parties. The separation between the haves and have-nots is full of meaning and a useful social analysis to distinguish between those in favour of the status quo and those who would favour change. The notion of a rentier state, which has been described in the social sciences and taken up by the political parties, takes into account the central role of hydrocarbon in the economy and social redistribution.[60]

The absence of institutionalisation (organisational or in a programme) of the pro-reformers makes it difficult to identify them. In contrast, the multiple diagnostics of the current situation in Algeria are targeting reforms to be undertaken in a concrete manner.[61] The indicators to evaluate reforms must measure the systematic (or otherwise) character of these tools.

The World Bank, United Nations Development Programme (UNDP) and European Union (EU) define a good elite as an ethical leadership that comprises the values of democracy, justice, respect for human rights, credibility, responsibility, duty, freedom of speech, development, altruism and integrity. For its part, the UNDP's Arab Human Development Report defines good governance as that which "promotes, drives and supports human well-being, by developing capacity, choices, skills and liberties (both economic and social as well as political), especially in the case of the most needy and the most marginalised in society".[62] Moreover, it attributes "Arab decadence" to the absence of liberty, equality between the sexes, and democracy, and a lack of knowledge. Compared to other regions, the Arab world suffers from a "freedom deficit". Political participation is under-developed, institutions are under-developed, and the quality of those institutions involved in governance is poor. Freedom of expression and association are, however, more widespread than they were twenty years ago.

The Arab Human Development Report uses indicators that have not been used before. In its first version, the author, Fergany, proposed the construction of a more relevant measuring instrument than the human development index (HDI), as the latter clouds the complexity of the notion of human development, which is indissociable from human liberty. Fergany presents his personal attempt as a point of departure for more detailed research and more accurate statistics.

Conclusion

The example of Algeria suggests various means for the design of a new indicator in assessing democracy, political reform, economic transformation and good governance. It must allow for evaluations of different countries and, thus, must be rather generalised. It must also not be too abstract, and lose its contextualised meaning within regional and national situations. It should also take into account the transitional phase that many countries are undergoing. Algeria, which is often seen as an exceptional case, is not really exceptional. It is an authoritarian regime that opened up in the decade 1980-1990 and began a transition towards democracy and the market economy. Furthermore, the available indicators presuppose an implicit conception of democracy and economic liberalism that has become the standard for evaluating governance and public policies.

Finally, an indicator must measure the strategic elements of reform and good governance. The indicators used may appear purely formal and often associated with the conditionalities of the World Bank and development aid. Theories of transition distinguish three phases: the fall of authoritarian regimes is followed by democratisation, which must be consolidated in a third phase. Simple political liberalisation is not automatically followed by democratisation. Any indicator should evaluate the politics of passing from liberalisation to democratisation and then to consolidation. The components of the indicator would then feature the strategic elements that would lead to irreversible reform and change. The example of Algeria clearly shows that reforms are not irreversible and that democratisation may only signify liberalisation.

In fact, indicators should evaluate reform policies and not only the formal and legal aspects of governance. From a historical point of view, the problem is fundamental, to ensure a real change. It is similar to a revolution and should carry the necessary elements to reflect that condition.[63] There are five key indicators that evaluate political reforms and political governance. These include:

1. the status of religion involving freedom of worship and religious tolerance
2. training including programmes, teacher training, history, philosophy, and human rights
3. the family with emphasis on male-female relations, parenthood, child care and child abuse
4. State-citizen relations especially fairness before the law and autonomy or independence of the judicial system
5. equality with emphasis on protection and provision of social aid.

These five indicators are not intended to replace the classic indicators, such as the existence of a competitive electoral system, recognition of parliament's legislative function, political participation, the presence of a strong civil society, good governance of businesses, and rule of law. They complement each other and thus serve to better evaluate current and future changes.

Governance

'African Charter for Popular Participation in Development and Transformation', *IFDA Dossier*, no 79, December 1990.

'Chapitre 7: Les incertitudes de l'âge planétaire', *Le Grand Atlas de l'histoire mondiale*, Paris: EU France SA et A Michel, 1991.

'L'opposition dans les parlements africains', Actes du séminaire parlementaire régional sur Rôle et responsabilités de l'opposition dans les parlements africains, Ouagadougou, 15-16 November 1996.

African Leadership Forum, 'Africa and the Successor Generation', Summary Report and Papers presented at the tenth Anniversary of the African Leadership Forum, Cotonou, 26-28 November 1998.

A Benbitour, *L'expérience algérienne de développement 1962-1991. Leçons pour l'avenir*, Alger: Ed techniques de l'entreprise ISGP, 1993.

M Boukhobza, *Octobre 1988: évolution ou rupture*, Alger: Bouchène, 1991.

CEDEJ, *Démocratie et démocratisation dans le monde arabe*, Cairo: CEDEJ, 1992.

P Engelhard, *L'Afrique miroir du monde*, Paris: Arléa, 1998.

S Goumeziane, Le mal algérien: économie politique d'une transition inachevée 1962-1994, Paris: Fayard, 1994.

A Kapil, *L'évolution du régime autoritaire en Algérie*, Paris: CNRS, 1990.

D Liabès, 'Rentes, légitimité et statu quo: quelques éléments de réflexions sur la fin de l'Etat providence', Cahiers du CREAD, no 6, 1986.

A Ly, *La théorisation de la connexion capitaliste des continents: Point de vue d'un historien*, Dakar: IFAN-UCAD, 1994.

R Otayek, 'Démocratie, culture politique, sociétés plurales: une approche comparative à partir des situations africaines', *RFSP*, vol 47, no 6, December 1997.

J Pennef, 'Trajectoires sociales et carrières des patrons algériens', *ARSS*, no 41, February 1982.

G Salamé, 'Sur la causalité d'un manque: pourquoi le monde arabe n'est-il pas démocratique?', *RFSP*, no 41, June 1991.

M Touraine, *Le bouleversement du monde: Géopolitique du XXIe siècle*, Paris: Seuil, 1995.

World Bank, *Le développement au seuil du XXIe siècle: Rapport sur les développement dans le monde*, Washington: World Bank, 2000.

World Bank, *Can Africa claim the 21st century?*, Washington: World Bank, 2000.

A Yefsah, 'Armée et politique depuis les événements d'octobre 1988: L'armée sans hidjab', *Les temps modernes*, no 50, January-February 1995.

Y Dezalay and B Garth, 'Le "Washington Consensus": contribution à une sociologie de l'hégémonie du néo-libéralisme', *ARSS*, no 121-122, 1998.

Notes and References

1   Contrary to what was written in the article 'Elites' in the *Encyclopedia Universalis* (research on elites in the Third World "has led to rich, vivid monographs of contemporary history, which don't teach us very much about the sociology of elites"), there is a need to put in place "a new framework for Political Sociology, valid for both democratic pluralist societies as well as authoritarian societies or those in transition". See G. Lowell Field, John Highley, Michael G. Burton, 'A New Framework for Political Sociology', *Revue européenne sciences sociales*, no 88, vol XXVIII, 1998, pp 149-182.

2   W. B. Quandt, *Revolution and Political Leadership: Algeria 1954-1968*, Massachusetts: MIT Press, 1969; J Leca, 'Etat et société en Algérie', in Bassma Kodwani-Derwish (ed), *Maghreb: Les années de transition*, Paris, Masson, 1990.

3   L. Blin, 'Algérie: Les élites politiques', *Les Cahiers de l'Orient*, no 25-26, 1992.

4   Between 1986 and 1996, more than 400 studies of elites and dozens of new interpretations and revisions were published. More than a hundred researchers (historians, political scientists, economists, sociologists, etc) are undertaking research into the issue. G. Busino, *Elites et élitismes*, Paris: PUF, 1996, p 115.

5   *Democracy in Developing Countries*, Boulder: Lynne Rienner Publishers, 1991, vol 1, p 21.

6   For a bibliography in English, see Joseph Roland A. Ayee, 'Political Leadership and Developmental Democracy in Africa', Dakar: CODESRIA, Annual social science conference, 26-29 November 2002.

7   G. Chaussinand-Nogaret, 'Elites', in A. Burguière (ed.), *Dictionnaire des sciences historiques*, Paris: PUF, 1986; P. Bourdieu, 'La représentation politique: Eléments pour une théorie du champ politique', *ARSS*, no 38, 1982.

8   C. Charles, *Les élites de la République 1890-1900*, Paris: Minuit, 1987; G. Chaussinand-Nogaret, *Une histoire des élites, Recueil de textes*, La Haye: Mouton, 1975.

9   A chronology of the transition (1998-2000) has been published by A. Cheurfi, *La classe politique algérienne de 1900 à nos jours: Dictionnaire biographie*, Alger: Casbah, 2001; R. Benyoub, *Annuaire politique de l'Algérie*, Alger: imp ANEP, 1999; and the annual chronicles of the *Annuaire de l'Afrique du nord* (Paris: CNRS).

10 For an eyewitness account on the context and the team organising these reforms, see G. Hidouci, *Algérie: La libération inachevée*, Paris: La découverte, 1995.

11 A. Dahmani, *L'expérience algérienne des réformes. Problématique d'une transition à l'économie de marché*, Alger: AAN, 1998.

12 *Le Quotidien d'Oran*, 15 December 2002.

13 *El Watan*, cited in, 15 January 2003.

14 Interview with the French journal *Le Point*, reprinted in *Liberté*, 17 January 2003.

15 CNES report, 2nd semester 1999.

16 *Le Quotidien d'Oran*, 23 December 2002.

17 *Liberté*, 19 December 2002.

18 *Liberté*, 19 December 2002.

19 *El Watan*, 16 December 2002.

20 An international mission of the IFHR investigated this subject from 25 July to 1 August 2002. The report, entitled 'Formal pluralism and barriers to the exercise of trade union rights', is cited at length in *El Watan*, 23 December 2002.

21 For example, the National Council of Higher Education claims 8 000 members out of 19 000 teachers in the universities.

22 *Algérie-Hebdo*, no 12, 9-15 January 2003.

23 *Algérie Hebdo*, no 11, 2-8 January 2003. In the social domain (humanitarian and charitable actions, promotion and protection of women and children, helping children in difficulty, and health interventions), the Ministry of Employment and National Solidarity

has counted 1 183 associations, of which 1 085 are local and 98 national. Social associations represent 18%, humanitarian organisations 15%, medical associations 45% and others 6%.

24 Report 2002.
25 *Le Régional*, 12-18 December 2002.
26 *Le Quotidien d'Oran*, 17 December 2002.
27 *Ibid.*, 20 December 2002.
28 *La Tribune*, 1 December 2002.
29 *Liberté*, 17 December 2002.
30 *Le Quotidien d'Oran*, 20 December 2002.
31 The upcoming presidential election in 2004 has revived the reform project. The announcement was made in September-October 2002. The Ministry of Justice is setting up a committee to follow up on the recommendations of the National Commission of Reform and Justice. The Minister of National Education has announced that, as of the beginning of the 2002-2003 school year, the first school reform measures will begin. The Family Code has been re-examined from the perspective of creating a personal statute. The privatisation of enterprises must be sped up.
32 *El Watan*, 16 December 2002.
33 *Les Débats*, 22-28 January 2003.
34 *Algérie-Hebdo*, no 12, 9-15 January 2003.
35 *El Watan*, 28 December 2002.
36 A Cheurfi, *La classe politique algérienne de 1900 à nos jours: Dictionnaire biographique*, Alger: Casbah, 2001.
37 R. Benyoub, *L'Annuaire politique de l'Algérie*, Alger: Auto-édition, 1999.
38 L. Blin, N. Abdi, L. Rejais, B. Stora, *Algérie: 200 hommes de pouvoir*, Paris: Indigo-publications, 1992.
39 On the question of political generations, see J. F. Sirinelli (ed.), *Générations intellectuelles: effets d'âge et phénomène de génération dans le milieu intellectuel français*, Cahiers de l'IHTP, 1997; K. Mannheim, *Le problème des générations*, Paris: Nathan, 1990.
40 J. Berque, 'Préface', in H Sharabi, *Néopatriarcat*, Alger: Ed Marinoor, nd, p 10.
41 Ali Zay'our, *Psychanalyse du Soi arabe*, Beyrouth, 1977, cited by Sharabi, nd, p 62.
42 C. Lacoste-Dujardin, *Les mères contre les filles: Maternité et patriarcat au Mahgreb*, Paris: La Découverte, 1985.

43 Interview in the journal *Izuran-Racines*, no 37, December 2002.

44 *Jeune-Afrique*, no 2139, 19-25 January 2003.

45 *Algérie-Hebdo*, no 14, 23-29 January 2003.

46 "The child's first meeting with classical Arabic language or litera-ture is mediated by the sacred text (Koran) which must usually be learnt by heart. From the beginning, the child thus experiences a dissociation between learning and understanding. His first sponta-neous attempts at questioning and clarification (for example, of meanings, of understanding) are doomed to failure", Sharabi, nd, p 138.

47 *Algérie-Hebdo*, no 12, 9-15 January 2003.

48 T. Chenntouf, *Unité et pluralisme pendant la guerre d'indépendance d'Algérie au miroir des décolonisations françaises*, Paris: Société françaises d'histoire d'Outre mer, 2000, pp 283-306.

49 A. Bouhara, *Les Viviers de la Révolution*, Algeria, 2002.

50 S. Djillali, *L'Algérie, une nation en chantier*, Algeria: Casbah, 2002, pp 24, 28

51 M'hammed Boukhobza, *Alger-Actualités*, 8-14 October 1992.

52 *Mémoires du général Kh. Nezzar*, Alger: Chihab, 2000, p 135.

53 Cited by Cheurfi 2001, pp 10-11.

54 *La JFLN un passé glorieux, un avenir ininterrompu*, Algeria: ANEP, 1986; *Le FLN, instrument et alibi du pouvoir*, Algeria: Dahleb, 1990; *Le FLN a-t-il jamais eu le pouvoir?*, Algeria: El Maarifa, 1994.

55 *Algérie-Hebdo*, no 14, 23-29 January 2003.

56 Sharabi, nd, p 27.

57 For a history and critique of the concept of governance elaborated by the World Bank, see R. Charlick, 'Le concept de gouvernance et ses implications en Afrique', in M. Esoavelomandroso and G Feltz (eds), *Démocratie et développement: Mirage ou espoir raisonna-ble?*, Paris-Antananarivo: Karthala-Omaly si Anio, 1995, pp 17-42.

58 W. B. Quandt, *Société et pouvoir en Algérie*, Algeria: Casbah, 1998, p 174.

59 A good account is given in the work of G. Hidouci, who was him-self one of these reformers. See *Algérie: La libération inachevée*, Paris: La Découverte, 1995.

60 Algerian National Economic and Social Review, 'Avis: Stratégie nationale de développement économique et social à moyen terme',

8e session plénière, mai 1997; 'Rapport national sur le développement humain', novembre 2000; 'Projet d'étude sur la maîtrise de la globalisation: une nécessité pour les plus faibles', 17e session plénière; 'Rapport national sur le développement social', April 1999.

61 D. Liabès, 'Rentes, légitimité et statu quo: quelques éléments de réflexion sur la fin de l'Etat providence', Cahiers du CREAD, 1986, no 6; S. Goumeziane, Le mal algérien: économie politique d'une transition inachevée 1962-1994, Paris: Fayard, 1994.

62 UNDP, Human Development Report 2002, Deepening democracy in a fragmented world, 2002.

63 The Arab Human Development Report UNDP 2003 speaks of "Arab decadence" and emphasises "the disaster of development in the Arab countries".

Further Reading

B'Chir Badra, 'Réflexions sur le concept des élites chez le sociologue arabe', Revue tunisienne des sciences sociales, no. 53, 1978.

Cahiers du CERES, Elites et pouvoir dans le monde arabe pendant la période moderne et contemporaine, Tunis, 1992.

T Chenntouf, 'Les nouvelles élites et la refondation des Etats au Maghreb au 16e siècle dans Felipe II y el Mediterranéo', Barcelone Sociedad Estatal par la Commemoracion de lo Centenarios de Felipe II y Carlos V, vol 2.

T. Chenntouf, 'Le Maghreb poste colonial', Communication au 3è Congrés de l'Association des historiens africains, Bamako, 2000.

CRESM, La formation des élites politiques maghrébines, Paris: LGDJ, 1973.

CRESM, Elites, pouvoir et légitimité au Maghreb, Paris: CNRS, 1978.

D. Gaxie, Les professionnels de la politique, Paris: PUF, 1973.

P. Gremion, Le pouvoir périphérique: bureaucrates et notables dans le système politique français, Paris: Seuil, 1976.

A. Ben Haddou, Maroc: les élites du Royaume, Paris: L'Harmattan, 1997.

E. B. Hermassi, Etat et société au Maghreb. Etude comparative, Paris: Anthropos, 1975.

R. Ilbert, 'La surimposition ders élites: Les cadres de la décolonisation', in C. R. Ageron and M Michel (eds), L'ère des décolonisations, Paris: Karthala-CNRS, 1995.

A. Krichen, *La fracture de l'intelligentsia. Problèmes de la langue et de la culture nationale in Tunisie au présent*, Paris: CNRS, 1986.

J. Lacam, 'Le politicien investisseur: un modèle d'interprétation de la gestion des ressources politiques', *RFSP*, no XXVIII, 1988.

Ministère de l'information et de la culture, *De l'ALN à l'ANP*, Alger, 1979.

C. Monga, 'L'indice de démocratisation: comment déchiffrer le nouvel aide-mémoire de l'autoritarisme', *Africa*, no 22, July-September 1995.

A. Nouschi, 'Qu'est-ce qu'un bourgeois ? Qu'est-ce qu'un notable?', *Les Cahiers de Méditerranée*, no 45, December 1992.

M. Offerlé, 'Professions et profession politique', in *La profession politique. XIXe-XXe siècles*, Paris: Belin, 1999.

N. Peuvolaropoulou, 'Temps historique et générations chez K Mannheim', *L'homme et la société*, no 111–112, 1994.

D. Richet, 'Autour de la Révolution française: Elites et despotisme', *Annales ESC*, no 1, 1969.

Ezra N. Suleman, *Les élites en France: grands corps et grandes écoles*, Paris: Seuil, 1979.

P. Vermeren, *La formation des élites marocaines et tunisiennes. Des nationalistes au islamistes 1920-2000*, Paris: La découverte, 2002.

A. C. Wagner, *Les nouvelles élites et la mondialisation*, Paris: PUF, 1998.

NIGERIA

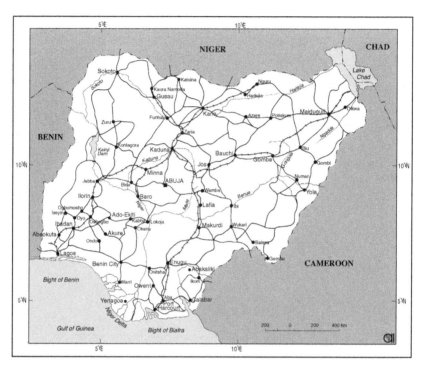

Source: Africa Institute of South Africa, 2005.

4. Evolution and Nature of Nigerian Political Elites and the Realisation of NEPADs Political and Development Agenda

Richard Iroanya

Introduction

After sixteen years (1983-1999) of brutal military dictatorship Nigeria returned to what may be called democratic governance in 1999. Bad governance, endemic corruption, ineffective public institutions, gross human rights abuse, and massive deterioration of infrastructures characterised the period of military rule in the country. The country regressed rather than progressed during this time and came very close to collapsing in 1993 following the annulment of the 12 June presidential election. Owing to these unfortunate developments, the country lost its leadership position on the continent as it was systematically ostracized from the community of nations both in Africa and the world. For instance, its membership of the Commonwealth of Nations was suspended due to the brutal repression that culminated in the conviction and execution of environmental activist Ken Saro-Wiwa and seven other Ogoni activists in 1995.

Since its return to democratic rule, Nigeria has tried to portray herself as a champion of democracy and to reclaim her leading role on the African continent. Thus, the country is actively involved in several bold initiatives that are geared toward solving the perennial political, social and economic challenges facing the African continent. Some of these development initiatives on which Africa's hopes are pinned are the African Union (AU), the New Partnership for Africa's Development (NEPAD), the Pan-African Parliament and the African Peer-Review Mechanism (APRM). Nigeria's active involvement in these development initiatives is not surprising to students of African politics. This is because since the country's independence in 1960, Africa has always been the cornerstone of its foreign policy.

Despite the presumed return to democratic governance, and active involvement in continental initiatives, Nigeria is still politically unstable. Structural conditions, which historically have prevented her from evolving the requisite political will necessary for political, social and economic development, remain largely unresolved. Among these structural conditions are ethnicity, which often results in electoral malpractices, corruption, nepotism, and despotic leadership. Others include, marginalisation, which has resulted in lopsided development, endemic poverty and the ever-present fear of military intervention into politics. Against this background, this chapter aims to examine the trends in the emergence of the present crop of Nigeria's political elites. The focus on elites is because they are "the chief decision makers in government, economic, military, media, labour, professional and cultural organisations in societies such as Nigeria".[1] More specifically, the chapter attempts to determine how the elites contribute to, or hamper, Nigeria's delivery on the political and development agenda nationally, regionally and globally. The hypothetical questions guiding this study are: can Nigerian political elites solve their national problems and muster enough proficiency to contribute to regional (AU/NEPAD) and global issues? Would the prevailing political situation in Nigeria and the role of the country's elites contribute or prevent the realisation of the aims and objectives of NEPAD?

To adequately address the above question, this chapter is structured in four main sections. The first section centres on conceptual clarification of the elite and the historical evolution of the Nigerian elites. The second section will address the various factors that prevent the development of political will and consensus among Nigerian elites to practise sustainable democracy in the country. The third section will examine the current socio-economic cum political situation in the country. This will be done against the background of democracy, good governance and rule of law, which are central to NEPAD. The last section will examine how members of the Nigerian political elites perceive NEPAD and what role they play towards realising its aims and objectives.

Clarification of Concept and Evolution of the Nigerian Political Elite

The concept 'elite' is used in this chapter in congruence with its discussion in the introductory chapter. Lasswell has observed that several kinds of elites exist in a society.[2] In the Nigerian context, the various groups of elites are not easily discernable, even by applying the 'plural elite group' approach. This is because Nigerian elites tend to overlap, converge and blend into a near perfect whole at the level of management and allocation of the country's scarce resources. Sklar tends to reach similar conclusion when he maintained that in Africa "elites fuse into a dominant group that include wealthy business men, senior administrators in both private and public sectors, seasoned politicians, professionals, and traditional rulers that represent main sources of power".[3] This situation creates the impression that a single elite group exists in Nigeria. The Nigerian political elites are defined in this chapter as: Nigerians who occupy positions of responsibility by whatever means, and by virtue of their positions make decisions that have far-reaching consequences on members of the Nigerian society. A positional identification of elites is used to include the National Executive Council (the president, Cabinet ministers and special advisers), state executive councils (governors, commissioners and advisers), members of national and state houses of assembly, local government chairpersons, top civil servants, heads of government parastatals and political party leaders. The subsequent sections will show how members of the Nigerian political elite evolved under various administrations in Nigeria, what factors led to their emergence, and why they have continued to dominate the Nigerian political scene.

The Evolution of the Nigerian Political Elite

The evolution of the Nigerian political elites took various forms, dictated by certain historical circumstances and events. For a better understanding of this process, this section is organised into specific periods in Nigerian political history. Note should be taken that Nigerian history is extensive and cannot be adequately exhausted in a discourse such as this. Thus, the pre-colonial and colonial periods of Nigeria's history have been left out, although socio-political problems, which originated from these periods, have continued to influence Nigeria's political process.

Evolution of the Elites in the First Republic (1960-1966)

The Nigerian nation was artificially created in 1914 as several scholars have shown.[4] The forceful integration of diverse ethnic groups and cultures by the British colonial administrators created several problems. One of these problems was, and still, is the lack of national integration or national identity in Nigeria. Through its 'divide and rule' system the British colonial administration encouraged the perpetuation of this problem by making no sustained effort to discourage it and foster national integration among Nigeria's diverse ethnic groups. This negligence was deliberate mainly because the system enhanced British economic exploitation of the country.[5] This would, however, have lasting implications for the newly independent Nigerian state. For instance, the evolution of its political elites and the art of wealth accumulation have followed the patterns established by the former British colonial system.

Although the colonial system discouraged national integration in Nigeria, it is important to stress here that the colonial administration did not create the Nigerian political elites, as it is currently constituted. The Nigerian political elites as currently characterized is, arguably a creation of the country's post-independent socio-political processes. This is because the concept of elite as employed here has its origin in Western history and thinking.[6] This assertion may be contrary to the views of some scholars who claim that Nigeria had discernable political elites at independence. It may also question whether pre-colonial Nigerian societies were totally egalitarian. Indeed pre-colonial Nigerian societies were certainly not egalitarian. Certain degrees of inequalities existed in them. For example, there were kings, chiefs, and titlehold-ers, who could be regarded as elites distinct from non-titleholders. However, the nature and functions of these pre-colonial 'elites' were quite different from the Westphalia type of political elites that have emerged after independence. Those pre-colonial prominent leaders did not metamorphose into the Western type of political elites that are under discussion here.

Thus, based on Western understanding of elites, Smythe and Smythe observed that at the dawn of Nigeria's independence in 1960, there was no "crystallised circle of elite families in any given Nigerian community".[7] The scholars further explained that there were "only individuals and their immediate families who were looked upon as elites[8] and most of them lived in government-reserved areas (GRA) and others lived in predominantly working class neighbourhoods".[9] They related very well with the people whose interest they repre-sented and were subjected to the same harsh colonial conditions as the rest of the people. These features are remarkably different from the present characteristics of those who constitute the country's political elites.

The "individuals" referred to by Smythe and Smythe were largely the so-called nationalist leaders who were at the forefront of the struggle for the country's independence. Prominent among them were people like Dr Nnamdi Azikiwe, Dr Michael Okpara, Chief Obafemi Awolowo, Chief Samuel L. Akintola, Sir Ahmadu Bello, and Sir Abubakar Tafawa Balewa. These people were leaders of the three main regions of the Nigerian federation, namely Eastern, Western and Northern regions. They were also leaders of the three major political parties of the first republic, namely the National Council of Nigeria Citizens (NCNC), the Action Group (AG) and the Northern People's Congress (NPC) respectively. These nationalist leaders, together with their followers, occupied prominent positions of authority at indepen-dence both at regional and national levels of the Nigerian political system. According to Smythe and Smythe, certain factors such as, urbanisation, Westernisation, education, foreign contact and popular media aided the emergence of these elites.[10] Another condition, which equally contributed to the emergence of this group of people, was the prevalent politico-economic ideology of the 1960s, which centred on state-directed development.[11] Since the state generates and allocates resources, it provided opportunity for public servants, politicians and their cohorts to acquire personal wealth.

Thus, politicians, public servants and business people capitalised on their positions in the country, to connive with those in power to set the process for the insidious formation, domination and perpetuation of elites in Nigeria. The desire to amass personal wealth resulted in intense competition for control of state resources among politicians. This was the beginning of the institutionalisation of large-scale corruption among public office holders in Nigeria. The competition for control of state resources was, however, more regionally based because the then regions were powerful and autonomous, and relied on revenue from agricultural products and natural resources to pursue a separate development agenda.[12] Revenue allocation in the country was based on the principle of efficiency characterised by derivation, revenue generation capability and fiscal efficiency. This principle gave the regions 50% control over their resources.[13] Emerging elites from ethnic minority groups who felt marginalised under the three main regions clamoured for the creation of new regions specifically for this reason. It should be noted that based on the nature of emerging elites at the time, it is possible to argue that those who clamoured for the creation of new regions at the time did so, not necessarily to protect the interest of their peoples, but for their own personal aggrandisement.

The First Republic collapsed in January 1966 due to intense political instability as a result of the division between the North and South, minority agitation, ethnic rivalries, electoral fraud, and manipulated population census. Suffice it to say, emerging elites at this time were more individualistic and exclusive in their thinking; more regionally inclined and loosely connected at the national level. Mustapha further observed that they also tended towards competition and authoritarianism.[14] Despite this, the process of national elite formation and coalescence into a dominant class in the Nigerian political system was set at this time.[15] The military that took over power in 1966, through its undemocratic actions and policies, helped to fast track the formation, consolidation and entrenchment process of this group of people in the Nigerian society. The role of the military in this process will be examined shortly.

The Military and the Evolution of the Political Elites in Nigeria (1966-1979)

As has been pointed out in the last section, intense political instability in the 1960s led to the first military incursion into Nigerian politics on 15 January 1966. The military coup did not, however, resolve the country's political impasse; rather, it worsened the situation as uncontrollable events led the country into a civil war.

The Federal Military Government (FMG) under the leadership of Yakubu Gowon took a number of radical actions that impacted on the structure of the country's federalism and the process of its elites' evolvement, fusion and entrenchment in the Nigerian society. First, the military abolished the three regional structure of the country in 1967, and created twelve states in their place. With this development, a new context began to emerge in Nigeria. Suberu observed that, with the abolition of regionalism, Nigeria began to transform from a "peripheralised federal system into a centralised federation".[16] After the overthrow of the Gowon administration and the emergence of Generals Murtala Mohammed and Olusegun Obasanjo in 1976, an additional seven states were created, bringing the total number of states of the Nigerian federation to nineteen.

Second, the enactments in 1969 of Petroleum Decrees 51 and 9 were further actions taken by the military to ensure centralisation of power and resource control in Nigeria. By Decree 51 the central government was empowered to own, collect and allocate all oil revenues, issue Oil Exploration Licences (OEL) and Oil Mining Licences (OML). Decree 9 extended the right of ownership of oil and other mineral resources granted the central government by Decree 51 to include all offshore oil revenues as well.

Third, the military also introduced a new revenue allocation principle or formula in 1970. Hitherto, revenue allocation was based on the principle of 'efficiency', specifically tailored to distribute resources judiciously to the most productive or economically viable component units of the federation. The principle was characterised by "derivation, independent revenue, absorptive capacity, tax effort, and fiscal efficiency".[17] Under the principle of efficiency, the regions retained 50 per cent control over their resources as mentioned earlier. With the introduction of the principle of 'equality' by the military in 1970, allocation of resources was and is still based on, even development, national interest and continuity in government services. Other features of the principle include financial comparability, social development, national standard, equality of access to development and land mass.[18] Further efforts at centralisation of resources include the enactment of the Land Use Act of 1978, as intensified by the Land Use Act of 1980. These Acts gave the central government of Nigeria total ownership of all land in the country. Thus, legally it is only the government that has the right to allocate land to individuals, companies, and institutions, only the government can also issue certificate of occupancy.[19]

Fourth, a new revenue allocation formula was followed by the policy of indigenisation in 1972. This policy, alternatively called 'economic nationalism' was a vital component of the country's Second National Development Plan embarked upon by the military. It is instructive to note that the policy was a response by the military to sustained lobbying, which began in the immediate post-independence years, by indigenous Nigerian business people to be allowed to participate fully in the country's economic activities, hitherto massively dominated by foreign investors. The indigenisation policy was implemented through the Nigerian Enterprises Promotion Decree (NEPD) of February 1972, as amended by Decree 3 of 1977. It sought increased involvement of the state in economic activities of the country by buying shares in foreign-owned industries. It equally sought to assist Nigerians to acquire shares in several industries and to be integrally involved in the country's industrial development. Thus, foreign-owned companies were pressurised to sell off a certain percentage of their holdings in Nigeria to the Nigerian government, business people, civil servants and the general public. Under this policy Nigerians were given 100% control and ownership of retail, light manufacturing and low-technology service industries; about 60% ownership and control of technology-intensive industries and financial institutions such as banks and insurance companies. Lastly, Nigerians were allowed 40% control and ownership of high-technology manufacturing industries.[20]

Each policy enunciated by the military, in unique ways contributed to the process of elites' formation and consolidation in Nigeria. First, the centralisation of power and the creation of more states were purported to resolve ethnic minority demand for more regions, foster unity in the country and to 'bring government nearer to the people'. In practice, however, these attempts were in fact aimed at weakening the powers of the old regions consequent upon the political crisis of the 1960s. This is because as the regions ceased to exist, the states that replaced them were not as strong as the regions were. In fact, the states were mere administrative units of the FMG. Furthermore, the creation of states was also targeted at destroying the power base of the secessionist Biafra and wooing the support of political elites from ethnic minority groups of eastern Nigeria during the civil war. More importantly, after the civil war, state creation became a means of pacifying dissatisfied elites, as it provides them spheres of monopolisation in the distribution of the country's resources and also as means of admitting new members into the ruling class. It was never, and is not likely to be, a means of bringing government nearer to the people as often claimed. Nnoli eloquently expressed this view by stating that those who benefit from state creation are civil servants, "who become permanent secretaries in the new states, academics, and other professionals who become commissioners, chairmen of public corporations, and directors of various institutes belonging to their new states".[21] Other categories of people who also benefit from this exercise are contractors and business people, who monopolise official contracts in their respective states.

Secondly, by centralising resource control in Nigeria through Decrees 51 and 9 of 1969 and through the introduction of new revenue allocation principle and various Land Use Acts, the central government was made much stronger than the federal units. These decrees shifted the terrain of competition for political power and resource control from the regions or states to the national level. Thus, the central government became and has remained a converging point of various elites from different regions and ethnic groups of the Nigerian federation competing for shares of the country's resources. These elites were diverse in their professional, intellectual and socio-economic orientations. There were the military, politicians, civil servants, academics, business people, and even traditional rulers. For instance, although the military were in power, old politicians from the First Republic were appointed to important positions in the country. Some were federal commissioners, special advisers and consultants to both the Gowon and the Murtala/Obasanjo regimes.

Thirdly, the process of elite formation and consolidation and the development of common interest were facilitated by the end of the civil war, readmission of Igbo elites through the post-war policy of 'Reconstruction, Rehabilitation and Reconciliation' and the introduction of the Policy of Indigenisation. Although this policy was intended as a means of transforming the economy and redistributing the country's wealth in the interest of all Nigerians, its shortcomings were massively exploited by several emerging elites for private wealth accumulation. As Graf succinctly observed, "indigenisation exemplifies express state policies aimed at furthering the interests of the indigenous forming elites".[22] The programme did not succeed in transforming the economy or in redistributing the wealth of the country in the interest of all. Rather, it ended up widening the economic disparity gap in the country.

The evolving elites, through these policies, developed a common economic and political interest in the unity, and stability of Nigeria and a consistent, complex system of interaction and sustenance of themselves in strategic positions. Most times they reassert their claims to power at national level by whipping up primordial sentiments. This was unlike the 1960s when they were more individualistic and exclusive in their thinking and strategies, regionally inclined and loosely connected at the national level. Against this background Graf has argued that the evolvement of the Nigerian political elites from January 1966 to October 1979, and to the present, can be succinctly described as a 'triangular elite alliance', of the military, the civil service and various business groupings'.[23] However, as the scholar has brilliantly articulated, the military has for all intents and purposes remained the most dominant group within this 'triangular alliance'.

To conclude this section, it is important to state that the nucleus of the present Nigerian political elites was formed during this period. The military largely contributed to this process through issuing of military decrees and counter-decrees, and several development policies and strategies. Other means included manipulation of primordial sentiments and the prevention of the development of strong civil society organisations. As would be seen in subsequent sections of this chapter, elites who have evolved from the 1960s and 1970s, or their cronies, who include sections of the intelligentsia, journalists and professionals, have remained the main powerbrokers in Nigerian politics.

The Nigerian Political Elites and the Collapse of the Second Republic (1979-1983)

After twelve years of dictatorial governance, the military reluctantly handed over the leadership of the country to elected civilians in 1979. Through well-thought-out strategies beginning with the adoption of a new constitution (presidential), enactment of numerous electoral decrees, and rigorous party registration process, the military ensured its collective interests were protected before handing over power to elected civilians. Those who took over from the military were mostly the same crop of elites who were prominent during the First Republic, who also held prominent positions during the twelve years of military dictatorship and were in favour of military policies enumerated in the last section. Since they were party leaders, they had strong influence over those who were elected as governors, members of the national assembly and state assemblies, and also those appointed as commissioners and ministers. Moreover, retired military officers also began to make serious incursions into Nigerian politics as civilians at this time. For this reason Graf reasons that the Second Republic was a conscious creation of the military to ensure military elites continuity.[24] This section examines how this was achieved and why intra-elite squabbles led to the collapse of the Second Republic.

The military adopted a Presidential Constitution as opposed to the Parliamentary Constitution used during the First Republic. Under this system, which is still in use, the Office of the President became the most powerful position in the country. The system serves very well the interests of those who centralised the country's administration and resources control, as the component units of the federations depend on revenue allocation from the central government to survive. Knowing the implication of having a strong central government, the military ensured that members of the same crop of elites or their cronies came to power in 1979. This was achieved by restricting the number of registered political parties to five and by ensuring that the parties had similar manifestoes. These manifestoes did not differ radically from policies of the departing military administration. Furthermore, the military banned all forms of political participation outside the framework of registered political parties. Trade unions were not allowed to join or provide financial support to any political party. No one was allowed to contest election as an independent candidate.[25]

The five political parties that met the rigorous requirements for the registration of political parties were: The National Party of Nigeria (NPN), the Unity Party of Nigeria, (UPN), The Nigerian People's Party (NPP), The Great Nigerian People's Party (GNPP), and the People's Redemption Party (PRP).

The five political parties dominated the affairs of the country at the federal, state and local government levels. The NPN won the presidential election and controlled seven states out of a total of nineteen states then. The UPN controlled five western states while NPP won in three states. The GNPP won in two states and the PRP also won two states, in the northern parts of the country. The NPN and the NPP went into alliance, a replica of the ruling coalition of the First Republic between the NPC and NCNC, while UPN like the former AG, became the official opposition.

During the First Republic, Nigeria practised parliamentary democracy inherited from colonial administrators. The emergent political elites of the immediate post-independence years could be said to have failed because they were untutored in the art of governance under this system and were still learning on the job when the First Republic collapsed. It was expected that there would be continuity in the parliamentary system of government during the Second Republic so as to enable the politicians to attain a reasonable degree of mastery of the system. Rather than parliamentary democracy, the military opted for the presidential system of governance for the country – a completely new concept in the country's political history! Thus, some scholars have argued that Nigerian political elites of the Second Republic failed partly because they had no previous experience of a presidential system of governance or the benefit of sufficient time to learn more about the working of the system. Those who adopted the presidential system for the country may have been more fascinated by its name and success in countries such as the United States of America (US) than by a sound understanding of the working of the system. The internal dynamics of the Nigerian society appeared not to have been considered before the system was adopted. The impact of this new system on the Nigerian political process was that politics became a fierce contest in which only the fittest survived. Politicians employed all kinds of strategies, both legal and extra legal, to win elections and to intimidate opposition parties in their strongholds.

Politically motivated assassinations, arsons and lawsuits aimed at destabilising the country and preventing the NPN from ruling became the order of the day. Bills introduced into the National Assembly were hardly passed or assented into laws. This state of affairs was compounded partly by declining economy as a result of gross mismanagement and large-scale corruption by the civilian elites. Severe intra-elite squabbles, almost to the point of lawlessness both at the national, state and local government levels, necessitated the inevitability of a military coup on 31 December 1983.

The Military and Nigerian Elites (1983-1999)

The military component of the Nigerian political elites decided in December 1983 to remove President Shagari from power. This was despite the fact that the interests of the military elites were well protected under civilian leadership. Major-General Mohammadu Buhari took over the leadership of the country after suspending some sections of the 1979 Constitution, and dissolving all democratic institutions such as the presidency, national assembly, and state houses of assembly. Among the reasons cited by the coup plotters for the overthrow of the civilian administration were: mismanagement of the economy, corruption, gross indiscipline, and deteriorating social infrastructures in Nigeria. A critical look, however, at the composition and policies of the Supreme Military Council (SMC) and the Federal Executive Council (FEC) reveals that there was no radical change of government. The Buhari-Idiagbon regime retained the same policies enunciated by the Shagari administration with little modification. The only new thing introduced was a kind of barrack discipline encapsulated in the 'War Against Indiscipline' (WAI) campaign. This can be seen from the fact that certain sections of the elites who were active in the country's politics in the 1970s and who for some reasons were excluded by politicians in the Second Republic bounced back into the main stream of Nigerian governance under Buhari's regime. Almost all his Cabinet ministers were once top civil servants, former members of federal or state executive councils and academics who had once been in government under the military.

Turner and Baker have argued that a conflict of elites' interests was the main reason for the coup of 1983.[26] In furthering their argument they maintained that political-business elites who dominated the ruling party (NPN) became very reckless in plundering the country's resources and in the process tended to marginalise the narrow military elites, who formed the core of the Nigerian political elites. For example, excessive competition for control of state resources, and loss of sense of direction demonstrated in the plundering of the economy not only destabilised the country's socio-economic system, but it also directly affected the business interests of retired military officers, especially those who were involved in agricultural production. The military equally felt that the Shagari's government was interfering with military operations. This was evidenced in the disagreement between Shagari and General Muhammadu Buhari over the handling of the Chadian invasion of Borno state in 1983. Buhari deployed his troops to repel the Chadian attacks and entered into Chadian territory, thereby effectively closing the border between Nigeria and Chad. When President Shagari ordered the withdrawal of the troops, Buhari refused to carry out the Presidential Order. He argued that the withdrawal of Nigerian troops would jeopardise the country's security. It was the quick intervention of the Army Chief of Staff, General Inua Wushishi that compelled Buhari to pull back the troops. It was not surprising therefore when Buhari overthrew Shagari later in the year.[27]

The Buhari-Idiagbon regime was not without its own internal problems that caused its downfall in 1985. The regime was, however, credited with restoring order in the country by arresting and detaining corrupt politicians, many without trial, and causing them to lose millions of nair in stolen money by effecting currency change. It had no coherent policy to address the country's socio-economic crisis inherited from Shagari. Thus, it began to lose favour among ordinary Nigerians and certain sections of the Nigerian political elites, and was eventually ousted from power on 27 August 1985 for three main reasons. First, it was discovered that the regime was partial in its fight against corruption. For example, under the Miscellaneous Offences Decree, people caught in minor criminal acts such as examination malpractices, and tampering with public property such as the National Electric Power Authority (NEPAD) or Nigeria Telecommunications (NITEL) equipment were arrested, hurriedly tried by military tribunals and sent to prison for as long as twenty years. Whereas former public officers implicated in financial scandals involving millions of naira were reappointed to ministerial positions. Second, its leadership style deprived Nigerians of their fundamental human rights. For instance, the government did not tolerate strike actions by workers and any form of demonstrations or public protest. The regime used the National Security Organisation (NSO) to harass, intimate, arrest and torture critics, protesters, student activists and striking workers. By October 1984, the total number of civil servants retrenched by the regime had reached 200 000.[28] Under Decree 4 of 1984, which was enacted to protect public officers against false media reports, journalists were arrested and detained for being critical of the regime's dictatorial rule.

Third, a clash of interests between the politico-military elites impacted negatively on the regime. Consequent upon divisions and disagreements over policies among members of the SMC, Buhari and Idiagbon became suspicious of ambitious military officers who were core members of the coup plot that toppled Shagari. They were kept under close watch and isolated from the main decision-making circle of the regime. Southern elites equally felt marginalised by the regime as important positions went to Nigerians from core northern states of Kano, Kaduna and Sokoto, and of the nineteen members of his SMC, thirteen were northerners.

The isolated faction within the regime, however, allied itself with, and gained strong moral and financial support, from businesspeople and retired southern military officers who still had a degree of influence in the military. This was evidenced from the fact that retired officers such as General Olusegun Obasanjo, and Major-General James Oluleye began publicly to criticize the regime's policies, especially its policy of counter-trade or trade by barter. It was a trade strategy aimed at exchanging oil for technology, raw material and spare parts required in the country. The policy was the regime's alternative for International Monetary Fund (IMF) loans, which it had rejected in 1984. Critics of the policy believed that the negative effects of the policy on the Nigerian economy far outweighed its benefits.[29] For instance, counter-trade encouraged corruption as the Aboyade Commission appointed by the Babangida regime discovered in 1986. The most vocal critics of the regime were retired military officers; their criticisms were in most cases interpreted as tacit calls on the military to effect a change of government in Nigeria. It was therefore not surprising that on 27 August 1985, Babangida and his cohorts capitalized on the unpopularity of the regime among Nigerians and certain sections of the elites to stage a palace coup.

The Nigerian Political Elites under the General Ibrahim Babangida Regime (1985-1993)

One major task that every military regime confronts when it comes to power is the mobilisation of the support of the elites and the masses as a means of legitimizing itself. The Babangida regime was very successful at this task. The regime in actual fact was elites-centred. It took certain bold measures to galvanize the support of both the military and the civilian factions of the Nigerian political elites. For example, the regime reorganized the Supreme Military Council (SMC) and Federal Executive Council (FEC) and renamed them, respectively, the Armed Forces Ruling Council (AFRC) and National Council of Ministers (NCM). It also tried to unite the various factions within the military by reappointing five former members of the SMC in the deposed junta into the AFRC, and ensured that the AFRC was composed of only military officers. Furthermore, six former ministers under Buhari such as Professor Tam David West (a top academic) were also retained in ministerial positions as part of the reconciliatory effort of the regime. Through this strategy Babangida was able to galvanise the support of the top echelon of the military institution.

In turn, the regime equally attempted to address the north-south dichotomy in the country by appointing southern elites to strategic positions such as the Chief of General Staff. Other retired military officers, mostly from the south, such as General Alani Akinrinade, were also co-opted into the regime as ministers. Prominent civilians representing trade unions and other groups in the society were also included. They were not totally new to government, as some had held positions before under other military regimes, especially in the 1970s. These civilian ministers were carefully chosen because they represented various interest groups that strongly opposed Buhari's regime.[30] It further sought to legitimize itself by repealing some of the unpopular decrees and policies of Buhari-Idiagbon such as Decree 4 of 1984 and by announcing on 13 January 1986 that it was prepared to hand over power to elected civilians in 1990. As a further attempt at ensuring the support of the Nigerian political elites, and in the process consolidate his powers, Babangida released corrupt former civilian governors and ministers in Shagari's government who were been detained without trial by the Buhari-Idiagbon regime. Shagari himself and former Vice-President Alex Ekwueme were also acquitted of corruption charges and released in 1986.

Various other economic and political strategies were employed by the regime to expand the elites' class, and sustain its support and resource accumulation. For instance, through its privatisation policy, the regime allowed both military and civilians elites unrestricted access, control and eventual ownership of public parastatals. Through its Second-Tier Foreign Exchange Market (SFEM) policy also, members of the Nigerian political elites had unrestricted access to the country's treasury. SFEM was designed to allow market forces to determine the exchange rate of the Nigerian local currency (naira) and the allocation of foreign exchange. In order to ensure the success of the policy, the government allowed the introduction of Foreign Exchange Bureaux de Change for trading in foreign exchange from the informal sources. This financial policy did not achieve the intended objectives. Rather, it became a means through which both serving and retired military officers and their civilian counterparts became emergency financial experts, specialising solely in mortgage and merchant banking or the so-called finance houses.

These new financial institutions were only interested in foreign currency trading. Thus, according to Lewis and Stein in their study conducted in 1993, 61% of retired military officers had a strong stake in financial institutions in Nigeria.[31] Through ministerial and gubernatorial appointments, and the creation of states and local governments, the regime expanded the elites' class and consolidated its grip on power and capital accumulation.[32]

To ensure continued elites' domination of the country in the proposed third republic, the regime set what Jibrin has described as "very expensive and virtually impossible preconditions"[33] for the formation and registration of political parties. This was reminiscent of the party formation and registration process of the 1970s in preparation for the Second Republic.

Some of the preconditions for party formation and registration included the following: the establishment within three months of functional party offices with at least three paid staff in all of the 435 local government areas of the country; and the supply of 25 copies of the membership list containing names, contact addresses and photographs of at least 200 members from each local government in the country. In addition the parties were to pay N50 000 registration fees. In the run-up to the 1993 presidential and parliamentary elections, only thirteen parties claimed to have met those conditions. However, consequent upon Babangida's hidden agenda on the transition programme, no party qualified for registration. The disqualified parties were said to have failed to meet the 'vision and objectives' of the Babangida regime. Against this background, the regime established two new political parties, namely the Social Democratic Party (SDP) and the National Republican Convention (NRC). It still emerged that these parties were dominated, once again, by the same crop of elites that had existed since the country's independence in 1960 and their protégées. The general elections of 1993 were contested under the banners of these two political parties.

While the regime sought to achieve elites' cohesion, wealth accumulation and support, it did not make sustained efforts to mobilize the support and integration of ordinary Nigerians in the country's political process. The regime tended also to exclude non-commissioned and junior officers of the Nigerian army in its governance. Although the regime repealed Decree 4 of 1984 and abolished the National Security Organisation (NSO), it soon replaced the decree with others and in the place of NSO it established the State Security Service (SSS), which continued to harass, intimidate and kill political opponents. Opposition to the regime by disenchanted Nigerian masses intensified as a result. Moreover, certain sections of the civilian elites such as academics and trade union leaders became very critical of it. This was after much manoeuvring of the transition process had shown that the military component of the Nigerian political elites under Babangida was not prepared to return power to civilians. A brief look at the transition to civil rule programme will help clarify this issue.

The regime enunciated a transition to civil rule programme in 1986, which was to commence in 1990. At the beginning it showed some serious commitment to the programme. For instance, it established a Political Bureau that called for a public debate on the type of political system to be adopted for the Third Republic. It equally called for public debate over the IMF loan. This was an attempt to get the people to become involved in the country's political process. Most importantly, the regime banned all former public office holders from 1960 to 1989, from participating in Nigerian politics of the proposed third republic.[34] As a sequel to this, the regime created a national Directorate of Social Mobilisation and Political Education (DSMPE), which was charged with the responsibility of inculcating a new political culture consistent with democratic governance into Nigerians and especially the new breed of politicians. It also convened a Constitutional Drafting Committee that produced the Third Republic's Constitution, otherwise known as 'The 1989 Constitution'. Moreover, in the phased transitional programme, local government chair, State Governors, members of state assemblies, and National Assembly members had all been elected. The last phase of the transition was to be marked with the election of the country's president. These seemingly bold initiatives would later turn to be strategies for self-succession. Events that later unfolded in the country showed that Babangida had no intention of handing over power to elected civilians. For example, the transition programme was repeatedly altered. Banned politicians were later un-banned, and about three different sets of presidential candidates were disqualified at various times in the truncated transition to civil rule programme. Unlike the promise he made to Nigerians in 1986 not to stay in power beyond 1990, Babangida stayed in power three years longer than necessary. He was forced to 'step aside' in 1993 as a result of violent demonstrations that marked people's reaction to his annulment of the presidential election on 12 June 1993, purportedly won by Moshood Kashimawo Olawole Abiola of the Social Democratic Party (SDP). Under the Ibrahim Babangida regime, the Nigerian elites' class expanded with the creation of new states and local governments and massive retirement of relatively young army officers. The members of the political elites also consolidated their economic accumulation and domination of the country's politics through the regime's economic policies such as privatisation.

Elites under Sanni Abacha and Abdusalam Abubakar Regimes (1993-1999)

As has been pointed out in the preceding sections, increased violent demonstrations over the annulment of the 12 June presidential election forced Babangida to step aside from power in order to avoid further degeneration of the political crisis into civil war. Before stepping aside, however, Babangida inaugurated an Interim National Government

(ING) under the leadership of Chief Earnest Shonekan to complete the transition programme he started. The ING lacked legitimacy from both constitutional and social viewpoints. Surprisingly, General Sanni Abacha, who was supposed to retire from the force with Babangida, was left in the ING as Minister of Defence. When he eventually wrestled power from Chief Earnest Shonekan in November 1993 it did not come as a surprise to several observers of the Nigerian political scene. According to several analysts, Abacha merely took the hidden agenda of the Babangida regime to its logical conclusion – the perpetuation of military rule by other means.[35] Having been involved in all the successful military coup plots in Nigeria since the 1970s, Abacha wanted to rule Nigeria at all cost.

The timing of the coup plot was, however, very wrong due to the political crisis in the country and considerable divisions within the military itself, and between military and civilian members of the Nigerian political elites. As a result of this development the regime could neither command the total loyalty of military officers (both serving and retired) nor civilian components of the Nigerian elites. Consequently, the regime became crude, and ruthless in dealing with both military and civilian members of the elites class and the masses who opposed its dictatorship and plan of self-succession in civilian governance. For example, the regime arrested and incarcerated General Oladipo Diya and Major-General Abdulkareem Adisa who were top members of the junta for plotting to over throw the regime. Former Head of Sate, General Olusegun Obasanjo, was also detained among those accused of plotting to overthrow the regime. Civilians were equally accused of coup plotting simply because of their opposition to the Abacha regime in particular and military dictatorships in general. These people were mainly journalists and civil right activists. The ruthlessness with which the Abacha regime ruled the country made Chinua Achebe to remark that he was 'probably the most brutal in his line of soldiers'.

Since the regime could not galvanise the support of the military and civil elites even with strategies such as state creation and transition to civil rule programme, it formed a new clique of mostly junior military officers who terrorised senior officers and civilians. Among the various security outfits created by the regime to terrorise Nigerians were the Office of the National Security Adviser (ONSA) under a retired police officer, Ismaila Gwarzo; and the Office of the Chief Security Officer to the Head of State (OCSOHS), with a Special Strike Force Unit, under the control of Major Hamza Al-Mustapha. There was also the Directorate of Military Intelligence (DMI), State Security Service (SSS) and National Intelligence Agency (NIA). These organisations engaged in extra-judicial killings of people the regime felt were threats to it. Among the notable figures it killed was Ken Saro-Wiwa and seven other Ogoni leaders who were protesting against political marginalization and environmental degradation of the Niger-Delta region. Those who were not killed were sent to prison, or detained without trial. Several members of the political elites simply went on self-exile to avoid the regime's death sentence or imprisonment.

Sensing that the majority of those opposing the military junta were based in southwestern cities of the country or were of southwestern origin, the regime resorted to whipping up ethnic sentiments specifically to attract support from Nigerians of northern origin. Among prominent people of southwestern origin whom it arrested and detained were Chief M. K. O. Abiola (who later died in detention), retired General Alani Akinrinade. Arguably, this strategy of wooing ethnic support did not work as effectively as the regime had intended. This is because opposition from the north against the Abacha regime was also strong. This forced the regime to arrest and detain prominent northerners such as Alhaji Abubakar Rimi, and General Shehu Yar' Adua, (then a presidential aspirant who later died in detention). Moreover, prominent members of the civilian elites from eastern parts of the country such as Dr Alex Ekwueme (Vice-President of the Second Republic), unequivocally denounced the regime's transition programme and the attempt at Abacha's attempt at self-succession as "immoral, unethical, politically unjust, and capable of destroying the unity of the country".[36] Similarly, various political and civil society organisations that vehemently opposed Abacha's dictatorship and concertedly called for a return to democratic governance were multi-ethnic in their memberships. Among such organisations were the Group of 34 (G 34), United Democratic Front of Nigeria (UDFN), Committee for the Defence of Human Rights (CDHR), Campaign for Democracy (CD), Civil Liberty Organisation (CLO) and several others.

Some analysts have argued that the regime was provoked into autocracy by the recommendation of the Constitutional Conference it convened in December 1994 as part of its transition to civil rule programme.[37] The conference had recommended, among other things, that it hand over power to civilians in January 1996. However, the conference was forced by the regime to rescind its recommendation and grant it five years to complete its transition programme. It was after the conference had rescinded its decision that the regime began another transition programme similar to that of Babangida. It established a National Electoral Commission (NECON), which called for the formation of political parties. Unlike the Babangida regime, which formed two political parties, Abacha called for multi-party democracy. Five political parties were eventually registered to contest the general election. It turned out that these parties were in fact owned and funded by the regime and were integral parts of its self-succession strategy. This is because the political parties without exception endorsed Abacha as their presidential candidate. Moreover, several new pro-Abacha organisations, possibly funded by the regime, intensified their campaign for Abacha to succeed himself. This development finally confirmed fears of pro-democracy activists that the regime had no intention of returning the country to democratic governance. It also led to the intensification of agitations for democracy in the country.

By June 1998, when Abacha died, the country was almost on the brink of war following sustained violent demonstrations. General Abdusalam Abubakar, who took over the leadership of the country, embarked on a quick transition to a programme of civil rule. His administration dissolved Abacha's Provisional Ruling Council, proscribed the five political parties and abolished the various notorious security outfits the regime had used to terrorise Nigerians. Moreover, the administration released all those in detention suspected of coup plots and conducted local government elections on 5 December 1998, and gubernatorial and state assembly elections on 9 January 1999. On 20 February 1999 the regime conducted elections for the national assembly and on 27 February 1999, the presidential election was held. General Olusegun Obasanjo, former military head of state from 1976 to 1979, was inaugurated as the second executive president of Nigeria on 29 May 1999. He was elected under the platform of the People's Democratic Party (PDP). Nigeria held its second general elections in 2003 and Obasanjo was re-elected the country's president.

Elites under the Obasanjo Regime (1999-2006)

The return to democratic governance restored hope in the country and encouraged popular support for the principle of democracy. Since coming to power in 1999, the government of President Obasanjo has tried to preserve the unity of the country. To the credit of the present government, popular participation in politics had been greatly improved especially during the first four years. Human right abuses have declined considerably compared to previous regimes. The government has also recorded reasonable success in certain areas of the economy and in its fight against corruption. But popular support for, and satisfaction with, the practice and availability of democracy has been declining noticeably. It does appear that many Nigerians have begun to lose faith in the ruling elites both at the national, state and local government levels.

The reasons for this are not far fetched. Many Nigerians feel that the dividends of democracy have not been forthcoming as expected, and in certain respects there tends to be no noticeable difference between the government and the previous ones. For example, the performance of elected legislators in Nigeria as members of the elite class has been dismal. The legislators spent a greater part of their first four-year tenure on impeachment debates rather than on passing Bills on areas of pressing needs such as poverty alleviation. Both the Senate and House of Representatives had their presidents and speakers, respectively, replaced at various times. Other issues that continue to consume the attention of the lawmakers relate to revenue allocation, rotational presidency and restructuring of the federation. The relationship between the lawmakers and the presidency has been strained to the extent that several attempts at impeaching the president have been made. The implication of this situation is that Nigerian elites are still deeply divided not only at the national level but also at the state and local government levels even in the so-called democratic dispensation.

There is little or no popular trust in public institutions such as the Independent National Electoral Commission (INEC). Elections have continued to be won fraudulently in the country. A glaring case of fraudulent elections in Nigeria was that of former governor of Anambra state, Dr Chris Ngige. His removal from office, however, has more to do with the crisis in the state in which he was involved in power tussle with those who helped to install him in office than a genuine attempt at fighting electoral malpractices. Corruption, thuggery, political assassinations, and arson have continued to form part of the country's political culture.

Despite the presumed enthronement of democratic governance in the country, military domination of Nigerian politics has to a large extent remained unchallenged. The new domination is no longer through the barrel of a gun but through ballot boxes. Adejumobi has aptly observed that retired military officers have become a powerful political force in Nigerian politics. This phenomenon, according to him, became noticeable under the Babangida transition programme, but has reached an unprecedented and disturbing level under the Abubakar political transition programme.[38] Although Adejumobi rightly observed that the trend reached an unprecedented level in 1999, the trend was noticeable as far back as the Second Republic. It can be recalled that retired army officers such as Samuel Ogbemudia were actively involved in the politics of the Second Republic. Another former military governor under the Gowon regime, Jacob Esuesen was also actively involved in the Second Republic politics of the old Cross River state.

Under the current democratic dispensation, retired military leaders are not only party founders and sponsors but also elected representatives and Cabinet ministers. The ruling PDP is dominated by retired military leaders. During the 2003 elections only retired military heads of state contested the presidential election. These were President Olusegun Obasanjo and General Mohammadu Buhari. As the 2007 presidential election is approaching, the two front-runners are also retired military officers such as General Ibrahim Babangida.

While not attempting to deny retired military officers their constitutional rights to participate in the country's political process, it is important to stress that this trend has several implications for the nascent Nigerian democracy. One such implication is that Nigeria has become indirectly 'remilitarized'.[39] The authoritarian disposition of the military makes retired officers involved in politics unable to adjust easily to democratic governance. Already, Nigerians are increasingly witnessing authoritarian and despotic tendencies in the policies and actions of the current administration. For example, the Nigerian parliament recently rejected a Bill intended to amend the constitution so as to enable President Olusegun Obasanjo to run for a third term. The failed attempt reminds Nigerians of previous attempts at self-succession made by Babangida and Abacha during their brutal regimes. Despotism is therefore natural in military leadership. Secondly, the involvement of retired military officers in Nigeria's political process does not only hinder the evolvement of social justice but also encourages the institutionalisation of corruption in the country. Continued military leadership of the country in the presumed democratic dispensation has not, for example, allowed for probes into the plundering of Nigeria's economy under various military regimes. This is despite numerous calls by Nigerians for the probing of General Ibrahim Babangida and several other retired military officers occupying strategic positions in Obasanjo's government. Rather than facing prosecution for numerous political killings, human rights abuses and corruption during his regime, Babangida, a staunch member and sponsor of the ruling PDP has officially declared his intention to contest the 2007 presidential election. Thirdly, as Adejumobi has suggested, involvement of retired officers does not provide an even playing ground for political contestations between "enfeebled civilian political class, who have been persecuted, suppressed and emaciated by long years of military rule and a crop of rich and powerful military retirees".[40] This fact was clearly demonstrated in the 2003 presidential, general, and gubernatorial elections where the military-dominated PDP pulled all its resources together to out-manoeuvre other political parties.

Current Political and Economic Situation in Nigeria and the NEPAD Agenda

As a result of the nature of the Nigerian political elites, the country has remained in the doldrums. It has been plagued by political instability, deteriorating physical and social infrastructure, unemployment, emigration and environmental degradation, among other things. The enduring political situation in Nigeria has led several scholars, organisations, institutions and governments to wonder if the country would continue to exist as one indivisible entity in the foreseeable future.

Nigeria has continued to experience social unrest, severe interethnic conflicts and criminal activities that most often result in the death of hundreds of people. In the Niger Delta region of the country, for example, several years of oil exploration and neglect by the Nigeria government have led to enduring poverty and environmental degradation in the region. Groups such as the Niger Delta People's Volunteer Force (NDPVF), Ijaw Youth Congress (IYC), and the Movement for the Survival of Ogoni People (MOSOP) and The Movement for the Emancipation of the Niger Delta (MEND), often express their dissatisfaction and frustration over this problem through violent demonstrations in the disruption of oil production. Apart from several separatist movements in the Niger Delta region, there are also several others in other parts of the country. These movements include Movement for the Actualisation of the Sovereign State of Biafra (MASSOB) and Odua Peoples' Congress (OPC). The country also continues to experience frequent strikes and counter-strike actions that paralyse economic activities by labour unions agitating for better working conditions and high cost of living. Moreover, many analysts still believe that despite attempts to curtail military incursion into politics, the military might still venture into Nigeria's politics at any time. The purported coup attempt of October 2004 involving four army officers, mostly Abacha loyalists, indicates that this may not be completely ruled out.

The majority of the Nigerian population lives in abject poverty, and unemployment and inflation are very high. These conditions have been worsening due to deteriorating social infrastructure, especially in urban areas. As a result of the huge gap between rural and urban areas in terms of development, there has also been a steady increase in rural-urban migration and the crime rate. Steady decline in the economy, lack of funding and proper management of resources have equally resulted in the deterioration of public schools. Nigeria's health sector is, needless to say, in total shambles. The country's health system is among the worst in the world, according to the World Health Organization (WHO) report. Its health system is ranked, 187 out of 191 by the WHO.[41] Nigeria's life expectancy of 38 years is also considered among the worst in the world and the rate of HIV/AIDS infections has reached alarming proportions. Owing to this appalling socio-economic situation in the country, Nigeria has continued to lose the best of her professionals and academics who are emigrating to the so-called greener pastures, especially to America and Europe. From the foregoing, therefore, it can be seen that Nigeria is, politically, socially and economically in a precarious condition. However, the country has continued to play a leading role in all African initiatives, especially NEPAD. It is against this background that the concluding section of this chapter will examine the perception of NEPAD by the Nigerian political elites, the role they are playing towards the realisation of NEPAD's aims and objectives and factors that may prevent the achievement of these objectives.

Nigerian Political Elites and Their Perception of NEPAD

NEPAD, according to the document that established it, is an African "Strategy for Achieving Sustainable Development in the 21st Century".[42] As a 'strategy' for sustainable development, the programme proposes to address several problematic areas in the African development process in equal partnership with the rest of the world. Thus, NEPAD has as one of its objectives, the development of democracy and good governance as well as, the sustainment of the culture of human rights, and good economic and corporate governance. Thus, based on the precarious condition of Nigeria politically, socially and economically there is no doubt that its elites perceive NEPAD as an innovative strategy for solving Nigeria's problems. NEPAD is therefore presented, especially by the top echelon of Nigerian elites who are in government, as capable of leading to the rewriting of the country's history and indeed that of Africa if its programmes are well implemented.

At the beginning of this chapter, however, Nigerian political elites were defined as more than simply government personalities. A positional identification of elites was used to include the National Executive Council (the president, Cabinet ministers and special advisers), state executive councils (governors, commissioners and advisers), members of national and state houses of assembly, local government chairperson, top civil servants, heads of government parastatals and political party leaders. The perception of NEPAD among these elites varies considerably. For example, in their study conducted in 2003 to ascertain the degree of awareness and commitment to the NEPAD agenda in seven African countries, Kotze and Steyn found that "Nigerian elites displayed a relatively high level of knowledge about NEPAD".[43] The "elites" Kotze and Steyn may have been referring to, were perhaps, mostly those involved in the NEPAD process. This is because the researchers also discovered that several members of the National Assembly were not even familiar with the programme. Again civil society organisations "displayed higher levels of knowledge surrounding NEPAD than their politicians and civil servants counterparts".[44] The NEPAD process has not been popularised at the state and local government levels, and most elites in the private sector are equally not aware of what NEPAD entails. Party leaders are more engrossed in party activities than in discussing NEPAD, which many have very little or no idea about and often tend to confuse with the African Union which is relatively well known, perhaps due to its association with the OAU.

As mentioned earlier, NEPAD is well known among sections of the Nigerian elites involved in its process. For example, President Olusegun Obasanjo is not only a co-protagonist of NEPAD with President Thabo Mbeki of South Africa, Presidents Abdulazeez Boutefika of Algeria and Abdoulaye Wade of Senagal, but has been Chairperson of the Heads of State and Government Implementation Committee (HSGIC). Nigeria is also Chair of several of NEPAD's committees such as Capital Flows Initiative Committee, Economic and Corporate Governance Committee, and Vice-Chair of the Infrastructure Committee. These committees are charged, respectively, with the responsibility of attracting capital into Africa up to US$64 billion annually; developing capacity among public sector officials pre-qualifying projects and development of public-private partnerships for funding and execution of projects under the NEPAD initiative.[45]

In order to popularise NEPAD among Nigerians, the government has created an extra-ministerial agency called NEPAD Nigeria Country Office, under the leadership of Chief Mrs Chinyere Asika (Senior Special Assistant to the President on NEPAD). This agency has been disseminating the message of NEPAD among Nigerians through its cluster programmes. These programmes centre on infrastructure, environment, urbanisation and population. They also focus on economic, corporate and political governance, agriculture and market access, science and technology, human resources development and health. The programmes are to be carried out at federal, state and local government levels through various strategies. For example, NEPAD Nigeria has ensured the creation of NEPAD Committees on Co-operation and Integration in Africa/NEPAD in both houses of the National Assembly. Members of these committees are to exercise oversight functions on the activities of NEPAD Nigeria. NEPAD Nigeria is also negotiating and entering into "strategic partnership with the private sector" and is increasingly facilitating the works of several non-governmental organisations (NGOs), community based organisations (CBOs), and youth organisations. Through the E-Africa Commission, Microsoft, and Hewlett Packard/ZTE have begun a pilot phase of the NEPAD E-School Programmes in twelve states of the federation. Coordinators of NEPAD programmes at state and local government levels have also been appointed, and the Nigerian government has committed enormous financial resources towards realising the aims and objectives of NEPAD Nigeria. For example, in 2005, the government provided N63 millions for overhead costs and an additional N15 million for capital expenditure.[46]

Nigeria has also adopted NEPAD's neo-liberal economic paradigm that encourages trade liberalisation, currency devaluation, subsidy withdrawal on petroleum and agriculture, private sector participation, and privatisation of public enterprises. Thus, under its National Empowerment and Development Strategy (NEEDS), the government has sold several state-owned industries and is pushing strongly for the privatisation of the country's power and telecommunications sectors. The current leadership has also embarked on the fight against corruption in the country, at the national, state, and local government levels. Nigerian elites are actively involved in peace processes in several African countries such as Sudan, Ivory Coast, the Gambia, Liberia, Togo and Zimbabwe. These efforts are no doubt, in line with NEPAD social, economic, political, peace and security agenda in the continent.

Efforts by the Nigerian elites to realize the aims and objectives of NEPAD notwithstanding, it is doubtful, if the NEPAD agenda can be realised in Nigeria. Several reasons support this assertion. First, the strategies adopted by NEPAD Nigeria to popularise NEPAD are still at their developmental stages. NEPAD therefore remains an exclusive theory of elites within the presidency.

As of 2005, NEPAD has not been launched in all the 36 states of the federation and most of the local government areas where the very poor people whose lives NEPAD is supposed to touch live. Ms Asika herself has acknowledged that one of the challenges facing NEPAD Nigeria is how to "communicate NEPAD effectively to different segments of the population".[47]

Second, while Nigerian elites are involved in peace processes in other African countries, Nigerians are living in insecurity as demonstrated by frequent violent clashes in the Niger Delta, in the southwestern city of Lagos and several parts of the northern region. These violent ethno-religious clashes are quite often instigated by factions of the elites in furtherance of their political and economic objectives. Again, the Nigerian elites' adoption of NEPAD's neo-liberal paradigm that strongly emphasises privatisation of public enterprises has not contributed to the economic well being of Nigerians. Rather, privatisation has caused untold hardships as a result of job losses and sharp increases in the crime rate and other social ills. At the same time, the elites have used privatisation as a means of private capital accumulation. This has been the case since independence in 1960. The fight against corruption embarked upon by the government is suspect too. This is because it is mostly those opposed to the government who are targeted while those strongly supporting the government are not.

Third, the Nigerian elites do very little to generate adequate funds internally to support NEPAD, but rely heavily on foreign donors. Ms Asika has noted that one of the challenges facing her agency is that: "NEPAD Nigeria is yet to receive financial support from international donor agencies". This may not be unconnected with the fact that since 1960, Nigeria has received financial supports amounting to billions of dollars for various development projects, which were not properly accounted for. These funds were in most cases never used for those development projects but were embezzled, misappropriated and siphoned back to European and American banks. The same leaders or protégées who could not account for the whereabouts of those development funds given to Nigeria by international donor agencies in the past are still very much around the corridors of power campaigning for funds to support NEPAD.

Fourth, NEPAD calls for the development of good governance characterised by "legitimacy, transparency, accountability and responsibility",[48] a government that does not only claim its legitimacy from popular elections, but also involves the electorate in its programmes and actions. Unfortunately, despite the enthronement of democracy in Nigeria there is still the problem of legitimacy because elections are not normally won in Nigeria but stolen through various electoral frauds by the strongest of the elites' factions. At other times leaders are selected through compromise to pacify certain sections of the elites in order to ensure the continued existence of the country. For example, the election of Obasanjo is generally regarded by many as an agreement by the military, international community and southwestern elites as a form of compensation for the annulled 1993 presidential election, which the late M. K. O. Abiola had purportedly won. The votes of the electorate are hardly taken into consideration under such arrangements. The end result is that elites who lead Nigerian government are very far removed from the electorate and so are hardly accountable to them. The rejected third term attempted by Obasanjo was also not the best example of democratic governance being preached by NEPAD.

Lastly, good governance as envisaged by NEPAD is one that must have strong, functional, effective and efficient public institutions for the protection of the rights and freedom of its citizens. It is also supposed to be a system that guarantees an enabling environment for sustainable economic development and participatory and therefore "ownership" of democratic reforms and programmes. However, as a result of military dictatorship, of which most elites championing the cause NEPAD in Nigeria were part and parcel of, there has been a steady deterioration in public service delivery in Nigeria.[49] Nigerians have lost faith in public institutions such as the bureaucracy, judiciary, police service, electoral institution and political parties. Moreover, to a large extent, these institutions have become sectionally, ethnically or personally shared among the elites. Rather than being used in the service of Nigerians, public institutions are used as "organs of patronage and clienteles network".[50] As a result, Nigerians cannot claim "ownership" of the reforms, actions and development programmes of the government as NEPAD envisages for them.

Conclusion

This chapter has examined the trends in the emergence of the present crop of Nigeria's political elites beginning from the first democratic dispensation of the country. The analysis began with the clarification of the concept of elites especially in the context of Nigeria. It sees the elites as those who occupy positions of responsibility by whatever means, and by virtue of their positions make decisions that have far reaching consequences on members of the Nigerian society. Even though different kinds of elites exist in several societies, the chapter has argued that in the context of Nigeria, they are hardly discernable because Nigerian elites tend to overlap, blend and fuse into a near perfect whole at the level of control, management and redistribution of the country's scarce resources. The involvement of the retired military officers in Nigerian politics clarifies this theoretical position. Civilian rule has been unsuccessful so far to break the political power of the military; the military elites have therefore reinvented themselves as civilian elites in Nigeria.

It has also demonstrated the characteristics that these elites have developed over the years in the process of their evolution. On the basis of this, the chapter argued that the elites in Nigeria have largely contributed to the social, political and economic predicament, which the country faces today. With respect to the political and economic agenda of NEPAD, the chapter has shown on one hand how Nigerian elites, especially those within the corridors of power, attempt to realise NEPAD's aims and objectives. On the other hand it has also shown how they hamper Nigeria's delivery on the NEPAD's political and development agenda. It concludes that based on the fact that the Nigerian elites are dominated by the military, the country's political culture has become military in nature. This therefore makes democratisation in Nigeria very difficult and it also encourages lack of transparency and therefore corruption. More over, the nature of the Nigerian political elites makes popularisation and implementation of the NEPAD objectives very difficult. Thus, NEPAD objectives may not be realisable in Nigeria, at least in the near future.

Notes and References

1   Kevin Tonkin, 'Elites and Democratic Consolidation in South Africa', Paper for the South African Political Science Association Conference, September 1995, p 1, quoted in E. Leistner, *African Predicament – Africa Wavering between past and modern time*, Pretoria: Mlalo Publishers, 2003.
2   *Ibid.*
3   Tita Korvenja, 'The Environmental Problems and Politics of Power: Review on the African Elite', *Nordic Journal of African Studies*, vol 2, no 1, 1993, p140, quoted in E. Leistner 2003, p 49.

4   *Ibid.*
5   Richard L. Sklar, 'Social Class and Political Activism in Africa: The Bourgeoisie and the Proletariat', quoted in E. Leistner 2003.
6   Korvenja 1993.
7   *Ibid.*, p 49.
8   A. Chife, *The Political Economy of Post-Cold War Africa*, Queenton Lampter: Edwin Mellen Press, 1997, p 62, quoted in E. Leistner, 2003.
9   *Ibid.*, p 62.
10 John Ayoade, quoted in D. Rotchild and N. Chazan (eds), *The Precarious Balance: State and Society in Africa*, London: Westview Press, 1988 p 100.
11 Erich Leistner, quoting Jennifer Seymour Whitaker, *How Can Africa Survive?*, New York: Harper & Row, 1988, p 37.
12 K. B. Hadjor, *On Transforming Africa*, New Jersey: Africa World Press, 1987, p 11.
13 Claude Ake, 'Why is Africa not Developing', *West Africa*, no 3538, 17 June, p 1214.
14 Claude Ake, 'What is the Problem with Ethnicity in Africa?', *Transformation,* vol 22, 1993, p 9.
15 Leistner 2003.
16 Chife 1997.
17 Ake, p 1212.
18 Wole Soyinka quoted in *Rapport* (Johannesburg), 10 October 1999, p 4 (translated and cited by Leistner 2003).
19 George B. N. Ayittey, 'Letter to the Editor', *Policy Review*, no 35, winter 1985, p 9, quoted in Leistner 2003.
20 Ikime Obaro, *Groundwork of Nigerian History*, Ibadan, Nigeria: Heinemann/Historical Society of Nigeria, 1980.
21 'Nigeria, The Journey So Far', available online at http://www.marxist.com/Africa/Nig_journey_sofar.html.
22 N. Okwudiba, *Ethnic Politics in Nigeria*. Enugu: Fourth Dimension Publishers, 1978.
23 B. J. Dudley, 'Western Nigeria and Nigerian Crisis' in Panther-Bricker (ed.), *Nigerian Politics and Military Rule: Prelude to a Civil War*, London: University of London Press, pp 161-197.
24 *Ibid.*
25 B. J. Dudley, *Instability and Political order: Politics and Crisis in Nigeria*, Ibadan University Press, 1973.

26 *Ibid.*

27 Joseph Richard, Democracy and Prebendal Politics in Nigeria: The Rise and Fall of the Second Republic

28 D. Abubakar, 'The Rise and Fall of the First and Second Republics in Nigeria' in F. U. Okafor (ed.), *New Strategies for Curbing Ethnic and Religious Conflicts,* Enugu: Fourth Dimension, 1997.

29 C. Ake, *Is Africa Democratizing?* Ikeja, Lagos: Malthouse Press, 1996, p 13.

30 *Ibid.*

31 George B. N. Ayittey, 'The Political Economy of Reform in Africa', *Journal of Economic Growth,* vol 3, no 3, Spring 1989, p 17.

32 Ake 1996.

33 Nereus I. Nwosu, 'The military and political instability in Nigeria, 1985-1993', *African Notes,* vol 21, Nos 1/2, 1999, pp 65-75.

34 Wale Segun Banjo, *The Internationalization of Ogoni Crisis,* Lagos Afreb Publishers, 1998.

35 M. J. Balogun, 'Promoting Good Governance Through Leadership Recruitment Training – A critical review of trends in Nigeria', UNECA, Addis Ababa, 1994 CA/MRAG/94/1TP.

36 Eghosa Osaghae quoted in Garth Le Père and Anthoni Van Nieuwkerk, 'Nigeria: Wither the Transition', in *Global Dialogue,* vol 3, 3 Dec 1998.

37 Ake 1996.

38 E. E. Anugwom, 'The Normalcy of Vice: The Public Sector and Corruption in Nigeria', in C.O Agwu (ed.) *Corruption in Nigeria: Critical Perspectives,* Enugu: Chuka Educational Publishers. See also J. O. Odey, The Anti-Corruption Crusade: The saga of a crippled Giant, Enugu SNAAP, D. Babarinsa 'A looter Continua' in *TELL* 7, 3 Lagos 1999 and Adigun Agbaje, Culture, Corruption and Development" in *Voices from Africa,* vol. 4, 1992.

39 Irin, 'Nigeria: Power Shifts to the South', West-Africa-irin-wa@ africaonline.co.ci-Nigeria power shifts to the south.http://www. africa.upen.edu/newsletters/irinw-22 2 99.html.

40 Wale Adebanwi, 'Yoruba power Elite and Contemporary Politics in Nigeria: The challenge of Obasanjo's Yoruba Presidency', available online at http://www.utexas.edu/conferences/africa2004/ database.

41 Peter J. Schraeder, 'Elites as Facilitators of impediments to political development?', Some lessons from 'Third wave of Democratization in Africa' in *The Journal of Developing Areas*, vol 29, no 1, October 1994, p 85.

42 E. E. Anugwom, 'Ethnicity, Politics and Elections in Nigeria: An Overview of Current trends', Occasional Paper, available online at http://www.ethnonet-africa.org/pubs/papeze.htm.

43 *Ibid.*

44 A. Adedeji, 'Cleansing the Augean Stables', in *Africa Today*, vol 5, May 1999.

45 Anugwom 2003.

46 *Ibid.*

47 *Ibid.*

48 Chife 2003, p 70.

49 C. Ake, *Democracy and Development in Africa*, Washington DC, Brookings Institution, 1996, p 1.

50 *Ibid.*

51 Waziri Adio, 'Tragedy of the Nigeria Elite', available online at http://wwwthisdayonline.com//archives/2002.

52 H. Kotze and C. Steyn, *African Elite Perspectives: AU and NEPAD*, Konrad-Adenauer, Johannesburg, December 2003, p 23.

53 *Ibid.*

54 *Country Report on Nigeria: Political Risk Yearbook*, vol 4, Sub-Saharan Africa. The PRS Group Inc. 2005, p 23.

55 Kanbur Ravi, *'The New Partnership for Africa's Development (NEPAD): An initial commentary'*, Politikon, vol 29, no 1, May 2002, pp 87-100.

56 Nthabiseng Nkosi, 'The African Union: Problems and Prospects', *Africa Insight*, vol 32, no 3, September 2002, p 59.

SOUTHERN AFRICA

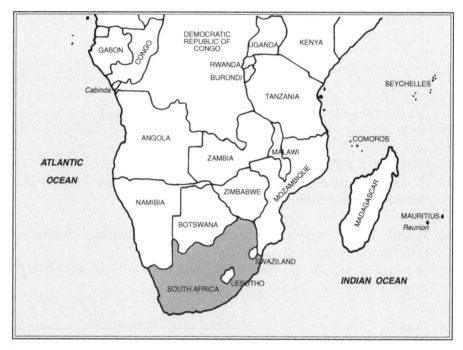

Source: Africa Institute of South Africa, 2005.

5. Political Leadership in South Africa and the Search for Equitable and Sustainable Economic Growth and Development

Susan Booysen

Introduction

This study investigates the political leadership in South Africa and its political will in and commitment to fostering sustainable and equitable economic growth and development. The discourse in this chapter is based on the premise that there is an interrelationship between political will and the creation of socio-economic conditions that lead to the advancement of citizens. In the final analysis, political elites increase the developmental benefits for both their political stewards and the general public, not simply for humanitarian considerations, but also for themselves and their parties to gain continued endorsement to remain in power.

In conditions of contemporary globalisation, with extensive national debt and faltering, primary export-led economies, political leadership encounters limits (and often growing limits) that are imposed on the scope of developmental policies and programmes, which might help them gain the political goodwill and support that are necessary to maintain their positions of power. South Africa is a small case in point, where macro-economic policies and private informal sector-driven approaches to employment and growth are designed to be friendly to the international financial institution guidelines and international investor sentiments. However, the combination of contemporary mobilisation and social protest trends with increasing levels of apathy and political despondency, indicate that these policies might eventually (in a 10-15 year term) fall short of ensuring the continuation of high levels of electoral endorsement of the ruling African National Congress (ANC).

In large measure, due to the extensive impact of forces of the international political economy, there is a lack in developing countries in general, of a scope for political will to assert itself in decisions that promote developmental and sustainable socio-economic growth. Yet, there is continuously emerging evidence of corruption and personal enrichment by African political leadership.[1] Simultaneously, the leaders themselves cite the lack of adequate resources to effect socio-economic transformation and a significant reduction of poverty.

The Bretton Woods institutions have often left African leaders with few options in the restructuring of their national economies. At least in the short term, structural adjustment programmes (SAPs) in many developing countries, have led to declining national socio-economic conditions, especially in precipitating higher unemployment and lower access to basic services. This would discourage the leadership to the exposure of the judgements of the electorate. However, with increasing conditionalities, which include holding regular, free and fair elections, leaderships are in varying degrees deprived of choice, hoping that the associated promises of aid and other forms of assistance might bring evidence of economic upliftment and therefore help them survive electoral judgement.

Political leadership in South Africa experienced variations of these programmes and conditions. The Growth, Employment and Redistribution (GEAR) strategy arguably constituted a variation of

SAPs, albeit in a self-imposed form. Economic expectations that were associated with GEAR were not realised. Yet, the ANC government was fortunate in that its implementation of GEAR coincided with early phases of post-apartheid-liberation governance. In these circumstances, high levels of support and legitimacy prevailed and the ANC had no inclination to avoid elections.

Privatisation and outsourcing are programmatic outflows of the International Monetary Fund (IMF) policies, which often serve as a vehicle for elite enrichment in the name of trickle-down policies, which might eventually reach the poor. Yet, at the same time, there is evidence in South Africa that, despite the growing African bourgeoisie and the apparent intensification of poverty, unemployment and class divisions, South Africans have been experiencing ground-breaking improvements in access to education and better lifestyles.[2] This chapter assesses the extent to which the socio-economic performance of the South African leadership affects its acceptability by the electorate and how that orientation shapes the style and substance of political leadership.

This chapter is presented in six parts. The first part examines the links between elections and socio-economic performance; the second part looks at the role of macro-economic strategies, while the third part assesses the impact of political leadership on wealth creation and poverty. The other sections examine the employment and unemployment divide and the indices of measuring economic performance. The last part looks at the institutional capacity to implement socio-economic policies.

Political Will and Sustainable Economic Growth and Development

This section discusses and maps the contexts and indicators of the South African leadership's political will to pursue substantive democratic policies and practices that would engender general economic growth and development. It examines the socio-economic state of the nation, with regard to core issues such as poverty, unemployment and empowerment and the leadership's political will to develop sufficient capacity to provide necessary social amenities and the momentum that would move the economy on the path of sustainable growth and development.

In the political domain, the identification of political will is a relatively straightforward matter. In the socio-economic domain, however, it is more complex to identify indicators of political will. The design of developmental policies is effected at one particular point in time; thereafter the stage of implementation follows. It is only over a period of time that it becomes clear whether:

- The political will to effect substantive democracy has adequately manifested itself in the results of policy implementation. Indicators of such a manifestation would include economic growth, job creation and the eradication or significant reduction of poverty.
- The political leadership displays the will to change tack and significantly supplement policy directions and/or the conditions and capacity for the effective implementation of policies, should the original policies not have had the desired effect.

A substantial portion of the analysis of the South African leadership's political will in the domain of economy and development in this chapter is channelled through the assessment of the impact of the government's GEAR strategy. This is the government's macro-economic vehicle for economic recovery and development, which has been implemented since 1996. Specific and explicitly stated economic targets were defined in the GEAR strategy. The strategy's achievements and failures with regard to development are well documented.[3] Furthermore, the period from 2000 has seen some recognition by the government that "whilst the macroeconomic policies were in place, there was much that was not being achieved" by the strategy. One of the consequences in the new millennium was the government's increased emphasis on the provision of a security net, and its accentuation of its social caring actions in leadership speeches and statements, which in 2003 benchmarked the extensive 'social wage' provided by the government. This is in the context in which a large percentage of South Africans, who qualified for components of the social wage, were not actively claiming, and often had not been empowered to claim. In his 2002 publication, Terreblanche calculated that almost 50% of those who qualified for some form of social assistance had not been receiving it.[4] The roll-out level was enhanced, and by late 2004, government gave assurances that the social security net was both being maintained and would be stepped-up in the 2005 national budget. This, against the background that it was approximately 4.5% of South Africa's gross domestic product (GDP) that would be expended on social assistance programmes.[5]

This study thus seeks to elaborate on the South African government's level of political will to advance democracy through a focus on its deeper layer of socio-economic development. In substantive and sustainable democracy, there is little room for the government to moderate concrete delivery whilst sustaining its power through sentiments of loyalty to, for example, a government based on liberation movement legitimacy. Such sheltered periods wear off. Thereafter, governments increasingly have to perform in the socio-economic domain in order to retain the political loyalty and electoral support of its citizens. Consideration of the advancement towards socio-economic development and substantive democracy of the population of any country, and in this case specifically South Africa, provides the essential longer-term set of indicators of political will needed to adhere to the spirit and processes of democratic governance. It is at the juncture where electorates threaten to abandon their political leaders, probably through elections, that the true test of the political will to maintain elections, functional legislatures and the rule of law arises. By early 2004, South Africa had not reached this point.

Linkages Between Elections and Socio-Economic Performance

This section assesses some of the main driving forces behind political leadership's support for constitutionalism, functional legislatures, credible elections, and predictable and legal successions. It hypothesises that, short of a dramatic turn of events at the ballot box, the political leaders of a governing party will retain commitment to democracy, to the extent that they expect to maintain power through the ballot. Sustainable popular development therefore would be an 'insurance policy' for voter support, and in turn, an assurance that leaders be prepared to expose themselves, without manipulation or rigging, to further rounds of elections. Support for credible, non-manipulated elections therefore, to a certain extent, depends on the certainty that the post-liberation 'political class' would be able to return to power. The return to power would be assured (or significantly guaranteed) through contentment of the electorate, which would hold off successful opposition assaults at the polls. It is mainly through extended, long-term discontentment with levels of socio-economic development being effected by the governing elites, corruption in their ranks, and the failure of the governing party to compensate for sub-optimal socio-economic change through general and campaign mobilisation, that such oppositional threats might occur.[6]

The South African political leadership, like its counterparts the world over, will do all in its power to avoid and postpone the juncture where a lack of economic performance leads to possible regime change through elections. Up to the third democratic elections of 2004, there was evidence that voter support for the ANC arose, irrespective of perceptions of ANC performance in key policy areas such as job creation and crime.[7] This might continue for a period, but not indefinitely. This critical juncture, however, is likely to arise, even if only in a decade or two. It is only then that the political will of leadership to subject itself to electoral verdict will truly be tested. In the extended interregnum, it is therefore the governing politicians' will to effect sustainable socio-economic development that holds the key to future questions of political will to uphold credible elections, constitutionalism, rule of law, and human rights.

Elections hardly ever deliver electoral surprises, except in the highly institutionalised two-party system. Incumbents and opponents almost invariably have clear indications of the likely results of a pending election. Leadership is either fully prepared before the election to hand over power, or it uses its power legally or illegally, constitutionally or para-constitutionally[8] before the election to resist getting to the point where it would have to hand over power. It might be that the governing South African political elite, in years to come, could reach a stage where it would have to prepare for handing over political power. However, in the interim, it is doing its utmost to avoid suggestions that such a situation might become a reality. The present ANC government in this juncture is performing dual positioning in order to avoid this situation. First, as a political party-movement, the ANC leadership 'plays the opposition' and ensures that the opposition's chances to mobilise and garner support remain or become minimised. It overwhelmingly achieves this through legal and constitutional action, including cooption, cooperation, absorption, ideological deligitimisation, etc. Second, it engages directly on the popular, voter front. In its capacity as government, it governs or strives to govern in a way that optimises socio-economic advancement and development.

The 'GEAR era' in South African politics profoundly impacted on assessments of the political will of the government elite. The period started in 1996, and by 2004, debate was raging on the extent to which nuanced suggestions of change were being phased into this macro-economic strategy. While the debate continued on the possible benefits, such as job creation, that the basically discarded Reconstruction and Development Programme (RDP) would have engendered, it was generally acknowledged that GEAR did *not* deliver the anticipated benefits. The government political elite was challenged with decisions on whether to stick to GEAR dogma, or to start changing tack. Up to 2002, there was only intermittent evidence of change. Thereafter, came an increasing emphasis on supplementary action. These included the 2003-2004 debate on South Africa's dual economy, and President Thabo Mbeki's specific inputs on creating the 'stairway' connections between the two economies:[9]

> We assess the implications of all these changes for South Africa's political leadership on the socio-economic policy, given the fact that one of the major policy manifestations has been the creation of significant middle and upper middle classes, when the gap between the rich and the poor has been widening.

Macro-Economic Strategy and the Political Will to Effect Sustainable Development

When considering the GEAR policy *vis-à-vis* the economic targets that were promulgated by government at the time of its adoption, a number of issues regarding objectives and ability to achieve sustainable development arise. There were notable shortfalls. Policy proposals that accompanied GEAR included a reduction of the budget deficit as a percentage of GDP; a restrained growth of the national debt, followed by a reversal of this growth; easing the interest burden on government debt; as well as the encouragement of foreign direct investment. Others included the privatisation of some state-owned enterprises; an increase in the flexibility of labour markets; in addition to the reorientation of government towards the creation of 'growth-enhancing policy frameworks', rather than the extension of direct state involvement.[10]

An assessment of GEAR performance based on 2001 and some subsequent statistics revealed some of the reasons why political elites increasingly recognised the need for supplementary action, assurances and new benchmarking of economic achievements, even under circumstances in which GEAR would not be changed. Roux highlighted the GEAR performance levels, providing a clear indication of both the strengths and the weaknesses of this policy (see Table 6.1).[11] The details indicate that GEAR resulted in major disappointments in terms of wage growth, real bank rate, government investment growth, private investment growth, non-gold export growth, foreign direct investment, GDP growth, annual job creation, and saving. Subsequent economic trends suggested that there could be improvements with regard to deficit reduction, government consumption, exchange rate, inflation, and the current account deficit. Yet, as suggested by Gelb, the South African economy appears to be firmly trapped on a 'low growth' path.[12]

In assessing South African economic trends, it is noted that a significant achievement of post-1994 government leadership was to turn previously consistent negative economic growth rates into positives. As noted by Roux, the average economic growth rate between 1993 and 2001 was 2.5% compared to an annual population growth rate of 2% (total population between 40.4 and 44.8 million), resulting in an annual average growth in real GDP per capita of 0.5%. The last time that South Africa recorded more than four consecutive years of positive economic growth was in the early 1970s. At the time of writing, statistics for 2003 were still incomplete. Select 2002 statistics include a 3.1% growth in GDP, effecting ten consecutive years of positive growth, and manufacturing growth reaching 5.4%.

Table 6.1: GEAR: Trends in Set and Realised Objectives 1996-2001 [2002-2003 updates where available in square brackets]

Gear Characteristics	Average GEAR %	Average Realised %
Fiscal deficit (% of GDP)	3,7	3,3 [Budget deficit, 2003:1%]
Average real wage growth private sector	0,8	4,1
Average real wage growth, public sector	1,3	2
Real bank rate	4,4	6,1
Real government investment growth	7,1	1,4
Real private investment growth	11,7	2,3 [12% of GDP 1994-2003]
Real non-gold export growth	8,4	6,8
Additional foreign direct investment	US $509 million	US $270 million
Results		
GDP growth	4,2	2,5 (0,1 in 1998) [3 in 2002]
Inflation (CPI)	8,2	6,7
Employment growth (non-agricultural formal)	2,9	-2,2
New jobs per year	270,000	-112,000[13]
Current account deficit (% of GDP)	2,4	1,1
Gross private savings (% of GDP)	21,2	15,2
Government dis-savings (% of GDP)	1,9	3,6

Sources: Adapted from Roux 2002 and Bond 2000; 2002 and 2003 figures from SA Yearbook 2003–04 and Gelb 2004.

Evidence of the Political Will to Achieve Substantive Democracy

The political elite adopted a number of macro-economic policies as a demonstration of democracy and good governance. Some of the positive measures taken to achieve the above objective include the following:

- Deficit reduction, government consumption, exchange rate, inflation, and the improvement of the current account deficit were the major GEAR-related indicators that the macro-economic strategy might have longer-term potential to increase jobs and ensure broad-based development
- South Africa improved its international credit ratings, indicating favourable international opinion
- The currency exchange rate first plummeted but then recovered, at least in part due to government interventions
- Despite serious shortcomings with regard to GEAR, the government was holding out the prospect that favourable international and national investor perceptions of the stability and investor-friendliness of the South African economy would deliver the pot of gold.

Evidence of Macro-Economic Policy Undermining Sustainable Development

Some of the views held along the lines of negativity and counter-productive macro-economic policies are analysed in the section below:

- GEAR is controversial in its commitment to ensuring that empowerment is broad-based
- Crucial GEAR targets were not met in the period spanning 1996-2004
- The growth rate was not sufficient to provide the necessary boost to the economy to allow for job creation
- The implementation of GEAR over five to six years did not create new jobs – South Africa experienced a variation of the phenomenon of 'jobless growth'

- GEAR resulted in major disappointments in terms of wage growth, the real bank rate, government investment growth, private investment growth, non-gold export growth, foreign direct investment, GDP growth, annual job creation, and savings.

The weight of this evidence indicates that the GEAR macro-economic strategy failed to deliver in several of the most crucial developmental dimensions of the strategy. Whereas crucial macro-economic indicators did fall into place, joblessness and below expectation growth rates plagued the strategy. There is analytical consensus that South Africa should be performing better than it is. It appears that additional political will is required to move South Africa towards a macro-economic framework that is conducive to substantive democracy.

Political Will and the Wealth-Poverty Gap

One of the tragic legacies of South Africa's structurally violent apartheid past is that human development and substantive democracy continue to be racially skewed, despite a range of efforts by the post-apartheid leadership to work towards the creation of equity. An important indicator of continued inequality is the Gini-coefficient (see Table 6.2). The coefficient for South Africa indicates only minor change between 1975 and 1996. In addition, a Gini-coefficient value of 0.69 places South Africa amongst the highest in this regard, in the world. From 1997 to 2002, the South African government estimated that the Gini-coefficient, excluding social transfers, moved from 0.68 to 0.59. The Gini, including transfers, went from 0.44 to 0.35.[14] (The Human Poverty Index in Table 6.9 provides an aggregate level overview of the depth of poverty in South Africa.)

Another indicator of inequality is the ratio of income of the richest 10% of the population compared with the poorest 10%. In South Africa, the share in income of the richest 10% of households is 42.5% greater than the share in income of the poorest 10% (see Table 6.3; also Table 6.4). Roux observed that the most noteworthy changes in South Africa's Gini-coefficient occurred *within population groups*.[15] The black-African Gini-coefficient rose from 0.47 in 1975, to 0.66 in 1996. With the advances of the new black middle class, this factor was likely to have shown a further significant increase in the period following 1996. This trend raises important issues with regard to future electoral stability in South Africa. A strong black middle class, with its position of strength largely attributable to ANC elite policies and actions, is likely to continue electoral support in future elections.

Statistics show a strengthening of the black middle class, even by the standards of the already dated 1996 figures. For instance, between 1991 and 1996, the number of black middle class households grew from 222 000 to 400 000; whilst the number of poor black households remained virtually unchanged (rising from 56% to 58%). The share of total income by population group equally indicates an overall advancement of the black middle class (see Table 6.3). African share of total income grew from 20% in 1970 (white share 72%), to 36% in 1996 (white share 52%).

Table 6.2: Gini-coefficient by Race/Population Group – 1975, 1991 and 1996; 1995-1998

RACE	1975	1991	1996	1995-1998
African	0.47	0.62	0.66	0.70-0.81
Coloured	0.51	0.52	0.56	–
Indian	0.45	0.49	0.52	–
White	0.36	0.46	0.50	0.75 to 0.67
All	0.68	0.68	0.69	0.73-0.80

*Value of 0 implies absolute equality and 1 absolute inequality.

Sources: Wharton Econometric and Forecasting Associated, as quoted in SAIRR 2001, p 374; statistics in right-hand column from Statistics SA, 'Measuring poverty in South Africa' in *SAIRR* 2001, p 374.

Statistics on poverty also indicate that it has been and continues to be black-African South Africans, in each of South Africa's nine provinces, who have fallen into the poverty trap (see Tables 6.4, 6.5 and 6.6). Provincial statistics show the extent to which it is also populous provinces, with large rural population sectors, that carry the highest 'poverty loads' (see Table 6.6). Poverty or minimum living levels were defined as, "minimum financial requirements for members of a family if they are to maintain their health and have acceptable levels of hygiene and sufficient clothing for their needs".

Table 6.3: Change in Income Deciles for Black South Africans, 1975-1996

Deciles of income	1975	1991	1996
(1=lowest; 10=highest)	All figures in percentages (%)		
1	87	92	90
2	87	92	93
3	86	90	91
4	86	86	89
5	90	83	86
6	86	77	81
7	75	69	72
8	51	48	60
9	7	22	39
10	2	9	22

Source: Wharton Econometric and Forecasting Associated in SAIRR 2001, p 375.

Table 6.4: Percentage Share of Total Income by Race/Population Group
(Italics in parentheses represent proportion of population)

Race	1970	1980	1991	1996
African	19.8 *(70.7)*	24.9 *(72.4)*	29.9 *(75.2)*	35.7 *(76.2)*
Coloured	6.7 *(9.4)*	7.2 *(9.3)*	6.8 *(8.7)*	7.9 *(8.6)*
Indian	2.4 *(2.9)*	3.0 *(2.8)*	3.8 *(2.6)*	4.5 *(2.6)*
White	71.2 *(17.0)*	65.0 *(15.5)*	59.5 *(13.5)*	51.9 *(12.6)*
Total	100	100	100	100

Source: Wharton Econometric and Forecasting Associated in SAIRR 2001, p 376.

Table 6.5: Change in Personal Disposable Income Per Capita by Population Group, 1995 and 2000

Race	1995 (ZAR)	2000 (ZAR)	Change (%)
African	4.122	7.567	83.6
Coloured	8.482	12.960	52.8
Indian	12.696	25.541	101.2
White	30.572	50.840	66.2

Source: Bureau of Market Research in *SAIRR* 2001, p 377.

Access to decent healthcare is one of the factors that might amend the effects of poverty. Simultaneously, the absence of access is a factor that could prevent otherwise increasingly socio-economically better-off South Africans from experiencing and appreciating general improvements in their developmental situation. It is in this context that the chapter refers to political leadership's records in respect of the HIV/AIDS pandemic and other healthcare issues. The high prevalence of HIV/AIDS in the South African population is set to have a far-reaching medium and long-term impact on both socio-demographic indicators and the economy. By 2003, an estimated 4.5 million South Africans were living with the disease. The numbers of infections had escalated since 1994.[17] AIDS deaths in 2003 were estimated at just fewer than 340 000, and were expected to rise to 424 000 in 2004, followed by 510 000 in 2005 and 779 000 in 2010. AIDS-related deaths as a percentage of all deaths in South Africa was estimated as 33.2% in 2001, 39.8% in 2002, and was expected to rise to 65.7% in 2010.[18]

In April 2002, the South African government issued its 'HIV causes AIDS' statement in which it moved away from the denial position that had threatened to emasculate ANC leadership for years. Government was engaged in political and Constitutional Court battles regarding its position on HIV/AIDS, and its refusal to provide anti-retroviral drugs on more than limited rollout bases. The Cabinet subsequently promised that it would start working on a national rollout plan. The implementation of this plan commenced in 2003. In early 2003, controversy again erupted with the government stalling on the implementation of the envisaged arrangement. The Treatment Action Campaign (TAC) implemented a movement of civil disobedience against government's non-signing and/or implementation of the framework agreement for a

Table 6.6: Poverty Levels in South Africa, 1996 – Comparative Trends, 2002

Province	Major population groups affected	Totals per province	Percentage of provincial population living in poverty	2002 incidence of poverty by % of households
Eastern Cape	4.4 m African	4.7 m	74 (81 of Africans)	48
Free State	1.3 m African	1.4 m	54 (61 of Africans)	48
Gauteng	2.1 m African	2.4 m	32 (42 of Africans)	12
KwaZulu-Natal	5.1 m African	5.3 m	63 (74 of Africans)	26
Mpumalanga	1.8 m African	1.8 m	64 (70 of Africans)	25
North West	2.0 m African	2.0 m	61 (65 of Africans)	37
Northern Cape	191 000 African	477 000	58 (69 of Africans)	35
Limpopo	3.8 m African	3.8 m	78 (80 of Africans)	38
Western Cape	423 000 African 649 000 Coloured	1.1 m	29 (50 of Africans; 29 of coloureds)	12

Sources: Adapted from Bureau of Market Research, Unisa. Econometric and Forecasting Associates in SAIRR 2001, p 371; 2002 data from Statistics SA 2000 in Roberts 2004, p 487.[16]

national prevention and treatment plan that had been negotiated and agreed upon in the National Economic Development and Labour Council (NEDLAC).[19] Mbeki also withdrew from the HIV/AIDS issue and delegated authority to Deputy President Jacob Zuma.[20] Questions about the scale and the consistency of the drug rollout marked the 2004 debates.

Another illustration of political will in the socio-economic sphere could be government policies and performance with regard to access to clean water. Government estimates included that from the period of 1995 to 2001, access rose from 60% to 85%; access to sanitation from 49% to 63%; and access to electricity connections from 32% to 70%. It also estimated that by 2003, a further 1.7 million urban households had gained access to clean water. Its total estimate for rural households acquiring access to these services in the period of 1994 to 2003 amounted to 1.6 million.[21]

Finally, continued extreme poverty and inequality within South Africa served to counter, and often cancel out, benefits that were derived from infrastructural developments such as water, electricity and telecommunications, which might have helped many of the impoverished citizens out of a vicious cycle of poverty and lack of access to services. Cashdan estimated that the rates of default in payment for these services stood at 23% in 1997, rising to above 90% in some townships.[22]

Demonstration of Political Will Towards Poverty Reduction

Some of the indicators that reflect positive efforts made by the political leadership to reduce poverty in South Africa are listed as follows:

- Within the 'black community' of South Africa, there was a leap in the Gini-coefficient, indicating more pronounced differences between rich and poor in this sector of the South African community (this could equally be categorised as a negative, but given that it indicates some form of deracialisation, the positive categorisation is used)

- The formation of a strong black middle class indicates that there could be additional favourable circumstances propelling the elite into secure and credible future elections
- The existence of a strong black-African middle class is further confirmed through the growth in the share of total income of black South Africans (this point could equally be categorised as a negative, depending on class perspective)
- Given the close links between healthcare and poverty eradication/development, the political leadership's dedication to work towards the full control of malaria, and better access to clinics, are factors that enhance its reputation in addressing poverty
- Improved access to education for a large cross-section of the South African population also favours the assessment of political will to enhance development
- The extended provision of access to water, electricity and telecommunications indicates a positive measure of will to address underdevelopment.

Indicators of Leadership's Unwillingness to Address the Problems of Continuing Poverty

Some discernible evidence of unwillingness by leadership to address the problem of poverty and to close the widening gap between the rich and the poor are summarised below:

- South Africa's Gini-coefficient remains amongst the highest in the world, with serious discrepancies between Gini-coefficients calculated for white and black South Africans
- Privatisation and outsourcing of services might have entailed putting these services out of reach of a range of poverty-stricken South Africans (although the commercialisation of public sector services had a similar impact)
- Government's vacillation on the HIV/AIDS issue put in serious doubt its will to ensure that South Africans do not become more susceptible to the cumulative effects of poverty
- The quality of education, lack of resources and under-deployment of teachers in schools seriously undermines the existence of

political will to provide quality education that would enhance future life prospects of the poor in society.

On the balance of evidence, as reviewed in this section, it appears that poverty reduction in South Africa lags, whilst the creation of a black middle class receives greater attention (or is easier to effect in prevailing conditions). Despite improvements in development, including heightened access to social services, poverty prevails and little overall progress has been made since the mid-1990s. It is problematic to argue that 'political will is absent'. Leadership in all probability does have the will, and because of this will, it has chosen a particular policy and ideological path to lead it towards the objective of development and significant poverty reduction. Some of the factors affecting the lack of success of the policy, especially those of an international or global nature, have also been beyond control of the leadership. The immediate next test of the government's political will lies in assessing the extent to which leadership possesses the resolve to amend and supplement existing policies. The advancement and extension of the security net within South African society is one tentative indicator in this direction; another might be the opening of debate on the role of the state in the country's economy.[23]

Political Will and South Africa's Employment/ Unemployment Situation

The rising rates of unemployment in the pre-GEAR and during the GEAR era, up to late 2002, and their effects on popular and voter perceptions of the political elite, could possibly be one of the core indicators of long-term electoral stability and continued elite support for competitive elections.

South Africa has been undergoing an extended period of consistent shedding of jobs, despite some positive trends with regard to economic growth and cuts in interest rates (see Tables 6.7 and 6.8). In one of the benchmark employment categories, namely the formal non-agricultural private sector, jobs in the decade 1989-1999 fell by 780 000, whilst public sector jobs decreased by 120 000 (the similar, but not identical data in Table 6.11 corroborates these trends). In one of the single biggest public sector cuts, jobs fell by 300 000 between 1996 and 1998. From 1975 to 1999, private sector responsibility for formal employment went down from 72% to 65%.[24]

Two categories of definitions of unemployment are commonly used, namely 'strict' and 'extended' (or 'broad'), with extended excluding informal sector labour absorption. One of the most important statistics therefore is that expanded unemployment in 1999 stood at 36.2%, and subsequently increased to 41.5% in 2001 and 41.8% in 2002. By this time, the strict definition's percentage came to an eight-year high of 30.5.[25] The expanded rate in 1999 per population group indicates the extent to which differential suffering was wrought by unemployment (strict unemployment rates in brackets) stands as follows: African 44% (29.2%); coloured: 23.6% (15.2%); Indian: 20.2% (15.6%); white: 6.8% (4.7%).[26] Official statistics (strict definition), based on the September 2001 *Labour Force Survey*, indicated that there was a total unemployment rate of 26.1%, peaking at 32.2 % for black-African South Africans, 20.5% for coloureds, 14.8% for indians, and 4,9% for whites.

By late 2002 (see details below), there was select evidence that the unemployment tide might have started turning. Statistics South Africa's *Survey on Unemployment and Earnings*, released in late 2002, indicated that up to September of that year, employment growth was positive for the first time in six years. It was reported that the economy had turned around with regard to job creation, stemming net job losses for the first time since 1996. One of the statements from government portrayed the optimism of government leadership "the policies that we have and continue to pursue, have helped us to push back the frontiers of poverty and open access to a better life".

This statement was partly based on the fact that the formal, non-agricultural sector had created jobs for the first time in twelve years (since 1989) in the second quarter of 2002.[27] Government also announced a number of measures to try and strengthen this trend, including a R3.6 billion injection into the Skills Development Fund, with R1 billion going into labour-intensive municipal infrastructure development projects, and R105 billion into other capital expenditures.[28] The subsequent Expanded Public Works Programme (EPWP) provided further measures to try and stem the tide of unemployment.

Table 6.7: Job Losses or Gains in the Period Between 1991 and 2000

Sector	Number of jobs lost (-) or gained (+) over the eriod	Percentage (%) change over he period
Mining	-310.280	-43.1%
Manufacturing	-275.268	-17.6%
Construction	-165.138	-42.6%
Trade	+ 84.090	+10.7%
Financial institutions	+ 8.943	+ 4.8%
Public sector	-182.424	-10.1%
TOTAL	-840.077	-15.4%

Source: Compiled from Roux 2002; *Quarterly Bulletins,* SA Reserve Bank 2002.

The enormous growth in the informal sector in South Africa, during the period since 1996, should be noted (also see Table 6.8). This sector is an important source of income for those without formal jobs, as there is no system of social security in the country that could sustain the unemployed. It is difficult to determine the exact size of the informal sector – one reason being that people may enter the informal sector to bridge a period of unemployment; some formally employed citizens also participate in the informal sector, while children are often employed in the informal sector. It is widely assumed that surveys underestimate the size of the informal sector. It is further known that the average income in this sector level is well below that of the formal sector, without any of the formal sector benefits. As highlighted by Barker, the informal sector is no solution to unemployment.[29]

In 2001, the Minister of Finance, in his budget speech, suggested that the decline in formal employment was being offset by the creation of 900 000 jobs from September 1996 to September 1999 in the informal sector. At the December 2002 ANC national conference, it was acknowledged that the informal sector did not have the capacity to bring about a substitute for formal employment, and that unemployment would continue to rise. The ANC conference also debated the feasibility of a "vastly expanded public works programme" as a solution to the unemployment crisis.[30]

Table 6.8: Overall Job Gains and Losses, 1996-1999 – Select Trends, 2002

	1996 (Persons)	1999 (Persons)	Change (% 1996-1999)	Increase/ decrease (1996-1999)	Select 2002 trends
Total employed	9.3 m	10.4 m	11.7	1.1 m	11.2 m
Formal sector (non-agriculture)	6.8 m	6.6 m	- 3,4	-228 000	Unemployed: 4.3 m
Agriculture	759 000	1.1 m	44.8	340 000	Other workers:
Informal sector	996 000	1.9 m	91.5	911 000	temporary, casual,
Domestic service	740 000	799 000	8	59 000	contract, seasonal: 2.1 m

Sources: Statistics SA, *October Household Survey 1999* in SAIRR 2001, p 362; right-hand column from the Policy Co-ordination and Advisory Services (PCAS) 2003, p 36.

Both historical factors and South Africa's modest economic performance over the last decade have contributed to poverty. A wide range of advances has been made over the past decade by the ANC rule. These advances include a significant increase in the number of children attending school; millions receiving a free meal every school day; access to primary healthcare being extended through the erection and operationalisation of a significant number of new clinics; as well as the electrification of a large number of houses, with 3.8 million connected to electricity. Others include rural access to pipe-borne water, with 8.3 million receiving clean running water; a large number of low-cost houses being built, including more than 5 million free houses; in addition to land restitution and redistribution, culminating in the issuance of hundreds of thousands of title deeds in urban areas.

It is important, however, to note that the inability of the South African economy to create jobs has been the root cause of a large number of other socio-economic problems. Despite the advances mentioned above, high unemployment has led to poor growth in the domestic demand for goods and services. It causes poverty, malnutrition, disease, and it affects the ability of the population to make meaningful use of improved educational services. It also cancels out advances in providing South Africans with water, electricity and telecommunication facilities. This is because in the same period, and often as part of the same processes, these services have become either privatised or commercialised, and their availability is subject to regular payments. The commercialisation of services has not only led to increased costs for poor households, but also contributed to job losses. Furthermore, outsourced public sector workers might retain jobs, but often suffer significant cuts in pay and working conditions.[31]

The 'social wage', comprising a range of grants and social services, was considerably extended in recent years. Social grants were increased twice in 2002, leading to a total of R1.5 billion that was made available to vulnerable members of society. By September 2003, approximately 6.5 million people received social grants, costing the South African state R2.5 billion per month.[32] Government estimated a total of 6.8 million beneficiaries.[33] These grants included the child support grant, disability (and HIV/AIDS) grant, old age grant and foster care grant, as well as some provision for free housing, limited free amounts of water and electricity, some free or minimally-charged healthcare, and land distribution. Given the "large social deficit", as dubbed by Roux, which South Africa currently experiences, the social deficit largely remains lodged amongst "black South Africans". In using a grant and general social wage approach to counter the social deficit, contrasting messages emerged from government leadership in 2004. On the one hand, there was emphasis on the enhanced rollout of, for example, the child support grant. On the other hand, by late 2004, tentative concerns were expressed that the high levels of social grant financing, in the future, might become unsustainable.

Intense debate prevails on the root causes of unemployment in South Africa. Select reasons for rises in unemployment include (and only some of these depend on the political will of the South African political elite; others were beyond their control) the following:[34]

- The South African economy changed to one that is increasingly based on the knowledge and services industries, with greater focus on technology, e-commerce, the Internet and services
- Changes in markets and the economy led to policies that impacted adversely on employment trends, including downsizing, rightsizing, privatisation and unbundling
- Globalisation and volatile international markets and currency trends created conditions in which employers favoured greater job flexibility, through the use of new technologies, which reduced the need for full-time labour, which led to alternative working arrangements
- On the supply side, the increasing number of women, students and unemployed availing themselves for temporary work facilitated alternative and informalised employment – processes of flexible labour became commonplace, whilst so-called home-based work also expanded
- Because of government regulation and demands imposed by equity action, employers increasingly made use of non-standard forms of employment in order to lower costs and avoid unionisation. The wage-raising effect of union membership was estimated by the World Bank at 35%, decreasing the number of jobs in the economy by 6.3%.

Indicators of Political Will to Minimise Unemployment

Some of the indicative efforts by the government of the day to create jobs and thereby reduce rising unemployment are summarised below. These include the following:

- After a prolonged period of job losses, 2002 brought tentative indications of a turnaround through modest but positive growth in employment in the formal non-agriculture sector. Although the trend was contested, government pointed out that between 1995 and 2002, the number of people employed in South Africa grew from 9.6 million to 11.2 million[35]
- Leadership made efforts to build employment initiatives through emphasis on partnerships, and the advancement of the idea of co-responsibility in job creation
- Encouragement of business, for instance through the system of financing of skills training, to equip the larger potential workforce with skills
- Facilitation of 'high black economic empowerment' by working on the assumption that growth in black business and the black middle class will, in due course, increase empowerment and employment
- Government emphasis on the improvements in the 'social wage', and continuous increases in grants to the unemployed, disabled, the sick and their caretakers, as measures that would contribute towards providing subsistence wages
- Recognition in ANC leadership/conference debates that supplementary job creation action is urgently required.

Evidence of Uncertainty in the Political Will to Address Unemployment

Some of the perceptions in South African society of a seeming failure on the part of leadership to effectively address the problem of poverty are documented and can be summarised as follows:

- There is little systematic evidence to prove that the leadership is resolute to move against some of the dated tenets of neo-liberal employment creation initiatives
- Severe levels of job losses would take a long period for the sustained reversal of previous levels of employment, simply to catch up. It would equally be difficult to generate employment that surpasses the number of new market entrants. There are few indications yet that the 2002-2004 turnaround would be either definitive or sustained
- Public work projects are few and still of limited anticipated impact, and more sustained engagement with the opportunities emerged belatedly
- Growth in the informal sector, which is largely unprotected and frequently exploited, could be counter-indicative of the political will to address employment
- Initiatives to enhance SMMEs are officially regarded as unable to reverse trends in unemployment
- Government resistance to the Basic Income Grant indicates reluctance to compensate beyond the level of 'social wage' initiatives for high unemployment rates.

With regard to job creation, or the reduction of unemployment, there appears to be political will amongst the leadership, but this will is evidently not bringing the desired results. The 2002-2004 indications of reversals of unemployment are tentative and still insufficient. Plans conceived by the leadership would need to be significantly extended in order to build systematic evidence of political will.

The Human Development Index in South Africa

The Human Development Index (HDI) for South Africa (see Table 6.10) offers indications of the highly ranked position that South Africa occupies, both on the continent and within the Southern African Development Community (SADC) region, regarding the continuous levels of high inequality within the country, and South Africa's relative economic decline from 1995 to 1998. The HDI of the United Nations Development Programme (UNDP) adds a number of socio-

Table 6.9: South African Human Poverty Index (HPI) and Indicators in the SADC Region, 1998

Indicator	South Africa's Position	Rankings of other states in SADC
HPI ranking	11 Second lowest poverty level out of 12 (DR Congo, Seychelles not ranked)	Highest: Angola 1 Lowest: Mauritius 12
HPI Index (HPI-1) value	20.2	Highest: Mozambique 50.7 Lowest: Mauritius 11.5
Percentage of population not expected to live beyond 40 years of age	25.9	Highest: Malawi 47.5 Lowest: Mauritius 4.8
Adult illiteracy rate (%)	16	Highest: Angola 58 Lowest: Seychelles 16.0
Percentage population without access to safe water	13	Highest: Angola 69 Lowest: Mauritius 2
Percentage population without access to health services	25	Highest: Angola 76 Lowest: Seychelles 1
Percentage underweight children under 5 years of age	9	Highest: Angola 42 Lowest: Seychelles 6 (different period)
Percentage population without safe water, and health services, and underweight children	15.7	Highest: Angola 62.3 Lowest: Mauritius 6.3
Percentage children not attaining Grade 5	35	Highest: Mozambique 54 Lowest: Seychelles, Mauritius 1

Source: UNDP, SADC Regional Human Development Report 2000: Challenges and opportunities for regional integration. Harare: SAPES Books, p 234, 2000.

demographic indicators, including life expectancy, the percentage of children in full-time education, and literacy to income indicators to derive an aggregate index for the country.

In a comparative context, the composite HDI value in pre-democracy days hovered around 0.660 in 1975 and 0.734 in 1990. By 1999, it stood at 0.702 and subsequently moved downwards to 0.684 in 2001, parallel with the declining life expectancy.[36]

Government leadership's efforts to improve the standard of living of South African people, with reference to poverty and development, falls short in several respects. As indicated by Roux, South Africa's development performance during the preceding two decades has been both disappointing and well below what might have been expected from a country with a relatively high GDP per capita. Roux specified that South Africa's development performance, in some ways, deteriorated during this period. In terms of 1999 statistics, South Africa had a GNP per capita or purchasing power parity (PPP) of US$ 8.908, life expectancy at birth (1995-2000) of 56.7 years, 1999 adult literacy rate of 84.9%, and 40.2% of male babies (commonly used indicator) likely to survive to the age of 65, 1995-2000. These statistics led to a 1999 HDI of 0.702, showing an improvement, when compared with the 0.648 value in 1975. The 1999 HDI, however, represented a decline of 2.8% from the average value for the 1995 to 1999 period. Roux further highlighted that South Africa was ranked 45th in the world in respect of GDP per capita, but only 94th with regard to human development.[37]

South Africa's world ranking changed slightly from 1999 to 2002, from 110th and 107th positions, respectively, out of a total of 173 countries. The 107th position was 19 positions lower than the 1990 ranking (out of 135 countries) and 15 positions lower than that in 1975 (out of 100 countries). From 1995 to 1998, South Africa's HDI declined by 5.23% compared with the SADC average of -5.30%. This was also the third greatest decline within the SADC region, after the Democratic Republic of Congo and Angola, both war-ridden countries. South Africa nevertheless retained its ranking as third overall in SADC (Table 6.10).[38]

Table 6.10: Human Development Index (HDI)

Comparison of South Africa's HDI Trends and Indicators with SADC States, 1998; Select updates where available	
Life expectancy at birth (years): **South Africa: 53.2** (1999: 56.7; UNDP figure for 2000: 52; 2001: 50.9) Highest: Seychelles: 71 Lowest: Malawi 40	**Life expectancy index:** **South Africa: 0.470** Highest: Seychelles: 0.71 Lowest: Malawi 0.242
Adult literacy rate (%): **South Africa: 84.6** (1999: 84.9; GCIS figures for 2001: 89) Highest: Zimbabwe 87.2; Lowest: Angola 42.0	**Adult literacy index:** **South Africa: 0.846** Highest: Zimbabwe 0.872; Lowest: 0.420
Combined 1st, 2nd, 3rd level gross enrolment ratio (%): **South Africa: 95** Highest: South Africa 95; Lowest: Mozambique, Angola 25	**Combined 1st, 2nd, 3rd level gross enrolment index:** **South Africa: 0.950** Highest: South Africa; Lowest: Angola, Mozambique 0.250
Real GDP per capita (PPP$): **South Africa: 8.488** (1999: 8.908) Highest: Seychelles: 10.600; Lowest: Tanzania 480	**GDP per capita index:** **South Africa: 0.804** Highest: Seychelles: 0.813; Lowest: Tanzania 0.284

Real GDP-A per capita (PPP US$): South Africa: **3.480** Highest: Seychelles 5.618; Lowest: Malawi 199	Real GDP per capita (PPP US$): South Africa: **0.643** Highest: Seychelles 0.730; Lowest: Malawi 0.124 (No statistics DR Congo, Mozambique)

1998 Values and Rankings HDI South Africa

SADC HDI (value)	SADC HDI-A (value)	Global HDI (value)	SADC HDI ranking SA (1995, 1997, 1998)
0.718	0.6665	0.697	3, 3, 3

1995-1998 Values and Rankings of HDI South Africa

	SADC HDI (value) 1998	SADC HDI-A (value) 1998	SADC HDI (value) 1997	SADC HDI (value) 1995
	0.718	0.665	0.725	0.758
Base indicator		Absolute change of -0,007 from 1997 to 1998	Absolute change of -0.033 from 1995-1997	Absolute change of -0.040 from 1995-1998

Sources: UNDP, SADC *Regional Human Development Report 2000: Challenges and opportunities for regional integration,* Harare: SAPES Books, 2000, pp 224-225; 1999 figures from Roux 2002.

Assessment of the Political Will to Effect Development and Equality

Some indicators that suggest positive democratic policy aimed at fostering development and equality in South African society, under the current political leadership are summarised below:

- South Africa possesses a favourable HDI ranking *vis-à-vis* most of the other SADC member states, as well as those in the sub-Saharan Africa
- The HDI for South Africa shows significant improvements with regards to the literacy and educational access measures
- Government continuously advances a range of growth, developmental and budgetary/fiscal initiatives to work towards development and higher levels of equality. These measures include charters and expenditure frameworks.

Indications of Insufficient Political Will to Effect Development

Some indications of unwillingness or relative failure to pursue development on the part of the political leadership have emerged in this study. A selection of negative or counter-development trends are highlighted below:

- South Africa's development performance over two decades is well below what might have been expected from a country with a relatively high GDP per capita
- South Africa's HDI ranking showed a comparatively steep decline in the period from 1995 to 1998, and beyond
- Life expectancy measures did not show adequate improvements in the period 1995 to 1998, and a decline in the period up to 2002 (HIV/AIDS might have played a role in these trends, and the impact is feared to become more severe)
- The positive overall HDI ranking veils large internal inequalities amongst the rich and the poor in South Africa. In 1999, 'white'

South Africa had a ranking of 19th in the world, whilst the country's overall ranking was 110th
* The HDI rankings confirm that despite South Africa's positive experience in the post-1994 period, regarding GDP and economic growth, there has not been a systematic developmental experience.

The HDI for South Africa graphically demonstrates the fact that, developmentally, South Africa is under-achieving. This is despite positive and comparatively good rankings in the SADC context. Given continuously high levels of unemployment and an expected decline in life expectancy, it is unlikely that South Africa's HDI will soon show significant improvement.

Institutional Capacity and the Implementation of Policy and Programmes

Many of South Africa's best intended socio-economic policy initiatives in the post-1994 period were undermined by a lack of articulation between policy and implementation strategies. There is also insufficient capacity of national departments to coordinate the implementation through staff training and development, as well as distended and/or inappropriately staffed departments. In addition, a lack of articulation between the national and provincial governments, and between the provincial and national spheres, has undermined some well-intended policies. Finally, inadequate capacity on the local/metropolitan government level, in addition to the leadership's premature assumption that the country was ready to implement 'developmental local government', led to doubts on whether political leadership had adequately considered the complexity of policy implementation.[39] The capacity shortcomings have been evident in both infrastructure and human resource development.

In order to interpret 'political will' in respect of capacity for implementation, the dedication of leadership to transform the bureaucratic structures, in line with the needs of the post-1994 South Africa, has to be assessed. Undoubtedly, great strides were made in, for instance, the integration of the former Bantustan and provincial governments, and formerly disparate local governments into new units. Whereas integration on a provincial level was accomplished within two to three years after 1994, the integration of the local government was implemented in interim form in the mid-1990s and in its final form on the eve of the 2000 local government elections.

Capacity problems on the provincial level are fairly widespread, but often concentrated in the poorer provinces. The Eastern Cape province is an example of this phenomenon. By 2002, central government intervened in the form of constituting an Interim Management Team to resolve intractable delivery problems in a number of the provincial departments.[40] Many of the problems of under-spending of allocated budgets in South African provincial government stem from the lack of capacity and project management skills within distributing agencies.[41] The extent of the level of this problem was indicated by the fact that, in 2002, for example, provinces under-spent their capital allocations by ZAR2 to 3 billion. In early 2003, Mbeki reported progress in actual provincial capital spending, which was up by 48% in the first nine months of the 2002 fiscal year.[42]

The implementation of the new structures for local government was continuing in 2004, with obvious implications for capacity in delivery. Local government capacity remained a major issue. Provincial and Local Government Minister, Sydney Mufamadi, in early 2003, found it necessary to call for strong and effective institutional structures in local government to fight poverty and realise sustainable development.[43] A major motivation for the new system was that it would ensure viable local government units. The new system was referred to as 'developmental local government'. It is widely recognised that the new municipal borders were hastily drawn and that a fragmented system was the result. In this context, service delivery often poses virtually insurmountable problems. By late 2004, problems with local level service delivery built up to protest level in several Free State towns. The incidence of dissatisfaction with service delivery on a local level, however, was much wider than these protests. Research showed that insufficient progress on the local level was closely linked to capacity problems.[44]

Local level mechanisms that were constructed to help ensure improved infrastructural delivery capacity included the so-called public-private partnerships (PPPs) and alternative service delivery (ASD). Cashdan argued that these mechanisms were unlikely to yield

the desired results in the context of "shrinking economic opportunities, the rising cost of living and increasing unemployment".[45] The
overall percentage owed in rates and services was 33% by 1998, and
has subsequently been on the increase, despite campaigns such as
Masakhane (Let's Build Together). By early 2002, more than half of
municipalities were reported to have been in financial difficulty, as
estimated by Cashdan. Local governments, by 2004, were in a continued state of crisis, combining low capacity for in-house delivery, with
outsourcing, public-private partnerships, restructuring and privatisation of service provider state corporations. Contributing to this crisis
was community inability or refusal to pay.

In short, the capacity for delivery and the capacity to work in terms
of community culture remained a far-reaching and formidable challenge on the local level. If the continued existence of seemingly
insoluble problems is an indicator of a 'lack of political will', then we
find ample indicators at the local level.

Indicators for Political Will to Build Capacity for Policy Implementation

Some of the efforts of the South African government to develop the
capacity of personnel, towards the implementation of socio-economic
policies geared towards sustainable development are hereby summarised. These include the following:

- Continuous efforts were made to restructure local government in
  order to make it effective for development
- Interventions were made by the executive, the ANC leadership
  and some provincial governments to ensure that provincial and
  local governance problems were resolved, even if these were regularly belated, such as in the Eastern Cape in 2002 and the Free
  State in 2004
- Design of methods of alternative service delivery and public-private partnerships, in order to help substitute for a lack of capacity
  in the public sector
- Improvements on the level of public spending in the provinces
  early in the new millennium

- Public hearings and other investigations were conducted into the lack of spending and the misdirection of public funds.

Indicators of Inadequate Political Will to Build Capacity for Implementation

Some of the failures of the leadership in capacity-building for effective socio-economic policy implementation include the following:

- Efforts to restructure local government in order to acquire an effective, capacity-rich local government has failed in many places, and there are too few initiatives underway with the potential to solve the prevailing problems
- Forms of alternative service provision remain ineffective in resolving a range of capacity problems in local government administration
- The training services provided were ineffectual, insufficiently penetrating the domains of provincial and local governments
- Overall, levels of public spending were still significantly behind allocated budgets, especially with regard to capital expenditure and infrastructural development. There has also been underspending of poverty relief funds by the government.

From 2002 to 2004 there was a sharply rising consciousness amongst political leadership that capacity for delivery had to be significantly enhanced. If political will, on the one hand, is measured by outcomes and results (rather than just stated commitment, strategic plans of action, and policy statements), then the conclusion would be that there is significant room for improvement when it comes to the political will to enhance capacity for delivery. Beside the consciousness of the extent to which the developmental needs of the population have to be satisfied on the local level, there was evidence of critical shortfalls in readiness to intervene and redirect policies, as well as strategies for local and provincial government structuring and human resource capacity-building. On the other hand, if policy frameworks measure political will, strategic plans, and delivery schedules, the South African government would fare considerably better.

Conclusion

This chapter proposed and analysed a set of standards for, and the role of, political will in providing substantive democracy, which is associated with socio-economic development in South Africa. Political will is a complicated concept, which makes its role in governance and socio-economic policy implementation rather intractable. Whereas the documents of the NEPAD, and the African Peer-Review Mechanism (APRM), for example, remain relatively vague on the empirical building blocks of 'political will for substantive democracy' in Africa, it places appropriate emphasis on sustainable development, developmental plans and the participatory processes through which these plans must be derived.

The approach of this chapter was, firstly, to assess the existence and extent of political will through the outcomes and results of government action. Secondly, it was to identify and consider policies and programmatic interventions, as an additional layer of evidence of political will. Thirdly, the existence of debate and general openness of government to consider policy alternatives in the face of sub-optimal performance of existing programmes was also identified, as some evidence of political will. It is important that there should be a demonstrated willingness of political leadership to engage with and to attempt to resolve developmental and socio-economic problems.

Overall, the chapter argued that there was a paucity of evidence of the political determination to experiment with new policy directions. Rather, government leadership expressed a willingness to supplement and perhaps deepen existing initiatives. There was also evidence of political will and determination to enhance capacity for the implementation of policies and programmes. This chapter argued that government has shown commitment towards the supply of social amenities such as water, electricity, and healthcare. This study also discussed economic policies, which were targeted towards the improvement of the economic status of the previously disadvantaged sectors of the society. Development initiatives, such as black economic empowerment (BEE) and the Growth, Employment and Redistribution (GEAR) strategy include some of the initiatives of government. The extent to which these programmes will transform the economic landscape of South Africa depends on the commitment of the political leadership towards not just the further development of existing initiatives, but in particular, the ability of these initiatives to extend, supplement and occasionally substitute existing policies and programmes.

The real test of the political will of the South African political and governing elite, as argued in this chapter, will come once the legitimacy of the ANC, as the liberation movement government starts thinning, under the burden of increasing socio-economic demands and the continuous inability to satisfy these needs to acceptable levels. At such a point of socio-economic crisis, voters could threaten to abandon their long-time political home of the ANC. This will pose the challenge to political leadership to display the political will to abide by the rules of elections and succession.

Notes and References

1   G. Scott, 'Who has Failed Africa? IMF Measures or the African Leadership?', *Journal of Asian and African Studies,* vol 33, no 3, 1998, pp 265-274.
2   K. Heller, 'Empowerment of Black South Africa: Up and Away', Guest Lecture, University of Port Elizabeth, February 2002; Annual Media Products Survey (AMPS), reported in *The Sunday Times,* 1 September 2002.
3   P. Bond, *Elite Transition: From Apartheid to Neo-liberalism in South Africa,* London/Pietermaritzburg: Pluto Press / University of Natal Press, 2000, pp 193-194.
4   S. Terreblanche, *A History of Inequality in South Africa, 1652-2002,* Pietermaritzburg: University of Natal Press, 2002, p 452.
5   T. Manual, 'Addressing South Africa's Social and Economic Imbalances – Budgetary and Fiscal Policy Considerations', Standard Bank Emerging Financial Markets Conference, Sun City, available online at http://www.finance.gov.za, 11 November 2004.
6   A different type of argument is advanced by N. van de Walle, *African Economies and the Politics of Permanent Crisis, 1979-1999,* Cambridge: Cambridge University Press, 2001, chapter 6. Van de Walle demonstrated that founding democratisation elections and the immediate subsequent periods of transition did not prescribe that the

economic performance of a series of sample countries would improve. Instead, the economies of old democracies and non-democracies somewhat outperformed those of the democratic newcomers.

7   S. Rule, *Electoral Territoriality in Southern Africa*, Aldershot: Ashgate, 2000, p 253.

8   S. Booysen, 'The Dualities of Contemporary Zimbabwean Politics: Constitutionalism Versus the Law of Power and the Land, 1999-2002', *African Studies Quarterly*, vol 7, nos 2/3, Special Issue: *Zimbabwe Looking Ahead,* 2003.

9   J. Battersby, 'Preserve the Goose and its Golden Egg', *The Sunday Independent* (Johannesburg), 31 August 2003, p 7.

10   See South African government, Department of Finance, *Growth, Employment and Redistribution: A Macro-economic Strategy,* Pretoria: Government Printer, 1996.

11   A. Roux, *Everyone's Guide to South Africa's Future*, Johannesburg: Zebra Press, 2002, p 237; also a major source for the trends indicated in the table below.

12   S. Gelb, 'An Overview of the South African Economy', in J. Daniel, R. Southall and J. Lutchman (eds), *State of the Nation, South Africa 2004-2005*, Pretoria: HSRC Press, 2004, p 384.

13   *South Africa Yearbook, 2003/04,* 2004, Pretoria: Government Communication and Information Service (GCIS), Johannesburg, 2004, p 58. This book points out that, in the same period of 1995 to 2002, the number of people unemployed grew by 2.4 million, because the number of people seeking work had increased.

14   Policy Coordinating and Advisory Services (PCAS), *Towards a Ten Year Review*, Pretoria: Government Communication and Information System, October 2003, p 90.

15   Roux 2002, *op. cit.*, p 208.

16   B. Roberts, 'Empty Stomachs, Empty Pockets: Poverty and Inequality in Post-apartheid South Africa' in Daniel *et al.* (eds), *op cit.*, 2002.

17   J. Netshitenzhe in *City Press* (Johannesburg), 16 March 2003, p 19.

18   Minister of Health, in response to a question in Parliament, *The Herald* (Cape Town), 21 March 2003, p 6.

19   *Weekend Argus* (Cape Town), 15 February 2003, p 2. Also see *Sunday Tribune* (Cape Town), 9 February 2003, elaborating on the thesis of government's lack of intention to sign the agreement. One of the government's concerns was the implication of signing an agreement by a multilateral institution such as Nedlac, and the

impact that this would have on the status of the South African National AIDS Council.

20 For an overview of government's changed position on HIV/AIDS, see Jimmy Seepe in *City Press* (Johannesburg), 1 December 2003, p 25.

21 PCAS, *op. cit.*, p 24.

22 B. Cashdan, 'Local Government and Poverty in South Africa' in S. Parnell, E. Pieterse, M. Swilling and D. Wooldridge (eds), *Democratising Local Government: The South African Experiment*, Cape Town: UCT Press, 2003, p 161.

23 See D. Everatt, 'The Politics of Poverty', in D. Everatt and V. Maphai (eds), *The Real State of the Nation: South Africa After 1990, Development Update*, Special Edition, vol 4, no 3, 2003, pp 75-99.

24 E. Slabber, 'Blacks Get Richer', *Finance Week* (Johannesburg), 25 February 2000, p 18; E. Slabber and T. Mazwai, 'Informal Sector Will Have to Create Jobs', *Finance Week* (Johannesburg), 29 September 2000, p 18; SA Reserve Bank in L. Vermeulen and R. Wiesner, 'Downsizing and the Survivor Syndrome: The South African Case', *South African Journal of Economic and Management Science*, vol 3, no 3, 2000, p 387.

25 Gelb 2004, *op. cit.*, p 425.

26 Statistics SA, as cited in South African Institute of Race Relations (SAIRR), *South Africa Survey, 2000/2001*, Johannesburg, 2001, pp 213, 334, 378.

27 Reserve Bank Governor Tito Mboweni in *Business Day* (Johannesburg), 2 December 2002, p 1.

28 *Mail & Guardian* (Johannesburg), 28 February 2003, p 10.

29 See F. Barker, *The South African Labour Market: Critical Issues for Renaissance*, Pretoria: J. L. van Schaik, 1999, pp 94-97.

30 See *Sunday Times* (Johannesburg), 1 December 2002, p 4. Two public works programmes already in place are 'Working for water' and Gauteng's 'Zivuseni programme'.

31 N. Makgetla, *Business Day*, 21 February 2003, p 11.

32 *South Africa Yearbook, 2003/04, op. cit.*, pp 550, 552. Also see Joel Netshitenzhe in *City Press* (Johannesburg), 16 March 2003, p 19.

33 PCAS, *op. cit.*, p 17. See p 26 for details on government housing subsidies, and the estimate stating that 6 million people had received housing in the 1994 to 2003 period.

34 Bullet point references: (1) Iraj Abedian, as cited in Hazelhurst, 'The Case for a New Mindset', *Financial Mail* (Johannesburg), 159(5), 2000, p 42; (2) M. Woodd, 'The Move Towards a Different Career Pattern', *Women in Management Review*, 14(1), 1999, p 22; T. Yanta, 'Job Losses: What Can Trade Unions Do?' *South African Labour Bulletin*, 25(2), 2001, p 13; (3) P. Brosnan, C. Allen, F. Horwitz and P. Walsh, 'From Standard to Non-standard Employment: Labour Force Change in Australia, New Zealand and South Africa', *International Journal of Manpower*, 22(8), 2000, p 749; (4) Brosnan *et al.*, 2000, *op. cit.*, p 749; (5) Vermeulen and Wiesner 2000, *op. cit.*, p 387; *The Economist* (Johannesburg), 31 October 1998.

35 *South Africa Yearbook 2003/04*, *op. cit.*, p 58. This source also points out that, in the same period, the number of unemployed grew by 2.4 million, because the number of people seeking work had increased.

36 D. Hemson and K. Owusu-Ampomah, 'A Better Life for All? Service Delivery and Poverty Alleviation' in Daniel *et al.* (eds), *op. cit.*, 2004, p 530-531.

37 Roux 2002, p 206.

38 UNDP, *SADC Regional Human Development Report 2000: Challenges and Opportunities for Regional Integration*, Harare: SAPES Books, 2000, pp 66.

39 For a background, see F. Cloete, 'Capacity-building for Sustainable Local Governance in South Africa' in Parnell *et al.*, *op. cit.*, 2002, pp 276-193.

40 For instance see *Business Day* (Johannesburg), 28 January 2003, p 3; *The Herald* (Cape Town), 2 December 2002, p 3; 17 March 2003, p 10; *Mail & Guardian* (Johannesburg), 22 November 2002, p 2.

41 Idasa, Provincial Spending Monitoring Project, 2001, 2002.

42 *Business Day* (Johannesburg), 18 February 2003, p 14.

43 *The Herald* (Cape Town), 21 March 2003, p 4.

44 S. Booysen, 'The Effect of Privatisation and Commercialisation of Water Services on the Right to Water: Grassroots Experiences' in Lukhanji and Amahlati, Cape Town: Community Law Centre, University of the Western Cape, 2004.

45 B. Cashdan, 'Local Government and Poverty in South Africa' in Parnell *et al.* op. cit. (eds), 2002, *op. cit.*, p 153.

SENEGAL

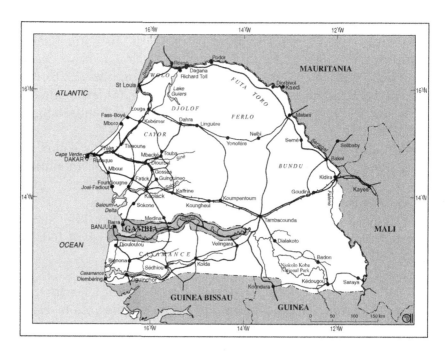

Source: Africa Institute of South Africa, 2005.

6. Political Leadership in Senegal: Clientelism and Monopolisation of Power

Serigne Mansour Tall[1] and Cheikh Gueye

Introduction

Africa's entry into the third millennium corresponds with a rethinking of the classical model of the functioning of the nation state. In most African countries, some of which are well endowed with natural resources, while others have a progressive political leadership, the basic options have been limited for the ruling class and economic decision makers. The continuing dependency, as well as the political and economic crisis, seem to have been strengthened in the past 40 years, and Africa is, as a result, always trying to catch up. Research into identity formation and political and social transitions has opened up a very interesting field of study for the social sciences in black Africa. However, such studies have been "Afro-pessimist" for too long, led by Africans who have been "educated" in Western schools and universities. Africa is thus "the world par excellence of all that is incomplete, mutilated, and unfinished".[1] This discourse and image reflect a conceptual, methodological and linguistic crisis in the social sciences in general, which arises from a reductive functionalism and an exclusive social utilitarianism. In consequence, the historicity of African societies is unknown,[2] as are the "foundations of what might be called their 'true lawfulness', 'true *raisons d'être*' and 'relation to nothing other than themselves'".[3]

However, the fragmentation of power that has accompanied the process of integrating Africa into the global economy needs to be examined, in order to understand what these societies really are and what they produce from a political perspective. Is the African Union (AU) and the initiative of Presidents Obasanjo of Nigeria, Mbeki of South Africa, Wade of Senegal and Bouteflika of Algeria respectively, which gave rise to the New Partnership for Africa's Development (NEPAD), a new way of bleeding states dry, or a truly new paradigm?

Nowadays, the question of the state, its reality and its composition is posed in most African countries in various forms. Even if it has only been a "pure import product" and an ineffective "foreign body", as Bertrand Badie would have it, there is still the question of how it can be legitimised. Globalisation, liberalisation, and informalisation seem to be the only constants in the development of contemporary Senegal. With Senegal often being held up as a model of democracy in the region, the reinvention of the state has become all the more important. Are the absence of coups and smooth political transitions indicators of the existence of a competent and accountable ruling class? Does multi-partyism correspond only with the existence of various parties? Can citizens really participate in the political procedures and process in a context of illiteracy and poverty? What is the point of an explosion of new print media titles when workers have only one daily meal and have no spare money to buy newspapers?

This chapter looks at the political systems and political elites in Senegal, in relation to the emerging developments and transformations within the country and paradigm shifts in Africa. The chapter is presented in five sections. The first section examines the economic context of the political leadership, the second part analyses the multi-party democracy in Senegal, the third looks at the extent of participation in the new dispensation, while the fourth section examines the perception of NEPAD among the political elite. The last section provides a conclusion and recommendations.

The Economic Context and Thoughts on the Reproduction of the Political Leadership

Agriculture

Senegal still has a predominantly agricultural economy. The main products are peanuts, millet, sorghum, rice, maize and cowpeas (*niébé*). Peanuts, the main source of income, cover 42% of arable land, and engage the majority of the active population with its production. Livestock farming is also important, although it has been affected by several years of drought since 1970. Moreover, incessant competition between agriculture and livestock farming over land use has led to the marginalisation of livestock. In the Ferlo and the Kolda region, where this rural activity is found, squatters are taking over land, leading to sometimes bloody conflicts with the farmers.

Fishing, which is an expanding industry, may become the new source of revenue for the country. Small-scale fishing, which has had slightly better yields than industrial fishing, is attracting a larger number of the population, who see it as an alternative when agriculture declines in the interior. However, resource pressures require conservation measures or sustainable management.

Non-Agricultural Sector

The manufacturing sector, in turn, is dominated by oils and phosphates. Indeed, the primary problem of the Senegalese economy is that it is overly concentrated in primary production, with declining profits and an over-exposure to the exploits of the world markets and droughts. Under the combined pressure of population growth, urbanisation and a slump in agriculture profits, the Senegalese economy has adapted to these vagaries of social and economic misfortune. Generally, the policy followed since independence has been to finance the development of the "modern" non-agricultural sector with international funds (bilateral and multilateral aid) and agricultural profits. With the downturn in global agricultural markets, the financial crisis and the poor intrinsic competitiveness of the Senegalese industry, this policy has failed. While the modern sector has stagnated, the agricultural sector has declined and the informal urban sector has grown accordingly.

Macro-Economic Policy

According to studies on employment by the central statistical office, the active population varies between 3 and 3.5 million, with the unemployment rate hovering between 7.5 and 11%. There are only about 60 000 civil servants and 80 000 workers in the private sector. In reality, informal sector businesses represent 60% of activities in the private sector, which contributes around 85% of the gross domestic product (GDP). The vast majority of the active population works in the informal sector, or is unemployed from time to time.

The structural adjustment policies introduced between 1985 and 1992 worsened the social situation, as the political elites could no longer ensure redistribution. "At the beginning of the 1990s, the state came across as a monstrous and ineffective structure in various donor publications".[4] To this sombre picture must be added the devaluation of the CFA franc in January 1994 in a bid to encourage exports.

The drying up of public financial resources means that political relations are being broken down. The state is increasingly using the land heritage as a resource in place of finances. But this situation is leading to dangerous conflicts over land, which threaten the stability of the country with their implications for ethnic, political and regional identity. This has in turn threatened the development of a united citizenry and led to increased jostling for position in the political parties and trade unions.

Citizenship and Multi-Partyism: The Unfinished Business of Senegalese Democracy

State and Non-State Role-Players

The rather grim economic outline raises the problem of how to reconcile a costly state and growing poverty among the population. It is difficult to find real institutional channels linking the post-independence Senegalese state and the society, which it represents. The state's frame of reference has long been limited to the diptych of clientelism and violence, or the carrot and the stick. The state is perceived as a foreign body. The destruction of public assets is perceived by the people as the destruction of someone else's assets. Civic engagement is weak. True citizenship is still a mere chimera, in spite of the peaceful transformation, which brought the Socialist Party to power between 1960 and 2000. The president has heavily criticised the indiscipline and lack of civic-mindedness among the Senegalese population. But what about the state? The public service is increasingly informal and complex, and comprises different actors – businessmen, public servants and politicians are developing contradictory approaches at the same time. The state is having difficulty in maintaining its duties as a result of the multiple contradictions it is experiencing. The political leaders are too often linked to religious chiefs and brotherhoods. For instance, the president owes his loyalty to the Senegalese Mouride (Sufi) brotherhood, and is suspected by the other brotherhoods of not remaining neutral.[5]

The Muslim brotherhoods do serve to regulate religious tensions and as a site of social construction, but their intimate links with the political rulers pose problems for the equitable management of relations between the state and its citizens. Political leaders in search of voters, who listen to the Marabouts (traditional, often religious leaders) when deciding where to cast their vote, are collaborating with the latter, endowed as they are with symbolic or real advantages, to the benefit of their group. The Marabouts, whether deliberately or involuntarily, channel the contesting desires of the opposition towards the ruling party. Their discourse is often centred on peace – God's choice of who is to wield power – and thus the uselessness of any opposition. But increasingly, the relations between politicians and the Marabouts, a group with varying ambitions, is changing. Their relations are in flux whenever an electoral contest approaches. Investments are set up, and steps are taken to court the religious chiefs, the "major voters", who give instructions to the crowds who hang on their every word. The promotion of religious chiefs reflects a resurgence of the traditional mechanisms for regulating the social order. However, this may lead to disputes with the state in future. A decline in support for the Marabouts has been seen as one of the factors leading to the former president Abdou Diouf's defeat in the 2000 elections.

Recent research in Senegal has focused on the so-called 'social contract', the gauge of Senegalese political stability, and the foundation of the legitimacy of the independent Senegalese state. During the past few years, it seems that groups other than political parties, such as trade unions, NGOs and associations, and notably Muslim regional brotherhoods, have constituted the true civil society, whose interactions with the state have, for a long time, ensured the stability and longevity of the state.[6] The Senegalese state, like most other states in black Africa, does not really arise from civil society.[7] It is set up outside of civil society, like a graft, which the latter must adapt to. It is increasingly independent of its clientele and is at times incapable of generating a legal and regulatory framework to oversee the executive branch of government. "The 'right' and 'legality' postulated by its administrative and judicial set-up serves more to legitimise its power than to guarantee its rights and responsibilities. This functioning is 'normal', because the modernity of the state is only a 'façade'. The base of its rooting in society is clientelism, which ensures a certain social cohesion".[8] Thus, what has been called a "success story" is certainly not one. The state does not transcend groups and communities. Rather, these groups and communities (brotherhoods, lineages, etc.) are becoming more distinct according to their social basis and appear to be more able to respond to the needs of ordinary Senegalese when faced with the crises of identity and of the state. While the lack or at least inactivity of an effective civil society in black Africa is often underlined by studies, in Senegal, it would be difficult not to consider certain dynamic groups, situated outside of the state but interacting closely with it, as a true civil society modelled on local values.[9] These groups, beginning as autonomous opposition bodies and then developing into legitimising bodies that interact with the state, have a greater capacity for mobilisation than that of the political parties or trade unions. Their way of functioning and their dynamic nature levels the state playing fields, where they continue to gain part of their resources through a tacit game of reciprocity. The historicity of the state is the product of an articulation of different legitimacies, which are interwoven, in an incessant double game of contest, complementarity and absorption.

Structure of Multi-Party Democracy

With Senegal's independence in 1960, the dual configuration linking two strong personalities with different political and social positions rapidly led to a political crisis, which, in time, gave birth to the presidential regime. Between this crisis and the current situation, Senegalese political life has developed from a single party to unregulated liberalisation, which has enabled the formation of nearly 70 political parties. On the whole, their ideological and doctrinal standpoints, and even their social development plans, are weak. The satirical press pokes fun at political parties, which are run from "telephone boxes". This proliferation, with around twenty active political bodies, has made the electoral consultation process much more complex. Alliances are only effective during electoral contests. The underlying motivation for such alliances is rarely ideological or programmatic. Rather, parties that do not possess the means to participate in elections, support other parties, with the hope of winning a few seats or increasing their influence in political decision-making. The simplicity of the process to officially recognise a party has led to their proliferation, even though the majority has not remained active after their creation. Only 11 political parties have seats in the three parliamentary chambers of the current legislature, with two independent members of parliament. Today, there is increasing use of the term 'parliamentary opposition' to designate the parties sitting in the assembly and which have a more or less active political role. The sources of funding of these parties is not public knowledge, and the state does not finance them, which means that it cannot control the origin of their resources. Generally, the members of parliament justify their voting as a block in terms of party discipline. In truth, the leader of the majority party is the only person who initiates decisions. The National Assembly is often called the 'chamber of applause and registration' by the press, especially when the absentee members are present during parliamentary sessions.

Since Abdou Diouf came to power in 1981, analysts have argued that there would be an expansion of the clientelist system, based on the results of elections since then. The adjustments of the state to the difficulties of political mobilisation and legitimisation have been analysed by Momar Coumba Diop and Mamadou Diouf, in a work titled *Senegal Under Abdou Diouf.*[10] The "technocracy" installed during the mid-1980s with the structural adjustment policy, which was presented as an alternative to the establishment of an "integral state", failed very quickly, according to them. Effectively, little could be done in the face of internal and external resistance, notwithstanding the interests of the International Monetary Fund and the World Bank, which wanted to make this a model for other countries to which their loans were destined. This failure was underlined by the disengagement of important sectors such as agriculture, a sector that has always kept the Marabouts and their peasant constituencies within the scope of the state. However, it would not be accurate to limit the electoral sphere of influence of the

Marabouts only to the peasant masses, as the brotherhoods have become urbanised and the new urban elites emerging from the informal sector are also an electoral targets for political leaders. Thus, while the ideological unity of the state does not appear to be fundamentally threatened, its fragmentation is growing, for various reasons.

Participation, Local Governance and Sub-Regional Integration: The Challenges for Democracy and Development in Post-Colonial Senegal

The Extent of Stakeholder Involvement in Decision-Making

The participation of actors in political decision-making takes place only through the representation of members of parliament; while they are elected in a democratic manner, their prominence on the electoral list depends essentially on their level within their respective political party. This is, in a nutshell, the debate between representative and participatory democracy. The lack of acceptance of independent candidates in legislative and local elections leads to the impression that the political parties are trying to monopolise power. The sharing of the management of public affairs with certain groups, such as the trade unions, is the result of a desire for control rather than that of real power-sharing. Moreover, "political interests are further dividing the union movement".[11]

Whether simply a fashionable concept or a political idea, governance as a legitimate public action, is a form of political organisation aiming to regulate the crisis of the nation-state, develop citizens in the most civic sense of the term, and develop controls for political leaders of integrity. As NEPAD stipulates, Africa must, on the basis of local realities, respect democratic value and belief systems, to the extent that these do not contradict laws and regulations. Deepening decentralisation gives the political elite the opportunity to move closer to its base, thus consolidating its clientele and at the same time, exposing itself to any demands and sanctions. But the important political decision of whether to decentralise, which was instigated together with the major administrative and territorial reforms of 1972, has not yet been properly established at the base. The transfer of skills has not been accompanied by a concomitant transfer of resources. For certain groups, the state has rather transferred its problems (in terms of health, education, etc.) than its resources. A call for autonomy is being made by the local populations. But the state has not yet transferred any resources to these peoples. Of course, the Senegalese cannot 'eat' decentralisation. In effect, decentralisation has no meaning for the people unless it is translated into a qualitative improvement in the living conditions of the masses, and improved access to basic social services. Nevertheless, the demands of the people are increasing and are being expressed more volubly and more often, notably due to the growth in the development of private, decentralised newspapers and especially radio stations, which broadcast mostly in the national languages. Thanks to their networks of correspondents, armed with mobile telephones and their focus on local information, these are becoming tools of awareness and conscientisation. A citizen's democracy has made great strides under their influence.

The Structure of Political Elites

The growing responsibilities of the president of the Rural Council, the institutional support given to the rural communities, especially the communes (which have increased from 48 to 60 in 1996) in partnership with the World Bank, and the creation of new local or regional collectives with councils elected by universal suffrage, have encouraged the rapid emergence of local elites, who are cashing in on their capacity to mobilise the people by demanding their incorporation into the national elite.

The local elite and the base are creating new challenges in all the major political issues. Some people are even returning to their original areas so as to play a new political role there. In other words, the emergence of new challenges is linked to the recomposition of local elites, especially in the rural areas. These local elites have played an important role in the mobilisation of opposition party support and non-partisan monitoring of the elections in 2000. The local elites had previously supported the Socialist Party, which was in power until the 2000 elections. It was only from within, by putting pressure on the endogenous elites, that an overthrow of the political status quo was possible. The elites that gave their loyalty to the Socialist Party did not accept the idea of regular polls, but rather simply expected to be kept in their positions of power. The recomposition of local elites and the role of the youth in monitoring elections are, along with the new institutional dispositions for transparency in elections, ensuring that polls since 2000 are free and fair.

In order to put an end to the disputes around the polls, a 1997 decree created the National Elections Observatory (ONEL) to ensure that they were transparent and fair, although the opposition was calling for an independent electoral commission. Whether this was a conceptual quarrel, a semantic quibble, or a real divergence of approach in terms of the supervision and organisation of the elections, it cannot be denied that a change of power was made possible after the organisation of elections, instituted by the Ministry of the Interior. The consensual audit of the electoral roll demonstrated that ONEL acquired a certain legitimacy even among the opposition. But ONEL is not a permanent structure – it runs only during elections. Another informal structure, the High Council for the Audiovisual (HCA) is an independent organ that attempts to guarantee equal access to the public media for the political bodies. The activities of these institutions in supervising the transparency of the electoral process are reinforced by certain civil society organisation, such as RADDHO (African Meeting for Human Rights), which played an important role in providing people with information and then in supervising the polls. There are thus both institutional and informal mechanisms to guarantee free and democratic expression in Senegalese elections, since those of 2000.

Spotlight on the New Political Leadership

At the moment, there are nearly a dozen daily papers that are relatively independent of political influence. The private press, which has grown considerably (especially the Walfadjri and Sud Com groups) in the past fifteen years, now plays an oppositional role. This was demonstrated in the last poll, when journalists released the results, as the ballot boxes were counted, district-by-district, using mobile telephones. This helped to prevent fraud or any other manipulation of the results.

In addition to the context that promotes free expression of beliefs and ideas, the birth of *Renouveau Démocratique* (Democratic Renewal) – a Senghorian body that has positioned itself after just a few months of existence as a 'third force' – seems to have created a new actor in the

Senegalese political arena. However, what damaged the Socialist Party the most, and may have led to its defeat, was the departure of Moustapha Niasse. The previous ruling party had, through an elaborate tangle of alliances and subterfuges, ensured its grip on power for 40 years. Observers were sure that it could only be threatened from within. The management of the issue of succession was the catalyst for a series of conflicts in and departures from the Grand Socialist Party, eroded as it was by the new political forces (e.g. Union for Democratic Renewal and the Alliance of the Forces of Progress.[12]) set up by its former members. A rebuilding of the Senegalese political landscape could not take place *ex nihilo*.

There are now more than 70 political parties in Senegal. But multipartyism is not enough, in itself, for the free expression of democratic choice. In addition, conditions must be conducive for effective participation in political life. Until recently, the immense majority of powers was monopolised by the Senegalese Socialist Party. Before the presidential elections of March 2000, it controlled all of the wheels of government, allowing its adversaries only a minority of seats in the National Assembly and a handful of wards in the big cities. The make-up of the National Assembly favoured the automatic voting of most deputies, who followed the lines laid down by their parties. Because of the overly partisan attitude among most deputies, the majority of whom do not seem to understand their role, democracy in Senegal has been more representative than participatory.

The monopolisation of elected posts and the exclusive nomination of supporters to managerial posts was for a long time an indicator of the problems underlying the Senegalese exception. Many of those who occupied their posts on the basis of their expertise did not dare support the opposition parties for fear of reprisals. The incorporation of partisan interests in the daily administration of the state, the concentration of power in the hands of the president, and the management of so-called political funds, for many years, militated against the building of a democratic culture in Senegal. After the transition, will there really be equal and transparent sharing of posts in the state? The witch hunt of former directors of public bodies, who were unable to transform and thus join the new administration, the expected consequences of the audits established by the new regime, and the uncitizenly behaviour of certain government officials, who have been mixed up in shady business deals, are not what the public expected after 19 March 2000. The audits appear to be going the same way as the law on illegal enrichment of 1981. What appears to be happening is that the new elites are promoting the principles of good governance at the beginning of their terms, but then choosing to create their own clientele to keep them in power. However, since 19 March 2000, the people now see the ballot paper as a weapon.

Rural leaders are also playing a role in maintaining their electoral clientele. Other social forces are emerging on the margins of or even within the state. The growing diversity of political beliefs and the liberalisation of electoral rules offer new opportunities for political parties which, for several years, have been attempting to grasp seats in the National Assembly[13] by any means possible, including introducing Marabouts onto the list of candidates. Marabouts are thus forming part of the National Assembly, at the heart of state power, by trading on their local legitimacy. The political cycle turns, and those who were initially considered important constituents to elect others, have now become the elected. Moreover, with the inanity of general political discourse, there is much support for an Islamic value system that is opposed to Western modernism, in a society that is losing its moral compass and becoming increasingly poor. Indeed, after the break-up of the Socialist Party, the second significant event after the 1998 elections revolved around a Marabout who founded a party around this idea and who campaigned for the 'Indivisibility of God'. It would not be an exaggeration to speak of the emergence of a fundamentalist Muslim discourse. The election of Cheikh Abdoulaye Dièye to the Assembly, as well as the attention which has been paid to him since the campaign, show that the masses may be sensitive to themes touching on French-style secularism or family law. The local political elites are calling for a new personal law enabling Muslims to be judged on the basis of Islamic prescriptions in matters of family law (succession, marriage, divorce), in spite of the personal opposition of the president to this project aimed at amending the family law, which has been in place since 1972.

The presidential elections of 2000 coincided with the maturation of the concept of *Sopi*, incarnated by a political leader favoured by the "pragmatic vote" (a vote for those who could win, i.e. the best-placed opposition candidates) during the first round. This is an unspoken regulation of the difficulties linked to the high number of political parties participating in the elections. It enabled the opposition forces to unite in an effort to defeat the Socialist Party to begin with, through the departure of the highly placed Moustapha Niasse, former prime-minister, and Djibo Ka, former minister of state. In addition, the consolidation of the political contest and the apprenticeship of an active citizenry had developed and strengthened a great deal since the elections of 1978, 1983 and especially those of 1988, with its wave of disputes around the results. Senegalese democracy needed only a democratic change of power to seal its democratic culture, at a time when the United States (US), usually a teacher of lessons, was having trouble ratifying the elections that brought George W. Bush to power. The "democracy of carriers of votes" – Marabouts, clients and other major constituents – was strongly tested, but it seems that the momentum was not maintained, as the new regime is shifting back towards these. Political elite clientelism has a long history in Senegal.

All spheres of society seem to have been affected by the changes, starting with the religious sphere. Senegal is largely Muslim, at more than 90%, with the rest of the population made up of Christians and a small animist minority. Senegalese Islam is organised in brotherhoods, with most believers following either the Tidjanes or the Mourides.

This religious sphere, which seems to have lost some of its mobilising power since the elections, risks growing in power again if the economic situation does not improve and if there are no more democratic leaders like Abdoulaye Wade, who can carry through the people's desire for change. In any case, a new political structure is difficult to envisage without the religious leaders or the values, which they want to promote. Abdoulaye Wade has just announced that the oath sworn by new presidents will henceforth begin with the words, "In the name of God and the people".[14]

Former President Diouf's defeat in the March 2000 elections was strongly marked by his tumultuous relations with certain members of the brotherhoods. The neutral silence of the Kalife-General of the Mourides, who gave no voting instructions, freed up the choice for the rural people who constituted the breeding ground of Diouf's party, the Socialist Party, during the previous decade, when he started to lose the support of the big cities. The opposition alliance, through the Front for Change (FAL), and the defection of some of the big shots in the Socialist Party (such as Niasse and Ka), were the final nails in the coffin of Diouf's regime.

Globally, we seemed to be witnessing a "calling into question of the 'political arrangements', which explained the weak distinction between the state and civil society, the sharing of tasks and the negotiation which underlay the 'success story' (Senegal's political stability)".[15] In response to the impotence of the Socialist Party administration, was the emergence of peripheral forces, with ample resources and patronage or which were built up from a concretisation of frustrations, in an attempt to free them. Among these were the brotherhoods, which have tried to expand their scope for autonomy by working more closely with the people, while continuing their support for the weakened state. This begs the question: Where is Senegal going?

Political Leadership and the Future of Senegal with Globalisation and Integration

The economy is still heavily dependent on agriculture and the whims of the weather. However, some progress can be seen in tourism and fishing, the two current motors of the Senegalese economy. In spite of the legitimacy of the new government, their desire to keep the management of public affairs to themselves reveals a propensity for exclusion and creates partisan and clientelist perceptions of the state. The National Assembly is still seen as a chamber of applause, rather than one of monitoring the executive, which calls into question the accountability of the political elites. The political leaders must be governed by a code of ethics and a declaration of patrimony before taking up office.

Legal dispositions such as the charge of "breaching the security of the state" destroy the independence of the judiciary. This disposition is a pretext to prohibit certain 'crimes' – such as student or workers' strikes, organised marches, newspaper articles, political declarations against the regime, and so on – under the curtain of an attack on the authority of the public order or on the authority of the state.

The many projects that have not yet been implemented – so-called white elephants – the monopolisation of certain roles by the ruling party, the closeness between the judiciary and the executive on certain political issues, the delays in selecting ministers, the catastrophic management of the peanut crop, can, for the post-changeover political leaders, be attributed to incompetence – perhaps linked to their lack of experience in managing the state, but nonetheless inexcusable. The leader's status is growing, but the brief passages that the current ruling party has spent in power in the "governments of enlarged presidential majority" do not seem to have provided its officials with the necessary expertise. This explains the recall of certain officials from the defeated party. This phenomenon, known as "political transhumance", which prevents the officials from developing a culture of opposition and makes them collaborate with those in power, shows the clientelist basis of political affairs in this country. Both those who left their parties after the defeat, and those who welcome them, appear to have little idea of what a state should be. Thus, the political officials, to avoid punishment and to maintain their positions, are staying close to whoever is in power. This leads the people to think that "all politicians are the same" and that there is no point in becoming politically engaged.

The Place of NEPAD in the Political Agenda of Senegal

It is possible that the development policies tended, until recently, to neglect society in favour of political leaders who would do anything to keep themselves in positions of power. The president is still leader of his party. This party can alter his position as judge, a position that he himself denounced when in the opposition. Once in power, to use his own expression, he is not willing to cut down the branch on which he is sitting, or more precisely, which enabled him to sit in the seat of power. Major infrastructural projects (such as NEPAD and the major projects of the heads of state) and institutional reforms repeated since the referendum, have only produced, at best, minimal results.

In the dialectics of cultural contingencies and the demands of economic development, NEPAD constitutes an opening for the African people's political and economic initiative. NEPAD should provide the opportunity to reverse the asymmetry between donor conditionalities and people's expectations. NEPAD is a major political marketing operation, a political challenge, and a new space for political mobilisation among Africans, and should instigate a moral re-arming of the masses, who could promote the consolidation of democracy by aligning themselves with an African model for the rule of law. It must, however, be prevented from becoming, as General de Gaulle told the United Nations, "a big machine". Unfortunately, NEPAD was created in a top-down manner, and has not yet been claimed by the African people as its own. It is an example of political mobilisation of African leaders around shared objectives. However, NEPAD is overly linked to the neo-liberal approach to politics, as it aims to mobilise private actors; whether abroad or in Africa, we still need the community development by the state. However, NEPAD does constitute a break with previous policies; it is a project aimed at society, and its development logic is centred on eight priorities: infrastructure, education, health, agriculture, information and communication technology (ICT), environment, energy, and access to the markets of the developed countries. NEPAD could enable African communities to create a presence through global networks but also to develop a global vision of development for the continent and an African position. The necessity of initiating this continental convergence, which is what NEPAD really is, requires a redefinition of the links between NEPAD and the other African sub-regional institutions (such as the West African Economic and Monetary Union (UEMOA); Economic Community of West African States (ECOWAS) and the Southern African Development Community (SADC) which have made some advances in certain areas. The issue of infrastructure – a central aspect of the NEPAD strategy – is a means of operationalising political principles, such as the free circulation of resources and people. Currently, the road between Senegal and Mali stops at the Senegalese border at Kidira, while railway traffic is facing difficulties.

Conclusion

Overall, the state's political elites seem to be filled with contradictions, which call into question several accepted realities. These include:

- *The historicity of the state:* the time frames of the state and the elites' strategies to reinforce their positions of power do not often correspond with a democratic culture. Here one can see an informalisation of the state, an institutionalisation of political transhumance (floor-crossing) and an end to sincere militancy, as well as the manipulation of constitutional provisions, according to personal and partisan interests – an administration at odds with the life cycle of the state.
- *The links between state and society:* a reconfiguration of these links and a restructuring of the forces at play in the political exchequer,

under the seal of clientelism and the personalisation of power, the reactivation of clientelist and regionalist patronage in the distribution of posts – with this region complaining that it does not have a minister, and having started a march or a newspaper article to denounce a local leader for having been demoted (for example, Kébemer and the director of hydraulics, or Podor and the eviction of the director of LONASE, the national lottery). In addition, the union leadership is considered a position for political rewards. All of this favours the sterility and reciprocal instrumentalisation of the links between elites and society. We will see a fragmentation of the identity of politicians under the influence of the brotherhoods, as they make inroads into the political field, as well as the emergence of leaders with a new profile: non-governmental organisations, informal businesspeople, emigrants, trade unions, and so forth. Can these actors play the role of a civil society?

- *The dynamism of emerging actors*: especially the religious and informal brotherhoods, those who have emigrated abroad, footballers, etc. – this sort of diversification of the sources of elites is new. Will it be possible to mitigate the "prolonging of sites of predation"?[16] It is necessary to listen to Africa, because "we knew how to speak about Africa, but we never knew, or most of us anyway, how to speak to it and especially listen to it".[17] Will there be a race between the new and former politicians?

- *NEPAD*: both an African club, a political challenge and a major political marketing avenue to set Africa up as a new destination for investments and not merely a source of resources for European and the United States markets. NEPAD must first be able to deal with the economics of setting up transparent mechanisms for the management of public affairs, such as bold policies in the struggle against corruption, as well as platforms for conscientising and creating civic awareness among both the elites and the masses. This is a new vision of the future for Africa. Should we fear a conflict of precedence among the five African presidents driving NEPAD? Are we risking hatching a plan aimed at technocrats disconnected from the realities and needs of the people? At the very least, NEPAD has the merit of mobilising Africans all over the continent to work for their own development.

It is clear that in the African context, the electoral process in Senegal is an exception. ONEL is independent of the government, its president is named by decree, and it plays a supervisory role. The Ministry of the Interior is limited to organising and providing logistical support during elections. The judiciary endorses election results. But the process of monitoring elections is the result of a long process of negotiations and compromises over several decades. Some of the results include:

- the identification of voters based on a national identity card when registering and during the polls
- the mandatory use of polling booths to promote the secrecy of the ballot
- lowering the voting age and creating awareness among the youth
- the participation of political parties at all stages of the electoral process
- access to the state media guaranteed by the HCA and the boom in private media outlets.

These gains from negotiating the electoral process must be consolidated and monitored. The changeover of power was the culmination of a long process of democratic expansion and the construction of a political citizenry. It must now trickle down to participatory, equitable and sustainable governance at local level.

Notes and References

1   Achille Mbembe, *On the Postcolony*, Paris: Karthala, 2001, p 1.
2   J. F. Bayart, *The Politics of the Belly*, 1989.
3   Mbembe 2001, p 5.
4   Momar Coumba Diop, 2002, p 12.
5   Interview with Serigna Abdou Aziz Sy al Ibn, spokesperson of the Tidiane brotherhood of Tivaouane during the annual Gamou (pilgrimage) of May 2003.
6   L. A. Villalon, *Islamic Society and State Power in Sénégal: Disciples and Citizens in Fatick*, Cambridge: Cambridge University Press, 1995, pp 12-13.

7   "Civil society is a vast ensemble of constantly changing groups and individuals whose only common ground is their being outside the state and who have acquired some consciousness of their externality and opposition to the state." Patrick Chabal quoted in *Ibid.*, p 24.

8   M. C. Diop and M. Diouf, 'Notes sur la reconversion des marabouts dans l'économie urbaine', *Année Africaine*, 1992-1993, p 328.

9   By 'civil society', we do not mean society separated by the state, but rather its relations with the state, i.e. in the intermediary space. Thus conceived, "civil society is at once an advanced space for society in the political arena and an area for the detotalisation of the state. Civil society is a space that protects against the state, but also a site of interaction and negotiation between the state and society." See F. Constantin and C. Coulon (eds), *Religion et transition démocratique en Afrique*, Paris: Karthala, p 19.

10 M. C. Diop and M. Diouf, *Senegal sous Abdou Diouf*, Paris: Karthala, 1990.

11 A. I. N'Diaye, *Le partenariat social en question: Vers de nouvelles relations de travail*, in M. C. Diop (ed.), *Le Sénégal Contemporain*, Paris: Karthala, 2002, p 422.

12 URD stands for the Union for Democratic Renewal; AFP for the Alliance of Forces for Progress.

13 The Senegalese Democratic Party has put forward no fewer than five Marabouts, in key seats, since the 1998 legislative elections. One of these was the former president of the Touba rural community, who was brought in a few weeks before the elections. His entry onto the list was at the cost of high-level officials from the party, who lost their seats after the elections. Most of them later formed a new political body, the Senegalese Liberal Party.

14 Quoted in *Le Soleil*, 21 November 2000.

15 Diop and Diouf 1990, p 29.

16 *Ibid.*, p 10.

17 Copans 1998, p 51.

SOUTH AFRICA

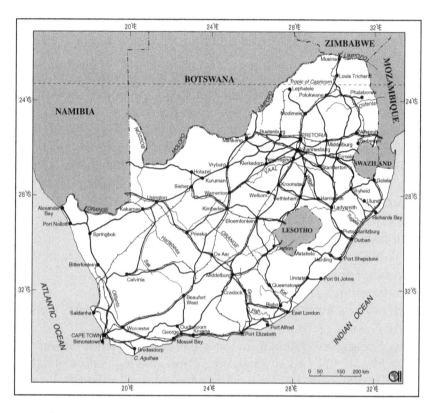

Source: Africa Institute of South Africa, 2005.

African Political Elites: The Search for Democracy and Good Governance

7. Political Leadership and Political Will Contributions to Democratic Governance in South Africa

Susan Booysen

Introduction

This chapter investigates the nature of political will of leadership in relation to democratic political and electoral practice in South Africa. It explores the complex manner in which political will relates to political power, good political governance, elections and commitment to participate in practices of fair and open contestation. Although the will to pursue democratic economic governance is the subject of a separate paper, political will in the political and economic spheres are inextricably linked, and will therefore also be referred to in this chapter.

The study is undertaken through both theoretical perspectives and empirical assessment and operationalisation. It explores whether or not there is significant evidence of the existence of political will amongst South Africa's governing elites. An important dimension of this study is the identification of indicators[1] of the existence of such political will, and, in contrast, indicators of the absence of, or doubts about, such will.

The chapter posits that there are *ideal* and *real* types of relationships between political leadership both in Africa and South Africa maintaining themselves in political power, and democratic governance (the latter defined as inclusive of democratic electoral and government practice, and sustainable, development-oriented socio-economic leadership practice). The *ideal relationship* entails that political leadership maintains itself in power via a combination of elections and democratic governance in the between-election periods. The power of political leadership is thus derived through the benefits that the population experiences. Beneficiation of the population would be the political leadership's primary driving force, and will facilitate the political leadership's retention of government power. The contrasting *real relationship* entails that political leadership frequently maintains itself in power through the outwardly evident processes of democratic electoral and government practice, or through oppressive and manipulative political practice (or a combination of these two sets of factors), whilst it pursues socio-economic practices that might have grassroots benefits (required in order to achieve the ultimate goal of staying in power), but, importantly, also benefit a relatively small political and economic elite.

The chapter therefore explores the ways in which successes and failures in the domains of socio-economic delivery and transformation predispose democratically elected political leaders in Africa, and South Africa in particular, to expose themselves to subsequent elections, or to elections that are continuously legitimate and credible, or 'free and fair'. It argues that political will to pursue legitimate and credible elections is affected by successes with past socio-economic and developmental governance. Political leadership, therefore, through its practices of developmental and transformation-oriented policies and programmes, can create the conditions in which sound electoral practice flourishes.

Exposure to Elections and Restricted Choices in the Economic Domain

The analysis recognises that the notion of political leadership's 'self-exposure to elections' has several possible connotations. On a continuum, election exposure can range from elections that are completely devoid of governing party intervention in the form of manipulation, to the limited use of state resources to advantage the ruling party, as well as interventions that include extensive stacking of the odds against the opposition and rigging. This exercise, as will be demonstrated in the rest of the chapter, could have implications for the tendency to unambiguously classify South Africa as one of the model cases of adherence to quality political and socio-economic governance in Africa. South Africa often 'leads the pack' and the government has overseen a phenomenal change of gear away from the racially and economically inequitable apartheid past, yet much remains to be consolidated. It is in this domain that the political will of the leadership will be tested.

South Africa is in the early phases of this process of prevailing electoral practices being affected by the relative successes of developmental governance. The analysis posits a two-phased argument, namely that the governing party in South Africa, the African National Congress (ANC), enjoys relatively uncomplicated positive ratings with regard to adherence to quality political and socio-economic governance, and that the real test of commitment for South Africa's political leadership will only emerge upon a realisation of electoral threat. A crucial interim test therefore would be the leadership's orientation towards 'emerging' or incipient manifestations of opposition.

Political will to promote sustainable and equitable economic growth and development (the latter being a major dimension of democratic governance), and willingness to enter the cycle of regular and 'free and fair' elections, is generally steered by the leadership's expectations of citizens' verdict through the quintessential 'next election'. Leadership, however, only has partial control over the socio-economic circumstances and conditions that are likely to affect socio-economic events and trends.

The notion of 'political will' is of extreme importance in contemporary manifestations and projections of South African politics. Much of this relevance derives from the fact that South Africa's democracy is still young and that the political economy is in a continuous transitional state. Despite a plethora of positive evidence that currently prevails, the *definitive* evidence that the political leadership has the will to ensure the endurance of initial democratic and socio-economic transformation, in many respects, does not yet exist. Reasons for this include the current period's evidence and counter-evidence with regard to the dimensions of political will. For virtually each instance of positive assertion of political will, the analyst can offer evidence of negative manifestations. This stresses the importance of systematic consideration of political will in South Africa.

The interrelationships that are highlighted in this section suggest that the analysis and measurement of the 'political will' of African leadership should be anchored in a combination of *internal* (personal motivations, group pressures and legitimation, and class-building) and *external* (international political economy, regional political-economic realities and state of domestic delivery) political and socio-economic factors.[2]

Political Will

Political will, for the purposes of this study, is the determination and capacity of leaders to define and promote a number of transformative projects. With regard to the *economy*, the search for evidence of political will is focused on transformative projects aimed at ensuring economic growth, equitable development, the enhancement of the productive base of the economy, the significant lessening of poverty, and improvement of the conditions of life and livelihood of the people. With regard to *politics*, this chapter argues that political will is manifested through a commitment to democratic governance, which includes a competitive electoral system and credible elections, a functional legislature, the institution of participatory democracy, the existence of a vibrant and strong civil society, the implementation of a framework of corporate governance and code of best practice, and the existence and practice of rule of law and constitutionalism.

'Democratic governance' is defined as, first, socio-economic practice, policies and programmes that lead to sustainable and equitable growth and development and, second, democratic political practice in elections and government. These two dimensions have equal status. The operationalisation of political will in the twin domains of democratic political practice and democratic socio-economic practice calls for the identification of specific sets of indicators. Political will, in other words, could be expressed through a series of specific, empirical measures.

In addition, the first category of expression, on the individual level, is through personal rhetoric, comprising speeches, statements, and personal policy declarations. Rhetorical political will, collectively, would be expressed through party and government policies, statements, etc. Another category of indicators of political will is at the level of actions and consequent results and change. It might even be argued that political will is most clearly indicated through past statements and actions that have resulted in positive political and economic practice and results (see Table 7.1).

le 7.1: Analytical Approach and Operationalisation

Democratic practice in government and elections		Equitable and sustainable economic growth and development	
Indicators		Indicators	
Positive trends	Negative trends	Positive Trends	NegativeTrends
Affirmation of political will	Political will questioned	Affirmation of politicalwill	Political will Questioned
Weight of evidence		Weight of evidence	
Balance of assessment of political will in South Africa			

There is a close relationship between the rhetorical and results-oriented expressions of political will. The two are intertwined, and from time to time indistinguishable. In comparing the two, however, it has to be noted that actions necessarily speak louder than words. Whereas this chapter will lend force to verbal expressions of political will, the realisation of political action that carries forward the political and economic empowerment of the citizens and inhabitants of South Africa will carry more weight.

Accordingly, the chapter will note the first-order expressions of political will (verbal and rhetorical), but the bulk of the analysis will centre on second-order expressions, namely the realisation of actions and change on the ground. For instance, instead of just noting constitutional, party political and individual leader expressions of commitment to participatory democracy, or constitutional provisions, this chapter will note what opportunities for participation in the policy-making really exist in the political system. As a further example, rather than assessing political will for socio-economic upliftment through the ideals of the Growth, Employment and Redistribution (GEAR) strategy, trends in employment creation and macro-level distribution of income will be used.

The central hypothesis of this chapter therefore is the following: The South African political leadership in government collectively displays significant evidence of political will for the betterment of South African society. This is manifested, on the one hand, in statements, policies and constitutional provisions,[3] and, on the other hand, in government processes and policy realisation that affect the quality of politics and life of South Africans. Whereas, on many fronts, there are debates about whether there is significant commitment on the side of leadership to make both procedural-institutional and substantive difference to the quality of life of citizens, the balance of evidence by 2004 pointed to the likelihood that indeed there is political will. However, much of the actual verdict on political will remains suspended, for reasons including the fact that South Africa's democracy and many of its policies were relatively young – and it would therefore not be possible to definitively pronounce on the level of confirmation of commitment to socio-economic transformation. The same is argued with regard to a controversial policy such as the GEAR macroeconomic strategy. Whereas by 2004, it was clear that this policy was not achieving most of its stated goals, it was still held by the government that the benefits would be forthcoming. For instance, in the 2003 Presidential State of the Nation Address, Mbeki pronounced that "the tide has turned" and surmised that, despite problems in the process, there was definitive evidence that the legacy of the past was being left behind. In the 2004 speech, Mbeki added substance to 2003 suggestions that his government was moving towards a developmental state.[4] These diverse leadership manifestations in contemporary South African politics indicate the complexity of addressing notions of political will and government leadership.

Political Leadership in South Africa

Political leadership in South Africa emerged via a series of jagged waves under frequently oppressive conditions. This section first presents a brief interpretation of the periods of apartheid, transitional and post-apartheid leadership. In the second place, it assesses the transformation of political leadership in the course of South Africa's continuous post-1994 transition.

The Periods of Apartheid, Transitional and Post-Apartheid Leadership

The extended period of liberation struggles in and of South Africa was characterised by, for example, oppression, banning, persecution, the elimination of leaders, and co-optation into security and pseudo-legitimate apartheid-connected leadership struggles. Despite measures by the apartheid regime to create its own leadership structure for black South Africans, the liberation movement and the ANC leadership, as well as other layers of associated leadership, thrived through struggle. Underground and exile leadership structures grew through the decades of banning and armed struggle. The military wing of the ANC, Umkhonto we Sizwe, and to a lesser extent the armed wing of the Pan-Africanist Congress (PAC), Apla, played important roles. In the 1980s an increasingly strong internal resistance movement – in the form of the United Democratic Front (UDF) and Mass Democratic Movement (MDM) – assumed pivotal importance in the collapse of the old order. The leadership in exile simultaneously set up structures, established international networks, and prepared for return and assumption of power.

In the period of negotiated transition, a new category of leadership was forged. This was a largely demilitarised, cooperative-consensual, and, of necessity, compromise-driven and conciliatory type of leadership. In this transitional period, leaders of both the ascendant and descendant orders first started negotiating, then agreed on an interim order, and then cooperative government followed this. They built new, shared leadership structures out of previously disparate organisations, cultures and ideologies. Many of the old ideological differences, for instance within the tripartite alliance of the ANC or within the National Party (NP), temporarily receded. The early post-apartheid days saw the reign of 'rainbowist' cooperation in a system of power sharing between the ANC and minority opposition parties, especially the NP – subsequently renamed the New National Party, (NNP).

The post-apartheid period also brought significant class reconfigurations to the South African political and economic elite. As Glaser points out, the leading politicians and dominant capitalists of the *ancien regime* threw overboard their loyalty to white power. Amongst Africans, and under the mantle of black economic empowerment, observers witnessed a burgeoning of the black bourgeoisie and professional elite, accompanied by an individualistic jettisoning of solidarity with the black oppressed.[5] The neo-liberal ideology suited the new classes – they could advance their own financial well being without guilt, because through empowerment deals they would help create growth and open the doors, albeit in a gradual way, to the black middle classes of the future. This approach obviously carried the sanction of the neo-liberal investor community. The extent of state involvement, and the effect of its partial and uncoordinated provision of a safety net, remained the topic of new leadership debates, into the period of analysis.

The Changing Constitution of ANC and Government Leadership

In South Africa's approximately ten years of democratic governance, there has been both some consistency around a core of political leadership, and a great deal of movement and change slightly further from the core. The new leadership structures of the internally constituted, early-1990s ANC comprised a mixture of leadership from exile (political and military), internal resistance leadership, reformed former bantustan and tricameral parliament members, and new recruits. Organisationally, the ANC comprised the three alliance partners, which, beyond the ANC, consisted of the Congress of South African Trade Unions (Cosatu) and the South African Communist Party (SACP) and the SA National Civic Organisation (SANCO). It was largely these components that constituted the formal new political leadership in post-1994 South Africa. Cabinet and provincial premier positions were largely filled from the ranks of the tripartite alliance, but with the ANC numerically predominant. The dominance of Xhosa-speakers in top leadership positions has often been alluded to, yet there has always been significant representation from other cultural-linguistic groups and from coloured, Indian and white ANC membership, including in top leadership structures.

Alongside this continuity, there was also change, which manifested itself, for instance, in the form of a relatively major Cabinet change upon President Thabo Mbeki's initial assumption of the presidency in 1999, turnover in the National Executive Committee (NEC) of the ANC, and vacillating relationships of influence of the tripartite alliance partners on the ANC. Political leadership in the form of political advisors and advisory councils to the president also showed important changes with the transition between presidents. The 2004 Cabinet and premiership appointments indicated higher levels of representation of both women and 1980s internal resistance cadres in the executive domains of South African government.

Furthermore, leadership changes were manifested in the form of change in the inclusiveness of the ANC government, both on the national and the provincial levels. For instance, in 1996 the National Party ended its participation in the Government of National Unity (GNU), the origins of which were determined in the 1993 Multi-Party Negotiating process. The Inkatha Freedom Party (IFP) retained its participation in the GNU until the 2004 election. The ANC approached other parties from time to time to join forces in government. The Azanian People's Organisation (Azapo) in parliament agreed, and gained, first, a deputy-minister's position, and later a full ministerial post. The Democratic Party (DP) declined. In the final run-up to the 1999 election, several MPs defected to new political homes. In 2002, the NNP joined forces with the ANC. Its then 'cooperative alliance' was manifested in terms of joint action to assume power: at first this occurred only on a metropolitan and local government level. In 2004 the relationship was consolidated – first through electoral cooperation to gain control of the Western Cape, and in the post-election period the announcement of the NNP's gradual absorption into the ANC. These arrangements were thus effected both through the floor-crossing legislation, which emerged in the context of disintegration of the Democratic Alliance (DA) (in the form where the DA comprised the

DP and the NNP)[6] and the 2004 election. In addition, the ANC consolidated provincial power by winning a small but outright majority in KwaZulu-Natal in the 2004 election.

Political leadership in South Africa in the post-1994 period was also characterised by political deployment into state departments. These deployees came to run government departments alongside the bureaucratic appointments. Their primary roles, however, were advisory, in support of the Cabinet members.

Gradually, in the post-1994 period, South Africa also witnessed leadership reinforcement through the redeployment of ANC cadres to sensitive positions throughout parastatals and the wider economy. For instance, there were appointments in positions in Armscor and Denel, the Independent Communication Authority of South Africa, and Telkom. Senior ANC politicians also moved into industry and big business. In a significant number of instances, high-profile ANC personalities became leading figures in black economic empowerment initiatives.[7] Names in this regard include former Gauteng premier, Tokyo Sexwale; former speculated contender for the ANC presidential candidature, Cyril Ramaphosa; Saki Macozoma, senior ANC functionary; and former premiers and ministers in the form of Popo Molefe and Valli Moosa.[8] These figures, alongside many others, helped lend an aura of achievement to the new ANC business class. They could be seen as trail-blazers for black economic empowerment in the era of tentative transformation of the racial face of big business in South Africa. The General Secretary of the SACP, Blade Nzimande, however, summed up concerns about the prevailing mode of black economic empowerment when he warned that the involvement of capital in empowerment initiatives is inclined to lead to black elite economic empowerment (BEEE), rather than black economic empowerment (BEE). He observed that, in practice, there is a tendency to equate BEE with the empowerment of a small black elite rather than with eradicating poverty and creating jobs for the mass of the people.[9] From time to time, other respected and influential parties and individuals, including former archbishop Desmond Tutu, have also aired these sentiments.

Beyond the 1994 change in regime, South African political and government leadership changed throughout the next decade as the ANC continued working through the process of effecting political and socio-economic change. In this process, the ANC remained the major spawning ground for emerging leadership. Within the ANC, there would be continuous contestation both for positions and its candidate lists and other primary sites of deployment. This contestation, however, would also entail political compromises, holding back on criticism, not feeding potentially critical information through to leadership, and sometimes providing sycophantic advice.

The Multiple Layers of ANC Leadership and Governance Alliances

Under both post-1994 presidents, ANC leadership assumed the character of a shifting entity with multiple, coexisting layers and domains of partnerships. The ANC became constituted as a multiple-alliance party or movement. In the process, a complex relationship between the ANC and its tripartite alliance partners arose. Core components of this shifting-alliance leadership structure were:

- A continued 'left-wing' alliance with the SACP and Cosatu
- A more conservative, affirmative but informal alliance with the South African National Civics Organisation, the ANC Youth League, and the Women's League
- A governing alliance with the IFP (up to 2004), the NNP (up to 1996; and again from 2002 on), as well as Azapo
- A party alliance with the NNP, and then tentative integration after the 2004 election
- A black empowerment business alliance with empowerment business groupings
- A high-level general alliance with South African and international business
- Leadership in its rhetoric increasingly emphasising a new 'alliance' (or 'social compact') with civil society, to help compensate for government not being able to achieve socio-economic transformation on its own.

Post-1994 South Africa witnessed a range of both corporative and delegated-to-business sharing of responsibility deals. For instance, several high profile business and investor advisory councils and groupings came into being – both in the term of Mbeki as deputy president, and as president. Former President Nelson Mandela had, for instance, the

Brenthurst Group, but these groups became more ascendant towards the late 1990s. Even though they were advisors, these groups were used by top political leadership to extend the circle of governing elites, to effect shared responsibility, and co-opt national and international big business into decisions that often were under attack in the domestic context. Under Mbeki, the International Investment Council and the South African Business Advisory Forum, were established as important consultative policy input mechanisms.[10]

As one of the illustrations of community consultation as a form of extending the leadership structures through direct axes into the community, one might refer to *imbizo*. *Imbizo* is about learning from the community, and potentially improving delivery, as well as for the governing party to demonstrate its links to the people. The president has an annual *imbizo* programme, which takes these consultative practices to a number of the provinces of South Africa.[11] There are also provincial *imbizo* programmes, and in 2004 the National Council of Provinces (NCOP) also took its proceedings into localised settings.

The central hypothesis of this analysis will be considered in the context that a range of political and economic elites in contemporary South Africa is being tasked with transformative roles. The government and ANC as government assumed a large part of this responsibility. However, given its predominant economic policies, which emphasise the creation of investor- and business-friendly environments, as these continue to combine with limited state capacity, the state claims limited autonomy and also assumes restricted responsibility. In much of the crucial governance assignments of, for instance, the late 1990s and early 2000s, government increasingly called on business to share in responsibility for employment, job creation, socio-economic transformation and social responsibility. The emphasis was on the limited state, often as ideological statement that would signal to the international investor community the likelihood of 'safe' investment territory. The reality focused on limited state capacity as a profound constraint on what might be within the reach of the South African state. In the State of the Nation and other important national addresses, there has been both an increasing emphasis on the people of South Africa assuming co-responsibility, for instance through volunteer action, and the state assuming higher levels of responsibility.[12]

These trends, which will be assessed below, indicate far-reaching changes in the nature and composition of political and economic leadership in South Africa in the period from the early 1990s to 2004. The transition to power moved the ANC from a combination of exiled and internal resistance and liberation politics into complex leadership configurations, which include the dimensions of intra-ANC leadership struggles for party or movement hegemony; efforts to maintain links to citizens and voters, both through electoral and non-institutional politics; a form of power-sharing and responsibility-diffusion with business, both national and international; maintaining a fragile but mutually beneficial liberation movement leadership dynamic with the other partners in the tripartite alliance; building and nurturing substitute fraternal organisations, which could hypothetically replace the tripartite alliance partners in the event of a severe falling-out; constituting political leadership alliances in various formats with most of the opposition parties; and encouraging shared responsibility with community organisations and localised ANC structures.

Continuous transitional politics therefore had as a corollary continuous changes in political leadership, but more importantly, switches in alliance partners. Political leadership partnerships therefore became increasingly complex, both structurally and ideologically.

Political Will and Democratic Practice

This section focuses on the operationalisation of the political will of the South African government leadership. The approach to operationalisation will be to identify and assess, over a wide range of indicators, the factors pointing to the existence of political will, and those indicating a negation of political will. It is important to note that, in the analysis that follows, political will with regard to democratic political practice, including in elections and government, is easier to assess than political will as manifested in equitable and sustainable economic growth and development. The reason is both in the nature of economic policies in general, and in the specifics of the policies that are pursued by the South African government. The emphasis is on limited state involvement in the economy, including in job creation, whilst providing a social security net. Economic policies, even if they work, take time to turn the fortunes of ordinary citizens around. The fact that certain policies amplify the lag between policies and positive effect does not necessarily indicate policy failure and lack of political will. It might be that the political elites sincerely believe that their policies are the best in order to effect sustainable development. Poor judgment and lack of willingness to follow constructive advice does not necessarily equate with lack of political will. In contrast, action on the prevention of corruption, or action to effect efficient, goal-oriented social delivery, does present a tangible and more immediate indicator of developmental political will.

This section maps the contexts and indicators of the South African leadership's political will with regard to the following fields of democratic practice in which political will might manifest itself: the electoral system, elections, the legislature, interaction between the branches of government, intergovernmental relations, participatory democracy, civil society, political intervention regarding corporate governance, the rule of law and constitutionalism.

Elections

South Africa in the period 1994-2004, and in varying manifestations, held sufficiently to overwhelmingly free and fair elections (despite violence in the run-up to the founding elections), regular and timely elections, only minor contestations of results, and an electoral system that articulates most of the leader needs of the time. Simultaneously, however, the spirit of elections as 'the only game in town' was affected through polarising election campaigns, campaigns to sow doubt about the credentials of some opposition parties, controversy about party political funding,[13] double messages on possible change in the electoral system, and between-election floor-crossing, which led to non-electoral shifts in power (see Table 7.2).

Whereas the proportional representation list system offers South African voters and leadership the benefit of proportionality, as well as fair representation of small political parties, the system in its application to South Africa suffered from the reality of distance between representatives (on all three levels of government, despite local government being 50:50 proportional and ward-based) and voters. Constitutionally, South Africa was required to reconsider its electoral system after the 1999 and 2000 elections. A task team under the leadership of Frederik

Table 7.2: Change in National Party Political Representation (1994-2004)

Political Parties	Elections 1994 (%)	Elections 1999 (%)	Defections 2003 (number of seats)	Election 2004 (%)
African National Congress (ANC)	63	66	266 to 275	69.7
Democratic Party / Alliance (DP / DA)	1.7	9.6	38 to 46	12.4
Inkatha Freedom Party (IFP)	11	8.6	34 to 31	7.0
National / New National Party (NNP)	20	6.9	28 to 20	1.7
United Democratic Movement (UDM)	-	3.4	14 to 4	2.3
African Christian Democratic Party (ACDP)	0.5	1.4	6 to 7	1.6
Pan-Africanist Congress (PAC)	1.3	0.7	Rest of the parties: 14 to 12	0.7
Freedom Front / Freedom Front Plus (FF / FF+)	2.2	0.8		0.9
United Christian Democratic Party (UCDP)	-	0.8		0.8
Federal Alliance (FA)	-	0.5		-
Minority Front (MF)	-	0.3		0.4

Table 7.2: Change in National Party Political Representation (1994-2004) continued

Political Parties	Elections 1994 (%)	Elections 1999 (%)	Defections 2003 (number of seats)	Election 2004 (%)
Afrikaner Unity Movement (AEB)	-	0.3		-
Azanian People's Organisation (Azapo)	-	0.2		0.3
Other	0.8			0.1 for each of seven minor parties

van Zyl Slabbert was appointed. Prior to its final report, released in 2003, the ANC at its 2002 policy conference advocated the retention of the proportional representation system because of its inclusivity and nation-building features, as well as its potential to balance representation.[14] The ANC also reasoned that it would win a disproportionate number of constituency-based seats, thereby having a smaller part of the PR list for balancing its own representation. It is important to bear in mind that the system of proportional representation places ANC core leadership in a powerful position to control the ideological orientation and decisions of both the parliamentary caucus, and its own National Executive Committee.

As in other places on the continent where similar situations prevailed, the ANC, as a strong ruling party, faced accusations of power hunger, warnings of the dangers of dominance by one very strong party, and the fears of what it would do with a two-thirds majority. The fact remained, however, that these electoral victories, as well as the movement's consistent rise in electoral fortunes, were achieved via the norms and standards of credible elections that offered the overwhelmingly unhindered opportunity to vote (except in certain areas in 1994, and that mostly not as a result of ANC action), an environment free of violence and intimidation, 'clean' electoral management, and the acceptance of results.

As regards South African opposition politics, party political contestation, and institutional versus movement and organisational politics, it is important to bear in mind that contestation frequently happens beyond the boundaries of elections and legislative bodies. Effective contestation and policy influence might equally in the case of South Africa be asserted through the tripartite alliance, cooperative and consensual decisions between government and business, and direct influence of the ANC over government decisions.

For example, the governing alliance on occasion came out in intense criticism of government. At its mid-1998 congress, alliance partner SACP received an ANC reprimand for its anti-GEAR outspokenness.[15] Factions in the SACP subsequently advocated contesting local government elections under the SACP banner.[16] When Cosatu and the SACP in 2002 emerged with increasingly outspoken leadership declarations, there was a concerted ANC campaign to isolate and minimise the influence of intra-alliance oppositional leadership.[17]

It follows, therefore, that the existence of a competitive and procedurally exemplary electoral system should not be unduly glorified. Further criteria that need to be employed include the transparency of processes of decision- and policy-making, public acknowledgement of the influences on and driving forces behind policy and political decisions, transparency and accountability[18] in bringing updates on policy implementation to local communities, and tolerance and facilitation of contestation by the range of oppositional forces.[19]

Given the multiple sites of governance and channels of influence in South African government, one also has to look beyond legislative and presidential elections to assess the legality and legitimacy of succession into executive office. First, it is important to note that the presidential successor candidate is determined by the ANC at its regular national conferences. Although this removes the election of the president from the nationally representative institutions of the country, this is fully compatible with international practice. Secondly, presidential succession and presidential terms that are constitutionally limited have become an integral part of South African popular and leadership political culture. A different system prevails with regard to provincial governance. In this sphere, the president, together with core ANC structures, decides on who the premiers of the ANC-controlled provinces will be. This practice has been contested by provincial ANC structures responsible for the election of provincial chairpersons.

These ANC chairpersons are often regarded as the persons that the premierships should go to.

Political Will and Competitive Electoral System and Elections

A wide range of indicators pointing to the political will of both ANC and opposition party leadership to participate in and facilitate the conditions for competitive party politics, and an associated electoral system, manifests itself:

- One decade of uninterrupted, on-schedule elections, for all three levels of government. The third national and provincial elections of 2004 were effectively implemented, and planning for further elections on all levels is in place
- Presidential succession procedures are in place at a formal governmental level
- There is a regularised acceptance of articulation between national elections and elections within the ANC structures
- The electoral system is widely, though not unanimously, accepted. Despite flaws, the prevailing system is conducive to participation by small political parties, which constitutes a large proportion of the political parties in South Africa
- Both the ANC and losing opposition parties accept election results
- A sound electoral management system is in place, reflecting a fair level of independence
- Acceptance in popular and ANC leadership political culture of a maximum of two presidential terms
- Succession into executive office is through predictable and prescribed processes, combining party political and legislatives sites of action.

Counter-Manifestations: Less Political Tolerance and Pressures on Liberal Contestation

In contrast with the formally strong practices of political competition and multipartyism, the South African political landscape also offers indicators of the possible undermining of multiparty competition.

These include:

- Election campaigns of the governing party strongly mobilise against some of the opposition political parties. Whereas this is inherent to campaigning, some of the effects have been polarising, militating against tolerance of political diversity
- The ruling party tends to demonise important aspects of the opposition (for example, doubt is cast on the patriotism and non-racialism of the major opposition party)
- The ruling party regularly tries to co-opt opposition parties. Successful cases include the IFP, Azapo and the NNP
- Flaws of the electoral system, especially a lack of accountability to constituencies, are not being addressed. Representative and followers of the governing party are primarily accountable to their party, rather than, in the first place, to the electorate
- There is a lack of transparency of party political and campaign funding, beyond the amounts allocated from public funds from the taxpayer-sponsored Represented Political Parties' Fund
- The non-electoral opportunity for floor crossing or defection, as well as the formation of new (micro) political parties with immediate legislative representation and funding undermine elections as the mechanism to achieve representation and power shifts.

South Africa has a competitive system of elections and representation of the electorate by means of political parties. Elections are legitimate and well run. Party politics are competitive. Yet, there are also continuous actions to co-opt opposition parties into government, or to delegitimise contestation of government policies. Co-optation could also be seen in the light of constructive and patriotic opposition. In the context of the absence of an electoral threat to the ANC, it could be argued that there should be higher levels of recognition and facilitation of non-institutionalised opposition politics. Despite these flaws, the weight of evidence is still in favour of tolerance of party political diversity and competitive elections, albeit dominated by the ANC colossus.

Functional Legislature and Relations between the Branches of Government

The contemporary real-life expectations regarding a functional legislature diverge from the textbook notions of functional legislatures. The textbook notion has it that there would be effective oversight of the executive by the legislature. Whereas the South African legislature – the National Assembly together with the National Council of Provinces (NCOP) – functions in the sense of regularly adopting new legislation, and voicing a wide range of opinion in the committees, there is widespread debate on the extent to which parliament does not exercise, or is not given the opportunity to exercise, oversight of the executive.

It is well recorded that in South Africa (and in fact, in many if not most systems around the world) many policy and high-powered political decisions do originate in parliament. However, political systems are executive-driven and executive-centred. For instance, the Office of the Presidency in South Africa equals, if not surpasses, the legislature in political impact and clout. Policy research points to the fact that political power in the South African system is concentrated not just in the executive in general, but specifically also in the presidency and a range of presidential advisers. Analysts and journalists point out that important areas of contested government policy often stay out of bounds of parliamentary debate, constraining the effectiveness of parliament as an oversight body.[20]

Cabinet and core ANC structures are also significant in their impact, albeit less so. Additional power is located in the cluster structures of executive government functions. The background is that the offices of the president and deputy president perform central directing and coordinating functions, with policy functions, and especially economic policy, anchored in the office of the deputy president.[21] From 1999 onwards, in the Mbeki era, the integrated Office of the Presidency assumed and extended these functions. The Policy Coordination and Advisory Services (PCAS) structures in the presidency were added as significant components of political decision-making.[22] Originally constructed with a view to "exert influence before policies are even conceived",[23] the PCAS did not supersede advisors' and ministerial and top-departmental policy-directing influences. Instead, the PCAS's major influence has been in the relatively low-profile monitoring of progress in delivery. As early as 2003, PCAS influence over the policy-process had probably been surpassed by the clusters.

Executive dominance is further strengthened through influential presidential advisors. The president has three Special Advisors, serving in legal, political and economic affairs. These advisors are to be distinguished from the broader Advisory Forum in the presidency, which includes all Special Advisors, the Minister in the Presidency, parliamentary counsellors, the heads of communication in the offices of the president and deputy-president, and the Government Communication and Information System Chief Excecutive Officer (CEO).[24] In contrast to the 2001 report on the new presidency at work, there was a continued chasm between the ideal, documented procedures and realities of determining policy directions in the presidency. The corps of Special Presidential Advisors overshadowed PCAS influence on policy. Other dynamics in the presidency contributed to the sense of a core of policy actors that needs to be functionally integrated into a well-oiled operation. The trends therefore are that parliament is influential in political oversight only indirectly through the ANC parliamentary caucus, or through the opposition parties using the platform and processes of parliament.

In addition, much of the effective decision- and policy-making powers reside in the top echelons of the ANC. This influence permeates structures and institutions of national governance – a natural political phenomenon, given the fact that all government departments have political appointees in their top echelons. There is also close individual overlap in positions and policy consultation between senior ANC figures and senior government figures. In these contexts, the standard perspectives on executive accountability to the legislature become superfluous.

To take account of these contemporary manifestations of the relations between the legislature and the executive, the analysis therefore has to assert new criteria of assessment. These centre on issues such as transparency, voluntary accountability by the executive to the legislature, encouragement and opportunity for the legislature to intervene in the legislative process, and willingness of both political parties and party caucuses in parliament to encourage open debate and possibly 'free' voting. The ANC caucus in parliament is known for intense debate within the caucuses, combined with a willingness to follow the guidelines of party leadership, once these have been promulgated. The

ANC in parliament is also characterised by its reporting lines into the Office of the Presidency. The president appoints parliamentary counsellors who serve as channels of communication, information and monitoring.

The South African constitution provides for parliamentary committees with firm powers of oversight and accountability. In practice, there have been a range of efforts to hold the executive accountable. In many instances where policy is relatively uncontroversial, assembly and committee debates might be intense, and members of parliament (MPs) feel satisfied that they have impacted on the legislative process. Different portfolio and standing committees, however, have had varied experiences. The Standing Committee on Public Accounts (SCOPA) has been regarded as the most powerful of these committees.

Yet SCOPA has had mixed fortunes in its efforts to enforce executive accountability. In the early 2000s it became embroiled in the contradictions wrought by systematic scrutiny versus political loyalty.[25] The issue revolved around executive interference and pressure regarding scrutiny of the controversial deal in which South Africa undertook to purchase huge amounts of military hardware. SCOPA eventually bowed to pressure from both the executive and the ANC parliamentary caucus. This was publicly perceived as executive interference that was compromising the independence of the committee.[26] The principle that a member of an opposition party should chair this committee has nevertheless prevailed, although more compliant opposition parties have recently chaired the committee. SCOPA, alongside the auditor-general, has also become one of the agencies monitoring bureaucratic and state-owned company contracts on tendering and awarding contracts.[27] Directors-general of public service departments are routinely interrogated in the portfolio committees of parliament.

In further strengthening of the notion of the 'party parliament', the operations of the parliamentary ethics committee are cited as evidence of the ANC closing ranks to protect its own, thereby undermining the expectations of neutral, constituency-based representation and oversight. Examples cited include the committee's decision to sanction Winnie Madikizela-Mandela for failure to disclose receipt of gifts only after it was a fact of court record, the committee failing to reprimand a cabinet member for making disparaging remarks on the integrity of the statutorily protected auditor-general, and vacillating on reprimanding and insisting on the resignation of Tony Yengeni, even after he was convicted of fraud.[28] Former Speaker of the National Assembly, Frene Ginwala, declared her commitment to a change in the rules, to ensure more decisive action and effective penalties. ANC erstwhile chief whip, Nkosinathi Nhleko, stated that there were "lessons to be learnt" from parliament's handling of the Yengeni case.[29] The 1999 Corder Report on parliamentary oversight and accountability was to be implemented, subject to adoption by an ad hoc joint sub-committee. In essence, the committee's report seeks to position the constitutional imperative of ensuring effective oversight "at the heart of all parliament's work". It was hoped that oversight would be recognised as an autonomous function, alongside parliament's legislative role.[30]

The policy functions of the parliamentary committees, however, were generally reduced both through their inability to exercise meaningful review of the PCAS unit in the Office of the Presidency, and through being subject to the parliamentary caucus of the ANC.[31] In the 2000-2004 period the manner in which parliamentary power, via the ANC caucus, was subject to national executive political oversight was demonstrated. There were instances, in the domains of gender (under former MP Pregs Govender, who subsequently quit parliament in order to pursue gender advocacy), and finance (led by MP Barbara Hogan) where parliamentary committees, from time to time, hold their own against the executive and sometimes the caucus. Beyond political factors, workload and time constraints are recognised as detrimental to effective oversight by parliamentary committee. In several instances, however, the committees did overcome the cluster of factors limiting effective oversight.

There are also forums and processes through which the parliamentary committees might be assisted to exercise oversight of the executive, government departments and statutory bodies. These include public hearings, and requesting oral and written reports.[32]

The South African legislature has had a brief but mixed history in terms of ensuring regular consultation with its constituencies. One of the shortcomings of the legislature (nationally, but also on the provincial and local/metropolitan government levels) has been the inability, and often unwillingness, of representatives to remain in regular and meaningful contact with their constituents. One of the debates has been whether the elected representatives have the time and means to effect the required contact. Both parliament and political parties have tried to made amends. Constituency weeks were introduced, and parliamentary proceedings were suspended in these periods, but with mixed levels of success. On the national and provincial levels, government has increasingly introduced the practice of the *imbizo*. The *imbizo* entails that the president and Cabinet members, or premier and members of the provincial executive, visit designated areas, have meetings with a range of constituencies, listen to problems and issues, respond and sometimes initiate action.

Indications of the executive not taking parliament and opposition as seriously as would be expected are evidenced on several fronts. For instance, parliamentary debates are hardly taken seriously, and often not by the governing party. Opposition parties (especially those not in some executive power-sharing or co-optive arrangement with the ANC) tend to be more serious about debates, because it is one of their primary forums for trying to affect policy and making themselves heard. The president, who is already surrounded by influential policy-making structures, does not systematically engage with opposition party leaders who are outside the governing alliances. A forum chaired by Deputy President Jacob Zuma, where opposition leaders were meant to interact with the executive, has been rendered dysfunctional.[33]

Political Will and Parliamentary Oversight

There are several strengths of the parliament of South Africa that contribute to an important role for parliament in government and thereby serve as evidence of political will to let legislative institutions exercise power in policy and government processes. These include:

- All major political parties are represented in the legislature
- The legislature debates and adopts legislation, in fully procedural ways
- Active debate prevails both in party caucuses and in parliamentary committees (albeit with strong tendency to defer to figures in authority and ANC caucus)
- Party questions and statements highlight issues in parliament (although these are also controlled by the party political whips)

- The training of parliamentarians receives attention
- The executive and the legislature almost invariably, because of the predominance of the ANC, work in a consensual and cooperative fashion – it is therefore nearly impossible to identify lack of accountability with poor or poorly informed decision-making.

Counter-Evidence Pointing to Executive Override and Ineffective Community Contact

Indications of the executive not taking parliament and opposition as seriously as would be expected manifest themselves on several fronts:

- MPs often feel overburdened, especially if they belong to the smaller parties. Some do not take their representative task seriously, avoiding or failing to pursue community and constituency contact
- Parliament in most of its policies and decision-making functions is overshadowed by the executive, and either does not have the authority or the political seniority to hold it accountable. Alternatively, it operates in a consensual hegemonic way to ensure that the interests of the majority party prevail (which, in party political terms, is perfectly legitimate)
- In cases of contested policies and other forms of political action, it is highly unlikely that parliamentary committee influence will prevail, should this differ from executive-centred guidelines
- Committees have frequently reported being frustrated by executive accountability, or the lack thereof
- There is subservience of the legislature to the executive, albeit within the context of party political intra-ANC consensus.
- There is an inability of members of parliament to convey constituency issues to the executive, especially if this pertains to grassroots problems with policy and implementation
- There is extensive evidence of centralisation and central coordination of policy, which might be advisable, but in the case of South Africa it has also stifled debate and engendered limited participation.

South Africa, in its brief democratic period thus far, therefore has had a largely positive, albeit mixed, history of legislative functionality. In a range of important respects, the executive arm of government has had far more power and effect than its legislative counterpart. There have indeed been trends of centralisation of power, with the presidency and Cabinet clusters emerging as paramount in this process. It is important to bear in mind that several forms of governmental devolution of power also prevail in South African government, alongside the trends to centralise that have been discussed. Devolution is evident, for example, in the powers that are afforded to the provincial and local spheres of government.

Civil Society

This section maps the existence, tolerance and promotion of a strong civil society, and presents preliminary assessments of the influence of civil society on politics, while the next part explores the twin dimensions of public and civil society participation in public policy processes, and the opportunities for civil society to exercise influence over these processes and thereby be part of a system of participatory democracy. This section explores the extent to which the South African government leadership fosters a climate that facilitates the existence of a vibrant and strong civil society, and is prepared to concede political influence to civil society. This is assessed in terms of both the absence of political elites restricting the operations of civil society (prescribing their non-interference in matters of government), and the space for civil society to set its own agendas, and implement programmes independent of the state.

The evidence indicates that there is space in South Africa for civil society to plan and act without intervention, but to a large degree this depends on the organisation or grouping's political stance with regard to cooperative participation alongside government. South African political elites hardly ever venture into the domain of personal and direct intervention with the operations of civil society, unless the organisation is engaged in political or socio-economic contestation of government policies and programmes. The state apparatuses are from time to time activated in order to delegitimise or undermine political dissent and criticism. It is important to record that the post-1994 political leadership, for example, has contributed to the encouragement of religious and cultural tolerance and reconciliation.

Civil society in South Africa has been characterised by an ebb and flow in political action in the period since the advent of democracy in the early 1990s.[34] After a preceding decade of continuous mobilisation and confrontations with the state, civil society receded in political engagement. Not only the South African National Civic Organisation (Sanco) and the South African Non-governmental Organisasion Coalition (Sangoco), but a wide range of other political organisations, underwent a period of redefinition and role finding. The erstwhile active right-wing cultural organisations seemed to fade. They remained in relative oblivion, until politicised right-wing organisation emerged, in the form of the 2002-2003 revelations of paramilitary planning for disruption and subversion. In contrast, leftist civil society remained relatively active through the period of post-1994 democracy. In the early 2000s, there was some resurgence in mobilisation, especially around community and social service issues.

Swilling and Russell note that the post-1994 state-civil society relationship has been institutionalised via a set of arrangements that display corporatist features.[35] This "corporatist pact" is driven by a confident and ascendant black middle class in control of state power, a well-organised non-profit sector, a well-organised corporate sector, and an international donor environment that favours funding of non-profit organisations. These developments stand in the context of the National Economic Development and Labour Council (Nedlac) Act of 1994,[36] and the Local Government Municipal Systems Act of 2000, both helping to institutionalise corporatist decision-making on national and local government levels.

In general, civil society in South Africa, comprising the citizenry as well as, for example, people's forums and NGOs, could be positioned on a tertiary level of influence on public policy-making (after the influence of the presidency and its advisory councils, the ANC and Cabinet). Most of civil society – probably excluding business – is among those clusters of policy actors that only sporadically have a direct impact on the processes of public policy-making.

Civil society configurations are nevertheless important actors at this level of influence. The ANC stresses the importance of people's forums in the development of its policies. Detailed analyses suggest that these forums constitute core aspects of needs assessment and implementation strategies, rather than being forums for the initiation of policy.[37] Examples of areas where these forums are important include feeding schemes and the development of projects in infrastructure. On the other hand, by the early 2000s, NGOs, including progressive trade unions, shared the perception that their influence on policy had been declining for a number of years.[38]

By 2001 initiatives were underway which promised to lead to the reinvigoration of NGO policy influence. Sanco, for example, promised to re-enter the policy-setting scene and has subsequently done so with the help of the ANC.[39] The resumption of an active and goal-oriented role would help resurrect Sanco and its affiliates as a powerful cluster of policy actors.[40] By 2003, Sanco had been receiving sustained support from the ANC, which was hoping to build a strong civil society partner, especially in the context of occasionally acrimonious relationships with alliance partners Cosatu and the SACP. The ANC Youth League fulfilled a similar role. Support for increased civil society action and enhanced space for participation in the processes of public policy-making came from a range of high-profile sources.[41]

Political Will and Civil Society

Some of the indicators that reflect positive efforts by the political and government leadership to encourage and facilitate participatory and consultative orientations towards civil society include the following:

- In several phases of the policy development process, consultation with civil society groupings is actively promoted
- There is considerable space for civil society groupings in the social domain to operate without state intervention
- Political leadership has made a notable contribution towards encouraging tolerance and reconciliation
- State-civil society cooperation has been institutionalised through a number of corporatist measures
- Political elites have undertaken far-reaching initiatives to facilitate the creation of a black economic elite
- The mass media are largely tolerated (albeit frequently criticised) in their independent actions
- Local level governance specifically encourages the engagement of civil society organisations, also in the domain of service delivery.

Counter-Evidence Stunting the Existence of Strong Civil Society

Some discernible evidence exists of reluctance by ANC and government leadership to engage with civil society on matters of policy divergence from the government:

- The state apparatus is often activated to ideologically delegitimise or undermine political dissent
- Debate prevails on the level of independence from the state of the radio and television colossus, the South African Broadcasting Corporation
- Political leadership has tolerated actions of victimisation against, for instance, the Landless People's Movement and the Anti-Privatisation Forum
- There is selective facilitation of civil society activism, depending on broad political orientation.

The leadership's record therefore varies – and largely so in terms of the nature and political inclination of the civil society grouping involved. The South African political leadership thus projects an uneven landscape of civil society participation and influence in matters of agenda setting, goal definition, and the formulation and implementation of policy. The next section moves beyond the existence, participation and broad influence of civil society organisations, and investigates the prevalence in South Africa of the political leadership's systematic engagement with civil society in order to render facilitation of participatory democracy – a process that systematically draws civil society into policy- and decision-making processes.

Participatory Democracy, Mechanisms for Access to the State, and Policy Influence

This section focuses on the extent to which the South African political leadership encourages and actively promotes dialogue, participation and partnership of citizens, civil society, and business in sustainable development.[42] The analysis also focuses on the way in which civil society has been asserting itself in terms of policy advocacy and influence. The orientation is not only to focus on the opportunities and structures for participation, but also on the issue of whether participation is systematically meaningful and procedurally accepted in terms of actual impact on policy.

The South African political leadership's emphasis on partnerships is a good indication of its engagement with civil society. However, it also has to be understood in an ideological context. Partnerships such as Letsema and Vuk'uzenzele ('arise and act') are projects to supplement the limited role that government argues it should have in development and poverty relief. Mbeki made this point in 2000, when he stated that government's partnership with the people would "help lay to rest the false notion that the government has the exclusive responsibility to create jobs and, therefore, that everybody should wait for the government to create these jobs". In his 2002 State of the Nation address, Mbeki added a role for "community development workers", in order to help the public service achieve direct contact with the people. In the subsequent period there was modest progress in the training of these workers and in getting their work to articulate with that of a frequently ineffective existing public sector.

Ordinary members of civil society – the citizenry, as opposed to organised civil society – at first in the immediate pre-1994 years engaged in processes, which under ANC government had become more participative and consultative. An effective system of participatory democracy was in place. Then followed a period of scaling down on mobilisation for engagement in policy formulation, granting government the time to *progress* with implementation. From the government side, limited resources for policy transformation and an insufficient institutional and skills base from which costly consultation processes could be handled served to constrain participatory democracy. More recently, citizens appear to have started signalling new but limited expectations with regard to consultation for needs assessment on policy formulation and implementation. Their wish is to be engaged in updates on policy implementation. They request forums, through which government can be directed in the implementation and delivery phases, and renewed consultation so that government becomes reacquainted with community needs.[43] These expectations occur in a context in which the citizenry predominantly still observes a sympathetic and legitimate government in power – one that is largely trusted to take care of their needs through the implementation of 'good policies'. Importantly, these desires for consultation are linked to their democratically elected representatives.[44] Furthermore, these needs only minimally pertain to consultation in the phase of policy formulation. Instead, they are linked to consultative information-sharing, updating, briefings and progress reports.

It is important to note that the South African constitution requires that the public be afforded opportunities for participation in the processes of government. The constitution requires that the public have access to and involvement in parliament. Individuals thus have the right to attend the meetings of Parliamentary Committees and all the sittings of the National Assembly and the National Council of Provinces. The constitutional provisions, however, do not automatically translate into participation. There is also recognition that the structured opportunities for participation are inclined to favour organised, NGO-anchored civil society. As de Villiers notes, the legislatures and the executive cannot simply sit and wait for the poor and the disadvantaged to come to them.[45]

With regard to organised civil society, analysis points to a three-pronged ideologically oriented trend with regard to the existence, encouragement and facilitation of participatory democracy in South Africa:

1. There is that part of politicised civil society that challenges government policies and mobilises around required changes to those policies. Examples include the LPM, the APF, Jubilee 2000, and the Treatment Action Campaign (TAC). Government often discourages civil society participation that is contestational and challenges its policies and programmes. The part of civil society that has challenged the national political leadership also uses the Constitutional Court as an avenue to affect government policy.

2. There is civil society that the ANC government endeavours to attract, or those organisations such as the church, because of the culture and constituency, where it has relatively guaranteed access. Among civil society organisations that the ANC government endeavours to attract are mainly business and the mass media. National and international business closeness is in many respects reminiscent of a mutually co-optive, cooperative partnership, rather than a government-civil society relationship.[46]

3. There is fraternal civil society, with ANC-linked organisations in the form of the ANC Women's League, the Youth League, and Sanco. These organisations have guaranteed participation through organisational structures linked to the ANC. At times, Cosatu would also be part of this category. However, in times of intensive contestation on issues such as privatisation, restructuring of state assets, black economic empowerment, aspects of foreign policy, or state action on anti-retroviral drugs, Cosatu would rather be positioned in the first of these three categories.

Thus, with regard to organised civil society and participatory democracy in South Africa, one notes a range of access routes: public mobilisation, mass media and public opinion; protest action; petitions; the Constitutional Court; consultative and advisory interest assertion and advice to government – amounting to forms of cooperative governance, as is the case with business and specialised farming interests – or fraternal organisational links.

From the side of left-alliance and left-civil society, individual unions within Cosatu and activist organisations such as Jubilee 2000 play a notable role in the expression of challenges to government.[47] Opposition from alliance partner Cosatu, particularly in the form of strikes and public demands, is often vigorous.[48] In 2000, members of the Cosatu-aligned Samwu in the city of Johannesburg were on strike, protesting against privatisation and job losses. Samwu urged members only to vote for ANC candidates opposing privatisation. The civil society mass base most harshly affected by the adverse side of macro-economic policies, however, remained largely unorganised and under-mobilised, and therefore exercised limited participation. The governing alliance on occasion came out in criticism of government. It was in the period of the mid- to late 1990s that rural civil society interests moved to the core of activities of political contestation (through the inclusion of NGOs such as the National Land Committee and the Rural Development Services Network within the Sangoco grouping). In 2001, the LPM together with the APF made a significant civil society contestational impact at the World Summit on Sustainable Development (WSSD).

The ANC government operated in a different mode of consultation and cooperation with civil society in as far as business-as-civil society was concerned. Near the core of civil society influence, we find the role of business groupings, including national and international investors, trade partner governments, donors and international financial institutions. In the era of commonly accepted neo-liberal globalism, the South African leadership in 1996 switched from its Reconstruction and Development Programme (RDP) to the Growth, Employment and Redistribution (GEAR) strategy, signalling the intention to create an investor-friendly, growth-oriented national economic environment. This policy change was controversial but not unexpected, and much subsequent sustainable development debate focused on the capacity of the GEAR strategy to effect its growth, employment and development targets.[49] However, the government commenced an era of high-profile and high-priority intra-elite cooperation between the economic and political sectors. The South African political leadership has thus not hesitated to consult and co-opt business and financial elites in a wide range of its core policy-making functions. Some of these co-optive elites are to be found in the National Business Council, the International Investment Council, and among the presidential advisers.

Partial abdication of responsibility and limited accountability result from the government's plans to move with international neo-liberal dictates, and create an investor-friendly fiscal environment in which business, growth and employment are expected to flourish. The South African economy has in many respects continued to falter, despite government following the advice of its business-civil society governance partners. The political leadership regards business empowerment, and in particular black business empowerment, as the cornerstone of black economic empowerment. Developmental and social security actions would take care of broader-based black empowerment. Again, political-ideological considerations of leadership have appeared to affect its resolve to empower contenders for participatory influence beyond the core structures of policy influence. For instance, in early 2003 government was putting the brakes on one of the institutional manifestations of black empowerment in its denial of statutory status to the Black Economic Advisory Council, in spite of a contrary recommendation by the Black Economic Empowerment Commission, led by businessperson Cyril Ramaphosa (seen as a rival to the president).[50] Another instance was the political leadership's stalling on a rollout plan for HIV/AIDS anti-retroviral drugs, because it would entail prioritising influence of Nedlac over its favoured National Aids Council.

Political Will and Participatory Democracy

Some of the indicative efforts by the government to facilitate participatory democracy and access to effective policy influence for civil society are summarised below:

- Especially in the early, post-1994 stages of agenda-setting and policy formulation, there was widespread encouragement and facilitation of participatory democracy – for instance in the domains of housing policy, land reform, and local government restructuring
- There has been far-reaching facilitation of national and international business participation in government policy-making processes
- The Nedlac structures created the opportunity for corporative decision-making processes involving government, trade unions and business
- Structures in the Office of the Presidency created influential forums for consultation and effective impact by business and investors on public policy in South Africa
- The Constitutional Court ruled in favour of a number of civil society organisations in their challenges to government regarding HIV/AIDS treatment, land and housing
- Parliament conducts public hearings in which both individuals and organised civil society can participate
- Government leadership conducts *imbizo* and *letsema* to provide platforms for civil society participation in the assessment of policies and policy implementation
- It is especially the fraternal organisations that are guaranteed participation, especially in the form of audiences with the political elites of South Africa
- There has been progress in establishment of government information centres, assisting in empowering civil society to meaningfully engage with government.

Counter-Evidence of the Political Elite Blocking and Limiting Participatory Democracy

Some of the perceptions of a seeming failure on the part of government and ANC leadership to effectively address the problem participatory democracy can be summarised as follows:

- From the mid-1990s on, there was a gradual contraction of opportunities for participatory democracy – as the policy process advanced into predominantly implementation phase access (limited)
- Government has turned a blind eye to (or has encouraged) the intimidation of organisations such as the LPM. The government has instituted counter-measures to undermine left civil society
- Government intervenes against township-based and anti-privatisation movements when these organisations engage in the illegal reconnection of services, without providing alternatives
- The number of *imbizo* programmes is still relatively low. The opinion is that where they do happen they make a difference – but that their occurrence is not regular and widespread enough
- The facilitation of opportunities for participation often does not translate into effective policy- and decision-making influence. These opportunities and their associated mechanisms for access are often virtually devoid of political effect. It is often the business and investor association part of civil society that is granted opportunity, and these organisations become semi-suspended from their civil society status – entering the domain of both corporative and co-opted governance structures
- The system of parliamentary hearings has limited and NGO-elite impact.

Opportunities for the exercise of participatory democracy therefore vary mainly along three dimensions: challenge-agreement with the central political leadership; the phase of the policy process and associated closure of opportunity for systematic participation once policy closure is conceptualised; and closeness of the policy inputs to the heart of government-business decision-making processes. Overall, there appears to be an approximate balance between positive and negative indicators of government's encouragement and facilitation of forms of participatory democracy.

Framework of Quality Corporate Governance

This section relates the growing levels of consciousness and action with regard to corporate governance, to the notion of political will to facilitate quality democratic governance. South Africa's political leadership has spoken critically of the corruptive effect of the private on the public sector in South Africa. Through both the King II report, and the institutionalisation of investigative and prosecuting units, a series of important advances have been made towards establishing frameworks and tentative mechanisms of implementation in South Africa. Thus far, prosecutions have centred predominantly on the contravention of tax laws and, for instance, illegal fishing or trade. Prosecutions have tentatively penetrated the top echelons of government and the private sector.

The South African political leadership, increasingly since the mid-1990s and the 1996 adoption of the GEAR macro-economic strategy, has been making great efforts to ensure a solid relationship between government and business. Indeed, it would appear that government has gone out of its way to create an environment in which national and international business would feel welcome, and would invest and assist the national economy in achieving the desired rates of, for example, economic growth and job creation. As part of its strategy to build on its image of 'minimally corrupt', and reassure business in terms of safety of investment environment, the South African government has also worked to ensure that there would be action to eliminate, prevent or minimise public sector corruption.[51] As corollary, there would also have to be good and honest corporate governance.

From the late 1990s on, public debates in South Africa have focused on the fact that corruption in the country often occurs at the point of interface between the public and private sectors. Thomashausen states: "Private sector corruption is often the root cause of public sector corruption. It is normally the private sector that is economically stronger, and in the position to penetrate even the most determined and upright resistance against corruption in the public sector".[52] He also notes that, more often than not, the corrupting party is working for a foreign or multinational corporation. Thomashausen distinguishes between traditional and contemporary conceptualisations of private sector corruption. Traditionally, it was addressed as a matter of good business ethics and practices and in terms of special legislation, "such as laws against unfair business practices and unfair competition". Since the end of the 1970s, however, both international organisations and individual states have been focusing on the need to counter private sector corruption in a proactive and decisive manner. The contemporary trend is to criminalise corrupt acts of private sector officials (even when committed outside national jurisdiction), and to provide special protection and immunity for employees reporting malpractices.

Increasing potential sites of corruption came to the fore in the enlarged range of public-private sector interactions that were associated with the cause of restructuring and refocusing the pre-1994 South African economy. It was, for instance, with the opening up of the public sector in South Africa with regard to black economic empowerment, preferential procurement strategies, restructuring of the public sector, growing outsourcing (especially at the provincial and local levels of government), and huge and multiple contracts for the provision of services and materials, that corporate governance increasingly became an issue for public-political governance, and unscrupulous actors took advantage of vulnerabilities that are associated with areas of growth and lessened 'policing'. Corruption nevertheless remained relatively contained. South Africa scores medium-well on international corruption indices.

A milestone in setting standards for corporate governance in South Africa was set through the South African government's appointment of the King Commission. The issue of corporate governance was first raised in South Africa in 1994, when the first of the King Commission Reports, King I, was published. That report highlighted the need for companies to consider their responsibilities outside the financial and regulatory environment. It was hoped that King II would address the continued practices of lack of transparency and disclosure. King II was described as being driven by "triple-bottom-line reporting". This refers to the expectation that companies over and above their traditional financial reporting should report on their social, economic and environmental practices.[53] This, according to King, is in line with expectations of institutional investors who expect measurement "which will enable them to draw their own conclusions about sustainability". Sustainability is affected by factors beyond the financial.

Corporate Social Investment (CSI) became increasingly emphasised in South Africa. In the 2002 financial year, for example, CSI came to R2.2bn in South Africa (up 7.8% from 2001). There was evidence that integrated sustainability reporting (a theme emphasised by King) was increasingly accepted in South Africa, especially by the big companies. The associated code requires companies to disclose what they do in terms of health and safety, the environment, racial and gender equality, and black economic empowerment.[54]

The South African government also took the initiative in establishing special investigative units. These included, at national level, the Asset Forfeiture Unit, the Heath Special Investigative Unit (to recover public funds lost to corruption and misadministration; the unit was subsequently disbanded and functions handed over to other units), the Investigating Directorate for Serious Economic Offences (to investigate and prosecute corruption, fraud, theft and forgery), and the Directorate of Special Operations or the so-called Scorpions (to investigate crime syndicates, serious economic offences, corruption, crimes against the state).[55]

South Africa still has a long way to go in terms of giving legislative effect to all aspects of private-sector corruption. However, King II, the special investigative units and prosecuting authorities, as well as a high level of public consciousness of the need to act against the private sector as one of the major corrupting agencies of the public sector, will probably help carry the anti-corruption campaign in years to come, and could contribute to South Africa's desired image of a site of quality governance.

Political Will and Corporate Governance

Several indicators suggest positive government leadership aims at fostering an environment of minimal corruption, both in the public and private sectors, as well as high levels of corporate responsibility:

- The South African leadership took the initiative in the appointment of the two King Commissions
- King I and II suggested a wide range of measures with regard to both traditional and contemporary considerations for quality corporate governance
- Increasingly emphasis is placed on the fact that anti-corruption action cannot just come from the side of the state

- There has been strong action against the private sector with regard to tax evasion and corruption
- Widespread Scorpion action against defaulting and defrauding business have made an impact
- The Special Investigative Units have equally been making inroads into corruption in the public sector
- Strong leadership action has been evident in encouraging, advancing and requiring social responsibility, including equity action in the private sector.

Lack of Commitment in Enforcing Corporate Governance

Equally, there are several indications of seeming reluctance or relative failure to pursue decisive action against public and private sector corruption. These indicators include:

- Politicians appear not to be closely monitored and checked in their declaring conflicts of interest, or personal interest in public sector contracts, or assets, and action follows belatedly. When this happens, it is often as a consequence of media exposés. Large numbers of government politicians, in all spheres of government, also pursue business careers
- Tentative action has only been evident with regard to allegations of corruption in top echelons of government. In these cases allegations arose against private sector parties that have strong financial links to the South African government
- Tentative and incomplete action against corruption pertaining to nepotism and advancement of self-interest in the awarding of provincial government contracts, for example in the Eastern Cape
- Uncertainty about commitment to social responsibility, especially in the form of restitutive action with regard to the apartheid past.

Should South Africa's political leadership be assessed in terms of its will to promote, implement and enforce codes of conduct, and corporate governance frameworks, it will receive a number of positive references. However, the balance of evidence shows that until further confirmation of determination to act is forthcoming, it will remain a tentative approval rating at best.

Rule of Law, Constitutionalism and Substantive Democracy

Constitutionalism, defined minimally, alludes to the principle that the exercise of political power shall be bounded by rules that determine the validity of legislative and executive action. The procedure according to which this action must be performed is prescribed, or the permissible content of the action is delimited. As De Smith notes, constitutionalism "becomes a living reality to the extent that these rules curb the arbitrariness of discretion and are in fact observed by the wielders of political power".[56] Shivji outlines the "new constitutionalism" that articulates with African orientations and contexts. He emphasises the following four pillars: the right to people's and national self-determination; the right to practise democratic self-governance and the participation of citizens; the collective right of people and social groups to organise freely for political, ideological and other purposes (including the right to resist oppression); and the right to security and integrity of the person. These pillars present to the people of Africa the "assurance of the legitimacy of their struggle".[57] Gutto refers to the fact that constitutionalism implies governance within the framework of the rule of law, justice and respect for fundamental human rights and freedoms.[58]

Government in South Africa occurs in terms of constitutional provisions and the law. Political leadership adheres to these requirements, even if they simultaneously follow procedures that are not constitutionally prescribed, but internationally accepted as normal politics (for instance the predominance of the executive over the legislature). Where government processes deviate from the formal rules as prescribed in the constitutional provisions, these deviations are therefore in line with governance practice the world over – also in constitutional and 'model' democracies of for instance the West.

In this context, it is important that the South African constitution upholds first, second and third generation human rights. The first-generation rights have obviously been easier to uphold than those of the second generation – the latter requiring fulfilment of socio-economic needs and rights such as in the domains of housing or access to medical treatment. In terms of equality of citizens before the law, the South African political leadership has managed to maintain a high-quality record. This record was only occasionally questioned – mostly by some advantaged whites and so-called 'coloureds' claiming 'inverse' discrimination due to equity action.

The South African judiciary is also regarded as independent. In South Africa, no government or person is allowed to interfere in the work of the courts.[59] The Constitutional Court is the court of final resort in constitutional matters. Appointments of judges, and especially Constitutional Court judges, are made through a transparent process, in which the Judicial Services Commission plays an important role.[60]

The ANC leadership has proved that it has the political will to respect and uphold the position of the Constitutional Court as the highest authority in the land. The Constitutional Court had been involved in a stream of actions testing the validity of national legislation, and, in the process, effected a range of changes which put South Africa high in the international rankings of, for instance, gender equality. The Constitutional Court in its range of judgements has ruled both against and in favour of government. For instance, on socio-economic issues, it judged against government in the Grootboom case on urban land and housing, and in confirming government responsibility to roll out plans for the treatment of HIV/AIDS. The Constitutional Court further imposed a constitutional obligation on government to implement second-generation human rights – for instance, in the provision of housing.[61] The government, however, has taken some time to give effect to Constitutional Court rulings. At the time of writing, implementation of the 2002 ruling on anti-retrovirals was still awaited. In the instance of floor-crossing legislation, the Constitutional Court ruled essentially in favour of government, but pointed out that minimal constitutional changes would be required in order to legalise floor-crossing. Friedman argues that the Constitutional Court in this instance could equally have developed a plausible argument to show that floor-crossing by politicians elected on a party list violated vital elements of South Africa's constitutional order.[62] Friedman states: "All this warns against taking for granted that the Constitutional Court is a reliable safeguard against government attacks on democracy." As motivation for the statement, he notes that the Constitutional Court did not have the courage to rule against government's strategic goals of political ascendancy in the provinces.

Indications in South Africa in the early 2000s were therefore that the political leadership had a dedicated, consistent willingness, and probably determination, to uphold both the rule of law and constitutionalism. In addition, the nature of the South African state as a constitutional state was strictly upheld in the first decade of governance.

A number of constitutional changes were effected. In a controversial instance in early 2003, which effected constitutional change to allow floor-crossing between political parties on provincial and national levels, the necessary parliamentary majority to carry the change was obtained with the assistance of several opposition political parties. A majority that exceeded the required two-thirds was obtained to carry these changes. It remained hotly debated whether this instance of constitutional change was inspired by political opportunism by the ANC – i.e. seizing an opportunity to inflict 'damage' on the DA, the major opposition party.[63] Whereas the ANC in 1999, with the aid of the Minority Front, achieved a two-thirds majority in parliament, it obtained a 69.7% majority in the 2004 elections. Yet, there were no indications of the ANC attempting to use this strength in order to implement constitutional changes.

The rule of law also goes beyond the political leadership's commitment to procedural democracy, and includes indicators of substantive democracy. When the Human Development Index is used to assess the political will of South Africa's political leadership, trends indicate modest advancement towards achieving substantive democracy. The percentage of the national budget that is committed to health-care and education is a further starting point in assessing the commitment of leaders to poverty eradication, improvement of people's standard of living, and generally, human development. Regarding political leadership will to allocate appropriate funding to education, it is worth noting that out of government's total developmental spending for 2003/04, the largest single chunk went to education.[64] South Africa has been achieving impressive levels of spending in these domains, but encountered severe problems in respect of implementation bottlenecks, reducing staff costs *vis-à-vis* enlarging operational costs and infrastructure development, and prioritising health spending in domains of intense society need (such as in HIV/AIDS).

Political Will and the Constitution

Some of the efforts of the South African government to give effect to and maintain the rule of law and constitutionalism are hereby summarised:

- South Africa is a constitutional state, and the supremacy of the constitution in interpreting and assessing the work of the legislature and executive is upheld
- Government is restrained in influencing the appointment of judges, or the president and vice-president of the Constitutional Court, although the president has authority over some of the appointments and racially corrective actions have been in evidence
- A bill of rights is an integral part of the South African constitution. This bill of rights contains first, second and third generation human rights. It is especially in the domain of first-generation rights that the political elite has implemented and has been maintaining high levels of freedom and enforcement
- The government has not interfered in the work of the Constitutional Court.

Problems in the Fulfilment of Constitutionalism and Rule of Law

Some of the failures of the government in maintaining and strengthening the rule of law and constitutionalism have also been evident. Indicators of these are the following:

- In several instances there has been low follow-through and lack of speed in the implementation of Constitutional Court rulings
- The constitution has been amended for party political gain, in the instance of floor-crossing (albeit with support of some opposition parties)
- The South African political leadership has over the decade of democratic rule generally made advances towards heightening the levels of human dignity and effecting development. However, there is also a range of problems
- The South African political elite has encountered a wide range of problems in effecting substantive democracy. Despite improvements in several macro-economic indicators, extensive poverty combines with unemployment to dramatically affect human development.

In the domains of rule of law, constitutionalism and human rights the South African government has notched up significant advances, especially in the historically and internationally comparative contexts. Important shortcomings, however, surface in the need to prioritise the implementation of Constitutional Court rulings. Furthermore, much intensified work is required for the leadership to move from intermittent to consistent, nationwide success in socio-economic development and in upholding second- and third-generation human rights.

Conclusion

Under the heading of 'The new political will of Africa leaders', the New Partnership for Africa's Development (NEPAD) states a range of commitments. These include that the political leadership will strive to achieve forms of democracy and state legitimacy that have been redefined to include accountable government, a culture of human rights and popular participation (Article 43). Article 47 emphasises the importance of participatory democracy, and states the requirement that development plans will be "prepared through participatory processes involving the people". In terms of the NEPAD declaration, African leaders will also take responsibility for, for example, "promoting and protecting democracy and human rights in their respective countries and regions, by developing clear standards of accountability, transparency and participatory governance at the national and sub-national levels" (Article 49).

On the basis of the assessment of South Africa's performance in the field of democratic political practice in government and elections, this chapter tentatively concludes that South Africa fulfils a majority of conditions that are stated in the NEPAD declaration. However, there are many indicators that point to issues and problems that occur from time to time, location to location, and issue to issue. In order to capture important nuances, that might also signal potential future developments, the NEPAD criteria probably would need to be improved. This case study of political will in South Africa provided a mapping of such possible extensions and refinements.

There were two questions that were of central concern in the commissioning of this chapter, with regard to the political elite of South

Africa. The first question was whether the current elite, the emerging political culture and existing political institutions are ready for the task ahead, namely committing themselves to an ethos of democratic political and socio-economic governance. The second question was whether there is sufficient political will among the elite for successful delivery of the new ethos and initiatives. On both these fronts, and in the context of the current era, the answer regarding South Africa is in the affirmative.

South Africa is an excellent example of a country that has had the opportunity to have a clean (because of the decisiveness of the break with the politics of the apartheid past) and demilitarised start. South Africa, however, was simultaneously unfortunate enough soon after its liberation to have become subject to the ideological pincer grip of globalised neo-liberalism (implemented by the national elite in the belief that it would bring socio-economic reconstruction) and the reality that state capacity (both structural and in terms of human resources) would for some time be inadequate in delivering the job creation and socio-economic advancement that had been expected in terms of the explosion of expectations that immediately preceded and followed the ANC's ascendancy to power.

On the balance of evidence, and especially with regard to democratic political governance – as opposed to democratic socio-economic, developmental governance – South Africa has a good record in relation to NEPAD standards, with space for improvement. It has to be noted that it is easy for the ruling elite at this early stage of spontaneous electoral majorities to comply with standards of quality democratic governance. Judging by socio-economic indicators, and the short- to medium-term potential for success on the substantive democracy front, the rest of this transition might be as arduous and extended as the struggle for the vote that was achieved in 1994.

The final conclusion takes two dimensions into account that move beyond the original brief. This first additional dimension may be found in the caveats amidst the positive ratings the South African political elite notched up on the political will scorecard. The approach that was followed in this chapter was to take full account of the debate relating to political will, real intensions, and bottom-line commitments of the South Africa political elite. The empirical analysis noted and explored both the affirmative and the counter arguments relating to political will. In the political domain, the main finding is that there is an excellent commitment of the South African leadership to the processes and procedures that are required by the African Peer-Review Mechanism (APRM). Alongside this commitment, however, were many of the realities of contemporary politics across the world – that there are 'kitchen cabinets', and 'real powers behind the throne', off-constitution enclaves where the real power lies and the final decisions are taken. This is equally true for South Africa. It is also equally true that the leadership uses all means at its disposal, beyond the electorally competitive domain, to insure and enhance its political dominance.

In the socio-economic domain, the findings regarding political will could be seen as more ambiguous. They are open to interpretation and variations in ideological slant. They are also open to "reasonable doubt because of the longer term that is required to prove economic policies to have had political developmental will" and "reasonable chances of the required outcomes" behind them.

This leads to the second additional dimension of political will that this chapter took into account. Here, and in bringing together the political and socio-economic dimensions of political will, the paper developed a likely sustainability orientation in assessing the South African political elite. It asked the question of whether electoral security for an incumbent party (not just South Africa, but *any* party incumbent) could be a prerequisite for compliance with the type of conditions that are posed in the APRM. It is unlikely that this condition is relevant to a contemporary assessment of the South African political elite. It is, however, a hypothetical statement that has to be factored into the time-dimension for assessment of the sustainability of affirmative political will. It is important therefore that peer review will only bring definitive, certain answers when it is implemented over time.

Notes and References

1   Indicators, a frequently used concept in this paper, are defined as measures that translate abstract, immeasurable concepts (such as 'political will' in the political and socio-economic domains) into

operational, measurable forms. See M. Carly, *Social Measurement and Social Indicators: Issues of Policy and Theory*. London: Allen and Unwin, 1981.

2 J. F. Bayart, *The State in AFRICA: The Politics of the Belly*, London: Longman, 1993; Patrick Chabal and Jean-Pascal Daloz, *Africa Works: Disorder as Political Instrument*, London: International African Institute, in association with James Currey, 1999.

3 Constitution of the Republic of South Africa, Act No. 108 of 1996. Also see S. Booysen and S. Louw, 'The South African Constitution' in *The Encyclopaedia of Sub-Saharan Africa*, New York: Charles Screiber's Sons/Macmillan, 1997.

4 J. Daniel, R. Southall and J. Lutchman, 'Introduction: President Mbeki's Second term: Opening the Golden Door?' in J. Daniel, R. Southall and J. Lutchman (eds), *State of the Nation, South Africa 2004-2005*, Pretoria: HSRC Press, 2004, pp xxvi–xxxi.

5 D. Glaser, *Politics and Society in South Africa*, London: Sage Publications, 2001, pp 129–131.

6 The DA was subsequently retained as name for the party comprising both the old DP and the range of NNP members who chose to leave their former NNP home.

7 Legislative initiatives that have assisted the process of black economic empowerment include the National Small Business Act of 1996, the Competition Act of 1998, the National Empowerment Fund Act of 1998, the Employment Equity Act, and the Preferential Procurement Act of 2000.

8 N. Makgetla also notes the pressures on government to continue this elite form of empowerment, given that high-income Africans earned 15% less in salaries than equivalent whites, and receive half as much profit. See *Business Day*, 21 February 2003, p 11.

9 B. Nzimande, *City Press* (Johannesburg), 23 February 2003, p 19.

10 For instance, regarding the first 2003 meeting, see *City Press* (Johannesburg), 16 March 2003, p 5. The IAC was set up in early 2000 to "draw on insights of distinguished international business leaders" (Essop Pahad, Minister in the Office of the President).

11 For an overview, see *Sunday Times* (Johannesburg), 5 January 2003, p 4.

12 For an analysis of aspects of this pattern, see Daniel *et al.* 2004.

13 Idasa's Judith February notes: "Although South Africa has strong anti-corruption laws, the lack of mechanisms to regulate private party funding has left a glaring gap in the political process." There was a campaign to have provisions regarding private party funding included in the Anti-Corruption Bill, due to be passed in 2003, but this did not succeed. See *City Press* (Johannesburg), 26 January 2003, p 19; National Democratic Institute for International Affairs, *Funding of Political Parties: An International Comparative Study*, October 1998.

14 *Financial Mail* (Johannesburg), 4 October 2002, p 28. The ANC argued that smaller parties would disappear, or be limited to small numbers of seat, should a constituency-based system be introduced.

15 South African Communist Party, Conference proceedings, Johannesburg, 1998; also see SACP, 23 June 2000, 'South African Communist Party Proposals for an International Left Platform', 15 June 2001, available online at http://www.sacp.org.za/docs/left-platform.html.

16 South African Communist Party, 1999, Interview with office-bearer, 19 February, Port Elizabeth. Also see the intense debate in several editions of *The African Communist*, 1998-1999.

17 See *ANC Today*, vol 2, no 40, 4-10 October 2002; ANC Political Education Unit, Contribution to the NEC/NWC response to the 'Cronin Interviews' on the issue of neo-liberalism, October 2002.

18 For a DA view on parliament and accountability, see R. Taljaard, 'Accountability is the watchword for Parliament', *Business Day* (Johannesburg), 7 September 2000.

19 S. Booysen, 'Opposition Politics in Democratic South Africa.' *South African Journal of International Affairs*, vol 2/3, no 2, 1996, pp 55-75; S. Booysen, 'A Complexity Perspective on Contestation in post-apartheid South Africa: A Comparison of Political Party, Social Movement and Alliance Opposition', Paper presented at the biennial research colloquium of the South African Association of Political Studies, 11-13 October 2002.

20 S. Booysen, 'Transitions and Trends in Policymaking in Democratic South Africa', *Journal of Public Administration*, vol 36, no 2, 2001, pp 125-144; for a 2003 update, see *Sunday Times* (Johannesburg), 23 February 2003, p 21; *Business Day* (Johannesburg), 20 February 2003, p 12.

21 See *Business Day* (Johannesburg), 4 April 1996.

22 Although in elaborated and institutionalised form, the PCAS structures were a continuation of a concept launched when Mbeki was Deputy President. South African Institute of Race Relations, *South Africa Survey, 2000 / 2001,* Johannesburg: SAIRR, 2001, p 508; 'Public Policy-making', in A. J. Venter (ed.), *Government and Politics in the New South Africa,* Pretoria: Van Schaik Publishers, 2001.

23 S. Jacobs, 'An Imperial Presidency?', *Siyaya!,* no 6, Summer 1999, pp 4-12; SAIRR 2001, p 508.

24 F. Chikane, 'Integrated Democratic Governance: A Restructured Presidency at Work', Special report, Pretoria, Office of the President, 2001, pp 16, 19, 20, 26-27.

25 See S. Jacobs, 'Under the micro-SCOPA', *In Session,* February 2001, pp 10-11. According to Gavin Woods, there are five elements that strengthen the hand of SCOPA in doing its scrutiny work. These are other portfolio committees, the government departments themselves, the Auditor-General, parliament and the media.

26 For this debate, see *Business Day,* 16 October 2002, p 5.

27 See *City Press Business,* 20 April 2003, p 1 on the investigation into Transnet's awarding of a scrap-metal contract to a particular empowerment company. The investigation followed after SCOPA expressed concerns.

28 For an overview of these processes, see *Business Day* (Johannesburg), 20 February 2003, p 12.

29 See *Rapport,* 9 March 2003, p 2; *Mail & Guardian* (Johannesburg), 7 March 2003, p 4.

30 For an overview of the process and recommendations, see J. February, in *Cape Times* (Cape Town), 31 March 2003, p 9.

31 Also see B. Hogan, *Business Report* (Johannesburg), 2 March 2000, on the issue of parliament being in danger of becoming a 'rubber stamp' on measures such as inflation targeting, due to MPs either not understanding the issues, or not being consulted. See SAIRR 2001, pp 504-506 for details on the range of parliamentary committees.

32 See R. Calland (ed.), *The First 5 Years: A Review of South Africa's Democratic Parliament,* Cape Town: Idasa, 1999.

33 The latter opinion is that of DA leader Tony Leon; general analysis from *Sunday Times* (Johannesburg), 23 February 2003, p 21; S. Terreblanche, *A History of Inequality in South Africa, 1652-2002,* Pietermaritzburg: University of Natal Press, 2002, p 469.

34 Civil society in this paper is conceptualised as the umbrella term for the organised (mainly voluntary associations and non-governmental organisations – the component that is commonly regarded as the non-profit sector) and unorganised civil society (the citizenry, especially as manifested on local community level). Conceptualisations regularly equate civil society with associational life, a collective force balancing excessive concentrations of power in the state. See J. A. Hall, 'Consolidations of Democracy', in D. Held (ed.), *Prospects for Democracy,* Cambridge: Polity Press, 1996, pp 281-282; D. Potter, 'Democratization in Asia', in Held 1996, p. 359. This paper acknowledges that tradition, but also notes the need for a broader conceptualisation. Authors such as Martinussen relate civil society to local community. See J. Martinussen, *Society, State and Market: A Guide to Competing Theories of Development,* London: Zed Books, 1997, p 191. This conceptualisation recognises that there is a component of civil society on the level of the local community, harbouring a collective political consciousness. This shared political consciousness is not expressed through associational life. Political parties (sometimes also regarded as civil society) reflect a particular political consciousness, but local-level political consciousness does not penetrate into those political forums.

35 M. Swilling and B. Russel, *The Size and Scope of the Non-profit Sector in South Afri*ca, Durban: Mott Foundation, 2002.

36 See E. Webster and K. Gostner, *Nedlac: Building Consensus in a New Democratic Order?* Report commissioned by CDE, Johannesburg, 1998.

37 S. Booysen, 'Public Policymaking in South Africa: Understanding and Enhancing the Processes of Public Participation', *Final Summary Report, Part I of Report Series,* Research Report, Johannesburg and Washington DC, October 2001, p 52; S. Booysen, 'Public Policymaking in South Africa: Understanding and Enhancing the Processes of Public Participation', *Full Background Report, Part II of Report Series,* Research Report for the Joint

Center of Political and Economic Studies, Johannesburg and Washington DC, October 2001, p 102.

38 Cosatu and the South African National NGO Coalition, *The Sunday Independent* (Johannesburg), 8 October 2000.

39 See *City Press*, 22 April 2001; *Mail & Guardian* (Johannesburg), 20 April 2001.

40 These remarks from SANCO came at a time when the organisation was under pressure to sever links with the ANC. Various political and civic leaders at the SANCO national conference questioned SANCO's relevance in championing the plight of ordinary communities because of its close relationship with the ANC and government. See *City Press*, 15 April 2001; also see *City Press*, 22 April 2001.

41 T. Mbeki, *A Nation at Work for a Better Life*, Pretoria: Government Communication and Information System, 1999; N. Mandela, in *Business Day*, 25 April 2001; African National Congress, *Election Manifesto*, Johannesburg, 1999; F. Ginwala, 'A Parliament for All People', *City Press* (Johannesburg) , 18 March 2001.

42 See *State of the Nation Address*, February 2003; also Drew Forrest in *Mail & Guardian* (Johannesburg), 14 February 2003, p 17.

43 S. Booysen, 'Changing Practices and Needs in Policymaking and participation: Government and Civil Society in South Africa, 1994-2002', Monitoring and evaluation of Public Policy Workshop, 23-25 October 2002.

44 It is only in the absence of both contact and delivery that the citizens in this study insisted on renewed consultation for the formulation of policies. See S Booysen, 'Civil Society and Participation in Public Policymaking in South Africa', Conference paper, Questioning civil society in Africa, Institute for Policy Analysis and Research, Kenya, 6-8 November 2001.

45 S. de Villiers, *A people's government: The people's voice*, Cape Town: Parliamentary Support and Idasa, 2001. Also see www. parliament.gov.za/pubs/participation/index.html.

46 S. Terreblanche, *A History of Inequality in South Africa, 1652-2002*, Pietermaritzburg: University of Natal Press, 2002: "(Government's) ability to implement comprehensive programmes for alleviating poverty and redistributing wealth is clearly constrained by its elite compromises with the corporate sector and its global partners"

(p 419). He continues: "The politico-economic system that has replaced white political domination and colonial and racial capitalism ... can best be described as a system of *African elite democracy cum capitalist enclavity*" (p 423).

47 Jubilee 2000 is a movement campaigning for the removal of the national debt of African nations. http://search. megaspider.com/ TopSearch.html$FS?Jubilee+2000.

48 R. Habib and R. Taylor, 'Political Alliances and Parliamentary Opposition in Post-apartheid South Africa', Conference paper: Opposition in South Africa's new democracy, 20-30 June 2000; D. McKinley, 'Democracy, Power and Patronage: Debate and Opposition within the ANC and the Tripartite Alliance since 1994', Conference paper: Opposition in South Africa's new democracy, 20-30 June 2000.

49 It was in already in 1994 that the RDP White Paper committed the state to a robust export-oriented growth strategy. The World Bank was involved in its drafting.

50 *Business Day*, 13 March 2003, p 2, in analysis of the State of the Nation address by President Thabo Mbeki.

51 In early 2003 the *Corruption Country Assessment Report* on corruption in South Africa showed that 62% of businesses believe that corruption had become accepted business practice. A total of 11% of those surveyed (compared with 2% in 1997) reported having experienced corruption. Public service managers interviewed claimed that up to 75% of staff is untrustworthy and involved in low-level corruption.

52 A. Thomashausen, 'Anti-Corruption Measures: A Comparative Survey of Selected National and International Programmes', Occasional Papers, Konrad Adenhauer Stiftung, 2000, p 5, refers to the fact that "corruption cannot be defined to its manifestations in the public sector".

53 See *Moneyweb*, http://m1.mny.co.za/C2256A8C00448C6B/$all.

54 *Mail & Guardian* (Johannesburg), 'Investing in the Future', 17 April 2003, pp 12, 18.

55 See *South Africa Survey 2000-2001*, Chapter on 'Security Services', pp 105-107.

56 Quoted in I. G. Shivji (ed.), 'State and Constitutionalism: A New Democratic Perspective', *State and Constitutionalism: An African Debate on Democracy*, Harare: SAPES Books, 1991, p 28.

57 *Ibid*, pp 39-46, and in quotation of the Algiers Declaration, p 46.

58 S. Gutto, 'Constitutionalism, Elections and Democracy in Africa: Theory and Praxis', Paper delivered at the Africa Conference: Elections, democracy and Governance, Pretoria, 7-10 April 2003.

59 See *In Session*, February 2001, p 15.

60 See O. Jacobs, 'Constitutional Court's Role in Reform' in W. James and M. Levy (eds), *Pulse: Passages in Democracy-Building, Assessing South Africa's Transition*, Cape Town: Idasa, 1998, pp 45-51.

61 *The Sunday Independent* (Johannesburg), 21 May 2000; Constitution of the Republic of South Africa, Act No 108 of 1996.

62 S. Friedman, *Business Day* (Johannesburg), 16 October 2002, p 9.

63 See *Business Day* (Johannesburg), 17 October 2002, p 11.

64 See *Mail & Guardian* (Johannesburg), 17 April 2003, p 4.

Conclusion

Africa faces the onerous task of renewed development at a pace that is expected to alleviate the negative effects of underdevelopment, such as poverty, disease and hunger, which have taken a heavy toll on the continent's human and material resources. That the political systems on the continent contribute significantly to the lacklustre performance and economic relegation which Africa faces, it is no secret to political and civil actors on the continent. Efforts at diagnosing the problem, to identify the causative factors of the political impasse which has crippled development on the continent, has been the subject of debate and intellectual engagement since post-independence years, which span over four decades. This problem still persists and has stimulated political policy and strategic changes, whose assessments and remedies continue to be interrogated nationally and internationally. It is the consensus of opinion that the political elites are part and parcel of Africa's problems and in this regard, should use their privileged positions to proffer lasting solutions to these problems. The extent to which this perception is correct, remains questionable. Furthermore, the degree to which the contribution of political elites, in shaping the political landscape of Africa and in providing the antidote to the virus that attacks the body politic and the development path of the continent, has become a subject of concern – hence the propriety and legitimacy of the investigation through this book.

Trends in the progression and dynamics of political processes in Africa, from Cape to Cairo, and from Senegal to Somalia, have been so rapid that even political pundits and historical archivists find it difficult to keep abreast of the changes. Investigating the dynamics of politics and the role of actors in the arena from the five cardinal countries of Algeria, Egypt, Nigeria, Senegal and South Africa, reveals a broad spectrum of processes of political metamorphoses; diversity in political ideology; veracity in social, cultural, and religious tenacity; as well as the interplay of all these to inform and guide contemporary, structural and institutional changes on the continent. These factors have profoundly guided political processes and influenced decision making and actions by the political elites, who are hereby placed in the spotlight.

The political arena throughout Africa, as depicted in the selected five states, shows a mixed investigation of political destiny, which in some has reached tyrannical levels. A spate of dictatorships characterises the state apparatus in which hegemonic rules perpetuated discredited leaderships in power, at the expense of true democracy. Egypt was reeling under the control of the pharaohs, which was later extended under the rule of Abdel Nasser. The pharaonic regulation persisted under Anwar Sadat, who saw himself as the last pharaoh to rule Egypt. The thawing of the political ice has been manifested in an attempt at democratisation, under the leadership of Hosni Mubarak. Yet, in the words of Egyptian political analysts and sceptics, pessimism is rife – in spite of the ongoing democratisation process, Egypt is still characterised by a dominant rule of the presidential establishment. Thus, all authoritative and influential bodies of the state machinery are formally or informally affiliated with the office of the president. This highly centralised system of governance demonstrates the perpetuation of the old paternalistic and pharaonic relationship in the country.

A strong military presence and participation, as well as hegemonic institutionalisation became a distinguishing feature of the Egyptian political elites from the era of Nasser to the present Mubarak regime. Although the sheer number of military figures in politics declined from historic to modern times, the military establishment remains the most important political structure within the state. Expanding military enterprises enjoy a separate budget comprising loans, external military grants and profits. Since the 1970s, the Egyptian military has played an expanding role in economic issues in Egypt, in what has been termed "horizontal expansion" in industries, agriculture and infrastructure. For lack of what an Egyptian political analyst termed 'deep public support and genuine political legitimacy', the Mubarak regime depends heavily on the military to provide him with security and support, thereby elevating them to prominent positions as members of the state elite.

Sadat wrestled power from the people and tried to control the whole political arena by establishing his own laws such as the Shame Law and the Law of Protecting Social Peace. He thus saw the democratisation process as his initiative and branded himself a democracy-giver. He once warned his political opponents that "democracy has sharp teeth", invariably expressing the double-edged nature of democracy. The constitutional amendment of May 1980 further exacerbated the hegemonic power structure, which President Mubarak currently exploits to full benefit. As both the president of the state and that of the ruling National Democratic Party (NDP), he uses his position to choose NDP candidates for the People's Assembly. Consequently, despite its enormous constitutional powers, the Assembly is seen as a mere rubber stamp in the hands of the president and his executive.

Egyptian political elites pride themselves in having reached a milestone in the political transformation and democratisation process. They believe that Egypt is practising a functional democracy with respect for human rights, freedom of speech and freedom of expression including a free and independent press. They arrogate to themselves, credit for the practice of democracy and good governance by citing the formation of youth and motherhood organisations to which they pour copious accolades as the foundation of democracy. They hold this view strongly on the ground that the organizations will empower the youth and families and in so doing form the nucleus and pillars of democratic dispensations and good governance at the grassroots.

The role of the Egyptian elite in continental politics and the question of the direction of their loyalty is still a matter of continued debate and need for rationalisation. Their views on AU and NEPAD initiatives are wide and varying. Many see NEPAD as a 'hot potato' that must be handled with care lest it backfires. Others regard it as a reincarnation of the monstrous Structural Adjustment Programme (SAP), which may again engulf African states in a new arm-twisting development path. The optimists among the elites support the government stance that as a home-grown initiative for which Africa claims ownership but seeks partnership from friendly nations and organisations, NEPAD stands a good chance of transforming the economic and political landscape of Africa if given the desired local and international support. Whether NEPAD is the ultimate instrument of unity and integration between the Arab North Africa and Sub-Saharan Africa with Egypt acting as the chain-link remains the speculation and expectation from Africans, south of the Sahara.

The Algerian case presents an account that is reminiscent of post-independence African politics, which is marked by commitment of enormous resources to win independence and the enthronement of regimes, which inevitably become dictatorial and which tenaciously and relentlessly cling to power. Three distinguishing groupings and phases characterise the political elite structure in Algeria. The first group is the generation of politicians who joined and played active politics in the decade of 1950-1960. They participated in the anti-colonial struggle and the war of independence and acceded to power in 1962. The second group is the new generation of political actors, who entered the scene in the 1980-1990 era. They had no experience of colonisation or the anti-colonial struggles in the country. Rather, they were the products of the Algerian educational system, who were schooled in the new programmes. Although heterogeneous in composition, they all aspired to power and posed dual problems between their integration into the mainstream politics and the emergence of a new crop of elites. The third generation of elites are entering politics in the context of multi-party democracy and are building their power base from associations, trade unions and political parties after the October 1988 riots.

Independence in 1962 ushered in a dramatic turn of events in the Algerian political scene. After 1954, the old political grouping lost legitimacy after they failed to take active part on the war of independence. Thus, they lost out on political service and top administrative posts eluded them having been reserved for those who had taken active part in the struggle for independence. The ex-*Moudjahidine* (combatants) were rewarded through special legislation that gave them access to universities and the civil service. The notion of 'revolutionary family' was instituted between 1993 and 1994 and the formation of National Organisation of *Moudjahidine* and other associations created in their wake. Furthermore, the children of the *Chahid* (martyrs) and descendants of the *Moudjahidine* further buttressed support for the activists.

At the time of independence, there were few elites in trade and industry. The few that existed flourished on the fringes of the state dominated economic sector and markets. The agricultural revolution in 1975 was the first real attack on the economic elites and the codes regulating investments and state monopolies on foreign trade further limited their powers. The traditional elites were diminished and disqualified by massive education of children through the use of state apparatus. Accused of being archaic and conservative, they had to make way for elites linked to the *Nahda* (Renaissance). This centralisation of resources contributed to an almost elimination of the elites of the colonial period. The political renewal was brutal and rapid. With good education in the wake of nationalism and independence, the new elites dominated all spheres of political life and dominated the social scene. With their exclusive political resources, they constantly sought ways to keep themselves in power and enjoy continued control.

A series of reforms marked the Algerian governance since independence. Started in 1979, the reform process encompassed political, economic and social changes aimed at revolutionising the geopolitical and socio-economic systems. Commencing in 1979 after the death of Bourmediène, the political reform of 1992-1993 addressed the issue of security as the government tried to deal with terrorism and violence. Between 1991 and 2000, social reforms took the form of setting up national commissions and committees as a matter of priority to reform the educational and justice systems as well as state structures. Economic reforms included the implementation of the structural adjustment plans through reduced state involvement in the economy and the privatisation of public enterprises, transfer of perpetual tenure on agricultural land was granted to workers and more liberal investment codes were promulgated.

The political elites in Senegal are characterised by a state of contradictions, best described by analysts as "an administration at odds with the life cycle of the state". The elites' strategies to establish their power base and the time frames of the state do not often correspond with democratic culture. There is a general tendency among the elites to informalise the state, institutionalise political floor-crossing, terminate sincere militancy, and manipulate constitutional provisions for their personal and partisan interests. The link between the state and society is dysfunctional, and efforts are expended towards its reconfiguration. The reform takes diverse dimensions including the restructuring of the forces at play in the political economy under the umbrella of clientelism and personalisation of power and the reactivation of regionalist and clientelist attitudes in the distribution of posts.

The emerging crop of political actors, who include religious and informal brotherhoods and those who have emigrated abroad are known to be very dynamic. The scenario heralds a new form of emergence and diversification of elites. Whether there will be a race between this new breed of elites and the old political practitioners, and whether the race will prolong the sites of predation, are questions that probe the minds of political analysts. The elites consider NEPAD as an African club, a political challenge and a major political marketing avenue to set Africa up as a new destination for investments and not merely a source of resources for European and the United States markets.

The Nigerian experience of political elitism is summed up in such agonising words and unsavoury expressions as 'perfidy', 'corruption and illegality', 'faces behind the dancing masks', 'deceit and distraction', the list continues *ad infinitum*. This demonstrates the enormity of the problem and the depth of the oblivion into which the elites have sunk the political system in the country.

The many stages and phases of political milestones, through which the country has passed in more than four decades of its post-independence history, have bred more and more sophisticated and incongruous cabal of political elites. They consist of trickles from the hangers-on of the post-colonial era; the emergent group from the pre-civil and the post civil war military dictatorships; the players in the military continuum of the early 1980s to 1999; and the entrants of the post-1999 democracy, who boast no positive revolutionary agenda but are mere loyalists and students of the corrupt past and serving political elites. The high profile but sporadic scuffles with corruption and the much talked about anti-corruption crusades orchestrated with discomforting amplitude, is nothing but a ploy by the political elite to give a semblance of a spirited effort at self-cleansing in the country. To the contrary, it is perceived as a political gimmick and mere window dressing designed to appease the international donors and development partners. The truth is that corruption has been oxygenated in the lungs of the elites, carried in their arteries to feed their body politic, and that it is only the de-oxygenated blood which runs in the veins to the periphery of the society that the so-called anti-corruption crusade targets. Education for which Nigeria is famous world-wide has not been spared the exploitation of the elite as funding and financial support for education and capacity building as well as other social institutions have been profoundly derided, the welfare systems have collapsed and social infrastructure is in shambles.

With Nigeria as one of the architects of NEPAD, and with the country's development instruments, including social and political infrastructure in the state of moral and political decadence as highlighted above, the country could not ask for anything better than the hopes and aspirations, which NEPAD holds for her development. However, the discomfort brought about by the debilitating attitude of the political elite in the country raises serous doubts about the capability and capacity of Nigeria to take advantage of the initiative. This scenario of hopelessness exists, notwithstanding Nigeria's strategic positioning in NEPAD, and the nation's generous endowment with diversity and immensity of spectacular natural and human resources. The inevitability of this pessimistic view is best captured in the eloquent scepticism observed and expressed in this study to the effect that

> many Africans and Nigerians in particular who thought that the post-1999 democracy in Nigeria would engender a plethora of positive outcomes and that the elites would for once see the enormity of the task and make a clean break from the past were mistaken as the binge continues unabated.

The Nigerian elites continue to seek selfish rather than national interests at the expense of transparency and accountability with untoward consequences on development.

South Africa represents the state with relatively greater vision for economic and political prosperity. It represents a model state on the path of development, which is well focused with a systematised plan of action by the political elite. The political elite through the government of the day has pursued the option of deepening existing initiatives rather than risk experimentation with new policy directions. The furthering of the Black Economic Empowerment (BEE), the Reconstruction and Development Programme (RDP) and the Growth, Employment and Redistribution (GEAR) initiatives are some of these model pursuits. The government and the governing elite recognise that the success of these initiatives in providing the development impetus and in serving as the launching pad of the country's economic emancipation will depend on the political will of the elites. To achieve unity in diversity, the country, through its elites, makes a commitment to remain progressive in its thinking and action and to use developmental initiatives to address the diversity in needs, culture and race in the country.

On its ascendancy to power, the African National Congress (ANC) distanced itself from its apartheid past. It adopted the philosophy that good political leadership would engender forms of democracy and state legitimacy, comprising accountability, a culture of human rights, and participatory governance. It is little wonder, then, that the South African political elite has enjoyed positive ratings and are notched up in the political will scoreboard.

The elite has shown excellent commitment to the processes and procedures of the African developmental agenda such as the New Partnership for Africa's Development (NEPAD) and the African Peer Review Mechanism (APRM). It is further noted that the leadership uses all means at its disposal, beyond the electoral and competitive domain to shore-up its political dominance. In this regard, the positive findings on political will become more ambiguous and open to other interpretations and ideological connotations. This stint of doubt stems from the uncertainty of the future and the length of time it takes to assess whether economic policies have been backed by elite-driven political will and developmental agenda. Analysts admit that the real test of the political will of the political in South Africa will come when the legitimacy of the ANC as a liberation movement government begins to thin out and wane and the burden of increasing social demands exposes government's limitations and inability to satisfy these various and varying needs to acceptable levels. It is then that the true test of democracy and loyalty will emerge. Time will then tell whether the abilities of political elites, to stand up to the exigencies of need and to display willingness to adhere to the rules of democratic processes and succession, will be achieved and maintained. Overall, the African political elites seem to have lost touch with the reality that it is the mandate of the people that counts. Instead, they have pursued the path of self-enrichment and strategic positioning to perpetuate their hegemonic governments and reap the concomitant benefits uninterrupted.

The views of the elites on the transformation of the AU and the initiation of the NEPAD retuned a compendium of mixed grills. On the one hand, the pessimists and critics query the propriety of the top-down approach to the initiative as well as the composition of leaders and states that initiated the political transformation. The proponents hold the view that NEPAD is a step in the right direction in the absence of any better alternative at the moment. They advocate that Africans should rally round the drivers of NEPAD and give it support as Africa's home-grown initiative for its development. They plead with Africans to accept NEPAD as the instrument of change for development by which Africa engages development partners for its development based on equality and mutual respect.

Lightning Source UK Ltd.
Milton Keynes UK
UKOW05f1627230916

283653UK00017B/233/P